THE JAMES GORDON BENNETTS

I am Yours Truly
James G. Bennett

From an engraving in *James Gordon Bennett and his Times*

The James Gordon Bennetts
Father and Son
Proprietors of the New York Herald

By
DON C. SEITZ

Author of
Joseph Pulitzer
Horace Greeley
The Dreadful Decade
Uncommon Americans
etc.

INDIANAPOLIS
The BOBBS-MERRILL *Company*
PUBLISHERS

First Edition

Printed in the United States of America

PRESS OF
BRAUNWORTH & CO., INC.
BOOK MANUFACTURERS
BROOKLYN, N. Y.

To
HENRY L. STODDARD

FOREWORD

After writing the lives of Joseph Pulitzer, recreator of the *World*, and of Horace Greeley, founder of the *Tribune*, it seemed to me there remained a gap in the history of nineteenth-century journalism, as far as New York is concerned, that should be filled with the story of James Gordon Bennett and his son, respectively proprietors of the *Herald*. One built up a great newspaper, the other kept it great until the time when age made him uncertain amid the confusions of the World War. Autocrat and satrap, the two Bennetts, they and they alone, owned the *Herald*. In enterprise and attainment, outside of public service, the *Herald's* record remains unsurpassed in American journalism. It has vanished in the embrace of the *Tribune*, leaving no trace of its merits behind. But the making of the paper was an amazing exploit, and the man who did it was more extraordinary than the two whose tales I have previously tried to tell. Had the son been less of a sybarite he would have excelled the father. Yet many of his achievements remain unmatched. Between them, the two Bennetts ruled the *Herald* for eighty-three years, the longest newspaper dynasty we Americans have known. They left no mourners when their hands grew cold. The elder was ostracized by the community, the younger by himself. The *Herald* was equally isolated and without friends. It compelled support by its energy and won its way by force. Buying and selling news was its business. In this it ranked supreme. The two strange men were enigmas to their contemporaries. It is they, rather than the

Herald, whom I hope to have now introduced to a wider understanding.

Thanks are due to Robert Hunt Lyman, Miss Claire Wallace Flynn, Robert E. Livingston, William Dinwiddie, George A. Cormack, Ralph D. Blumenfeld, James Melvin Lee and E. D. DeWitt for important assistance. Much information has also been derived from *James Gordon Bennett and His Times,* by Isaac C. Pray, New York, 1855.

D. C. S.

CONTENTS

LIST OF ILLUSTRATIONS

LIST OF ILLUSTRATIONS—*Concluded*

Facing page

THE JAMES GORDON BENNETTS

THE JAMES GORDON BENNETTS

CHAPTER I

THE FIRST REPORTER

UNTIL James Gordon Bennett the elder came into the field, journalism in America was personal. Editors dealt with their public and one another from the standpoint of the individual. Outside of his opponents the editor paid small attention to the things of life. It was left for Bennett to make the newspaper impudent and intrusive. To do this he became the first real reporter the American press had known. He must therefore be considered a recorder rather than a guide or commentator—not that he was deficient in either quality, but because he deliberately made reporting his choice.

Newspapers, as such, hardly deserved the name until this impertinent Scotchman came along and kenned the interest of mankind and womankind in their fellows. True, another Scot, Robert Burns, had written before Bennett's birth:

> If there's a hole in a' your coats
> I rede ye tent it;
> A chile's among ye takin' notes
> And, faith, he'll prent it.

This, however, though often applied to the ingenious young gentlemen who gather the news, did not refer to one of their kind, but to Francis Grose, the antiquarian, who noted the ways of the Scotch in his *Peregrinations through Scotland.*

Born in Banffshire, September 1, 1795, Bennett had, perhaps, read the sage suggestion of the great Doctor Samuel Johnson that "much may be made of a Scotchman if he be caught young."

However that may be, he evidently determined to do his own catching, for after a period of education at Aberdeen and travel on the Continent, some part of it through the family design to make him a priest, the Bennetts being Catholics, he came to the sudden conclusion to try his fortunes in America. Of his ancestry he once wrote mockingly:

Every record of the Bennetts was lost in a great freshet, previous to the year of our Lord 896, when they were a little band of free-booters in Saxony. I have no doubt they robbed and plundered a good deal, and, very likely, hen roosts, or anything that came in their way. They emigrated to France and lived on the Loire several hundred years. When William the Conqueror went to England, they were always ready for a fight, and crossed the seas. The Earl of Tankerville is a Bennett, and sprang from the lucky side of the race.

Another branch went to Scotland with an ancestor of the present Duke of Gordon (1836), and all, I believe, were robbers on a great scale. Latterly, however, they became churchmen, but never abandoned the good old Catholic Church, till I became graceless enough to set up for myself, and slap the Pope and Bishop Dubois right and left. I have had bishops, priests, deacons, robbers and all sorts of people in my family; and, what is more, we were bright in ideas and saucy enough in all conscience.

When twenty, he "cut loose" from Banffshire in 1815, floating around somehow in Glasgow and Aberdeen until April 6, 1819, when he departed for America, via Nova Scotia, impelled by the suggestion of a friend who was going, plus a deep interest in the country aroused by reading Benjamin Franklin's autobiography.

He arrived after a slow voyage at Halifax, where, with a puny purse, he took to school-teaching, then an ill-requited employment, and soon saved enough change to move on to Maine. Here another term in the town of Addison, across the bay from Mt. Desert, gave him the means to get to Boston, by schooner from Portland. The thrill of Boston as the starting point of the Revolution was deep upon him and he reveled in visiting its historic spots. "I felt," he wrote in after years, "the same glow in wandering over these scenes, as I did on the fields of Bannockburn, in my more youthful days. It was Liberty and Freedom struggling against pride and tyranny in both cases."

There was a good deal of conviviality in the Boston of Bennett's day but in this he refused to join. He was more than temperate in the use of liquor and tobacco. "I eat," he remarked to one who reproved him for his abstemiousness, "to live. I do not live to eat and drink."

Boston was not hospitable. When his pockets became empty, he found a shilling on the street that fed him for a day. A benevolent fellow countryman then gave him employment as a clerk in his store, whence he soon departed to become a proof-reader in the printing shop of Wells & Lilly. There the scent of printer's ink filled his nostrils. He liked the flavor, but despised proof-reading—one of the dullest and most responsible of occupations—and decided to adventure further. The impulse carried him to New York, early in 1822. After desultory employment on local sheets, he accepted an offer from A. S. Willington, owner of the Charleston, South Carolina, *Courier,* to take a hand in producing that respectable journal. In the *Courier* office he translated news from the Spanish papers, brought by sailing vessels from Havana, Spain and her rebellious colonies then being a center of interest. He wrote some things besides—including poetry.

The *Courier* was a fine paper, as the *News and Courier* is unto this day. Mr. Willington was enterprising and sent shallops far out to meet incoming ships, a method that was to be much used in later days by his young editor. There was nothing democratic about the *Courier* save the partisanship of its politics, and the youngster acquired in Charleston a strong southern view-point that ever after influenced his attitude in American affairs. The community itself was intensely aristocratic and hardly the place for an adventurer—least of all one with such newspaper ingenuity as Bennett afterward demonstrated he possessed.

His stay in Charleston ended in 1823, when he again turned his steps to New York. Newspaper conditions were not inviting and the young man announced his purpose to open a commercial school in October. There is no record that enough pupils responded to the call to carry out the idea. He thereafter fed himself with his pen. The *National Advocate,* a Democratic paper published by Thomas Snowden, with the backing of William P. Van Ness, gave him work. He wrote also for the *Mercantile Advertiser* and lectured on economic subjects, gaining all the while a knowledge of affairs and of politics that was to pay him large dividends in the future.

News was plentiful enough, but it was not the custom to print it. Accounts of social affairs were tabooed. The proceedings of courts could not be exploited. It was libelous to publish reports of bankruptcies. Murders were described in a half-dozen lines. Political proceedings alone earned space, and these were warped and twisted to suit the policy of the sheet. There were many papers,—nothing was easier to start or more difficult to keep going,—but they were partisan, or specialized organs that filled most of their space by cribbing from, or commenting on one another. New York had numerous dailies, small in size and circulation, that voiced the opinions of their editors, who clipped from exchanges and padded from the European mail. Correspondents served them from various parts of the country, but sent more of their own pedantry or opinion than news. Happenings of moment were recorded in paragraphs. There was no "working up" of stories and much that later became "news" was left unnoticed.

Such was the journalistic atmosphere into which our young Scotchman came. Inquisitive by nature, he was amply snubbed both in and out of the newspaper offices. He soon learned to conform, as the easiest way of getting along, and fell into the ways of his associates. While thus temporarily tamed, he grubbed along as best he could from one weak sheet to another until 1825, when he attempted to do something on his own hook by taking over entirely on credit a small

Sunday paper called the New York *Courier,* started by John Tyron. It took but a few weeks to empty his lean purse, and he turned the paper back to Tryon. The *National Advocate* and the *Mercantile Advertiser* again kept him moderately employed. His style of writing was what might be called florid—*vide* his report of the New York debut of Maria Felicita Garcia, who was to become famous as Madame Malibran:

> The overture was listened to with breathless silence. It was the first time that an Italian opera had been heard in this country. There was an enthusiasm in the public mind that surpasses language. At the conclusion of the overture, the whole audience burst forth in rapture and applause. I never applaud or make a noise at theaters. I leave that for loafers and blockhead critics to perpetrate; but at that moment I could hardly resist the contagion.
>
> The opera began; Figaro came forward. Every one was pleased—but the great attraction of the evening was yet to come. In a few moments Rosina came forward—the charming, black-eyed, modest, easy, exquisite Signorina! She was young and lovely. She wore a pink dress, trimmed with black. She came down to the footlights with exquisite grace, smiling like an angel from heaven as she came. The audience were in raptures. She opened her mouth—"una voce poco fa" burst from her lips in soft, melodious, exquisite tones. The whole theater was breathless—the ladies looking and listening—the gentlemen in raptures—the old French and Italian gentlemen in the pit almost melted into tears—and the venerable Da Ponte, sitting in the center, with his head uncovered, enjoying the glory and the delight of the scene.

For two years the *National Advocate* kept him fairly busy. He spread himself in a verbatim report of a celebrated bank fraud case, and wrote reports of the appearances of Thomas Abthorpe Cooper, William A. Conway, and William C. Macready, early English seekers after American dollars on the stage. In the spring of 1827 he ventured to Washington as a free lance and there picked up a place on the New York *Enquirer*. He had already secured a toehold in politics by attaching himself to the political fortunes of Martin Van Buren, bespeaking for him the successorship to Jackson which Van Buren attained, and Bennett traveled, thereafter, journalistically speaking, in that suave gentleman's train. He joined Tammany Hall and was a partisan Democrat for the moment. Of this association he once wrote:

When I first entered Tammany Hall, I entered it as an enthusiast studying human nature, as a young man would enter a new country, full of interest, and deriving advantage from every movement and every sight. I kept a diary during the whole period of my connection with that party, and the sentiments therein recorded, just as they occurred to me, still remain, and are the very sentiments which I entertain at this moment. I found out the hollow-heartedness and humbuggery of these political associations and political men; but yet I was so fascinated with the hairbreadth escapes and adventures that I could not disconnect myself from it until the revulsion took place between me and my partners in Philadelphia. After that period I regained my liberty and independence completely; and a fortunate thing it was for my prosperity that Van Buren and his men did behave so meanly and so contemptibly toward me in the year 1833. I then returned to New York, started the *Herald* with the knowledge I had of men and matters throughout the country, and have been successful ever since.

The attachment to Van Buren brought him into line with the Jacksonians, among whom he was one of the most fervent. He was present at the inauguration of Jackson as President, and reported the great occasion exuberantly:

The Chief Justice of the United States then administered the oath of office; and thus, in the sight of Heaven and the surrounding multitude, was Andrew Jackson declared the chief of the only free and pure republic upon earth. The welkin rang with music and the feeling plaudits of the populace, beauty smiled and waved her kerchief—the first spring birds carolled their notes of joy, and nature poured her various offerings to the Giver of all good. The very marble of the pediment seemed to glow with life—Justice, with firmer grasp, secured her scales—"Hope, enchanted, smiled," and the genius of our country breathed a living defiance to the world. What a lesson for the monarchies of Europe! The mummery of a coronation, with all its pomp and pageantry, sinks into merited insignificance before the simple and sublime spectacle of twelve millions of freemen, imparting this Executive Trust to the MAN OF THEIR CHOICE.

As a sequence it was given to Mr. Bennett to be the first person to put life into Washington correspondence. Here is his own account of it:

We happen to know a good deal of this business of letter-writing from Washington, for we were the first to give it its present light and amusing character in a series of letters published in the *New York Enquirer* in the years of 1827 and '8. Before that period a Washington's letter-writer simply gave the dull details of both houses, the abstracts of reports, or a few sketches of the speakers. In the letters I furnished the *New York Enquirer* in those years, then conducted by Mr. Noah, I changed the whole tone, temper, and style of Washington correspondence. Before my day, the late Mr. Carter had spent a winter or two at Washington, and gave a dull recital of what he had seen and heard, in the *Statesman* newspaper. In Philadelphia, Walsh, sitting in his easy-chair, wrote long, labored letters to himself, heavy, flat, stupid, and disagreeable.

It was in the winter and spring of 1828 that I wrote the series which appeared in the *Enquirer*. No one knew by whom they were written, either here or in Washington, but they were generally attributed to G. C. Verplanck. I remember very well how the idea of writing them originated in my own mind. In the Library of Congress I spent much of my time, poring over Jefferson's collection of old pamphlets, which no one, before or since, has perhaps looked into. Sometimes I would take a peep at the new publications of the day, and among them I found the recent publication of Horace Walpole's famous letters and correspondence, written during the reign of George II, and describing, in witty and agreeable badinage, the intrigues, politics, incidents, and explosions of that singular court. These letters were highly amusing, graphic, and interesting. I said to myself one day, "Why not try a few letters on a similar plan from this city, to be published in New York, describing, eulogizing or satirizing the court of John Q. Adams? I did so. All the political, gay, fashionable, witty, beautiful characters that appeared in Washington during that winter, were sketched off at random, without being personal or offensive to any of the parties—indeed, they were mostly all complimentary and pleasing to the parties.

These letters were published and became popular. They were copied throughout the country.

The fervid writer always had it in for the effete monarchies. He took on the most vivid thoughts of his adopted country and always made the most of them. Whatever principles the man had were on the side of liberty, so long as it covered white folk. He stood staunchly by Jackson. The *Enquirer,* under Major Mordecai M. Noah, had been waging a costly war with the New York *Courier,* run by James Watson Webb. Bennett suggested that the two join forces. This was done and the *Courier and Enquirer* became a sort of New York Thunderer for thirty years, under the headship of the blustering Webb. The consolidation left Bennett out. He puttered around trying to find capital among politicians for a venture of his own, but failing to get it, joined the *Courier and Enquirer* in the autumn of 1829, as associate editor. There were then in the metropolis eleven daily sheets and thirty-six of less frequent issue, serving 202,589 people. He continued to be more of a reporter than editor, making frequent trips to Washington and other points where things political were happening, and doing go-between work in politics. Jackson and John C. Calhoun, the vice-president, were at odds. The latter controlled the Senate and under his spell southern Democratic editors were readily confirmed to office, while those of the North were shut out. One of these was Noah. This bred some pretty stories, which Bennett wrote.

An unusual opportunity occurred in 1830 for the exercise of the reporter's peculiar talents for getting into trouble with the elect. On the morning of April seventh, Captain Joseph White, of Salem, Massachussetts, a man of wealth, who had annoyed two prospective heirs, Joseph J. Knapp, Jr., and John Francis Knapp, by remaining in good health at eighty, was found dead in bed, dripping with blood from a blow in the temple and thirteen stab wounds. Richard Crowninshield, Jr., and his brother George, were arrested as the actual committers of the crime, and the two Knapps, as having employed them to do the deed. Richard Crowninshield hanged himself in his cell. George proved an alibi. The two Knapps were convicted and duly executed. The State of Massachusetts called in the great Daniel Webster to assist in prosecuting the accused, who were all of good families.

It will be perceived that such a case had great merit for so rare a reporter as James Gordon Bennett. He regaled New York with choice accounts of the crime and the manner of the trial.

Reporting the court proceedings was not easy work. Perez Morton, the grim attorney-general, undertook to regulate the reporters. Bennett bumped him sharply. "He knows more of the technicalities of the law, than he does of the tactics of the Press," he wrote in a scathing criticism that continued: "It is an old, worm-eaten Gothic dogma of the Courts to consider the publicity given to every event by the Press, as destructive to the interests of law and justice.

"Is it possible," he went on, "that the publication of facts, or even rumors, can have any tendency to defeat the general operations of justice?" He further proclaimed: "The Press is the living Jury of the Nation." When this weighty thought reached Salem, the trenchant tribune of the Press was barred from the court room and all others were prohibited from taking notes, the Judge setting up a sort of interstate commerce rule that reporters could not be allowed to send their observations out of Massachusetts.

Bennett also wrote more than the court proceedings—bright sketches of Boston, Salem and Nahant. There was interest in all things about him and the skilful pen was never idle. During recesses in the long ordeal he looked up politics in Massachusetts and New Hampshire, becoming acquainted with Franklin Pierce, a bright young lawyer not long out of Bowdoin College, and little dreaming that he was to become president of the United States, largely with his visitor's help.

In 1831 Bennett was kept busy as a reporter and correspondent for the *Courier and Enquirer.* He went deeply into the merits of the United States Bank controversy in the Jackson interest, in which he overhauled the whole banking situation as it then existed. His chief indictment against the major institution was that it turned its great powers to political uses and exerted them to destroy one party and upbuild another.

In support of this charge he wrote:

. . . Let the mind, untinctured by prejudice—unawed by power—unbought by favors, look at the startling fact with steady attention, and unblanched gaze. What have we? An organized corps of presidents, cashiers, directors, clerks, tellers, lenders and borrowers, spread throughout the United States—moving simultaneously upon every given point—lending out money for hire, and distributing opinions for action—furnishing capital and thoughts at one and the same moment—buying men and votes as cattle in the market—giving a tone to public opinion—making and unmaking Presidents at will—controlling the free will of the people, and corrupting their servants—circulating simultaneously political theories, destructive of the constitution, and paper money injurious to every State Bank—curtailing and expanding at will discounts and exchanges—withering by a subtle poison, the liberty of the Press—and, in fact, erecting within the States of the Union, a new general government—an *Imperium in imperio,* unknown to the Constitution, defying its power, laughing at its restrictions, scorning its principles, and pointing to its golden vaults, as the weapon that will execute its behests, whenever it shall be necessary to carry them into action.

We repeat, therefore, as the Bank question of this State is finally settled by the passage of the city bank charters through the Senate, would it not be well for the legislature of New York to take the lead in following out the suggestion of the President, by commencing a rigid examination of the principles and policy involved in the United States Bank?

The lively young reporter had the old-fashioned newspaperman's delight in mixing up in things. One of these was the promoting of the political fortunes of William L. Marcy, who, as a result of Bennett's underground efforts on his behalf, secured the nomination for governor of New York, to which office he was duly elected. Marcy was senator from that state in 1832, and Bennett "worked" the *Courier and Enquirer* in his behalf. Colonel Webb was then impaled on one horn of the United States Bank dilemma and so not very Jacksonian. "In all this business," wrote Mr. Bennett in after years, "Senator Marcy wished to stand still between the two contending cliques, while I was to work the wires in Washington, and Mr. Webb was to fire off the big gun in New York. Senator Marcy and I, in Washington, used to laugh and chuckle most amusingly on the movements by which, through the *Courier and Enquirer,* we accomplished ultimately his nomination, checkmated his personal foes at Albany and elected him triumphantly, governor of the state for the first time. Before the summer was over, however, Mr. Webb bolted from the Democratic party on the United States Bank question, and came out against the re-election of General Jackson, including, also, the election of the very man William L. Marcy, whom he had contributed so much to bring before the public."

Bennett afterward confessed that he participated in the affair "like a political sinner as I was, as one of the electric wires between Washington and Albany." The thing came up to plague him in 1845, when he was making it warm for Webb and found he had been in a way disowned by Marcy, his former confidant. "It was," Bennett wrote, "therefore very unhandsome of him [Marcy] to have been as it now appears, writing letters to Jesse Hoyt, censuring me privately for the very thing which he approved and concurred in to myself personally at Washington."

He was taught then that journalism and political companionships do not go together, as many a correspondent has found to his sorrow.

In the early summer Bennett made a journey through central New York, analyzing political conditions. In September he dropped in on Washington and reported an Antimasonic convention at Baltimore. A Free Trade convention followed at Philadelphia in October. As a reporter he also found time to describe the doings of the Frenchman Chabert, who called himself the Fire King and at exhibitions given in New York entered red-hot ovens, swallowed boiling oil and handled molten lead without damage.

The Democrats won in the November election, and Bennett, then residing at No. 61 Broadway, represented the First Ward of New York in the incidental celebration. He had for colleagues such persons of consequence as Jesse Hoyt, Prosper M. Wetmore, Dudley Selden, Egbert Ward and Jacob S. Bogert. At the dinner Bennett proposed what was to be his last political toast:

"The democracy of New York—like the Tenth Legion of ancient Rome—the first in the field and the last out of it."

In welcoming the new Boston *Post,* freshly founded by Charles Gordon Greene, Bennett on the editorial page of the *Courier and Enquirer* laid down this view of what an editor should be:

> An editor must always be with the people, think with them, feel with them, and he need fear nothing. He will always be right, always strong, always popular, always free. The world has been humbugged long enough by spouters, and talkers, and conventioners, and legislators, *et id genus omne.* This is the editorial age, and the most intellectual of all ages.

In his editorial support of Jackson, as visible in the columns of the *Courier and Enquirer,* Bennett's style was breezy to say the least. Here is a sample:

> The impotency of the attacks which have been made upon General Jackson during the last three years by the Adams party, reminds us of an anecdote—"Mother," bawled out a great two-fisted girl one day, "my toe itches." "Well, scratch it, then." "I have; but it won't *stay scratched!*"
>
> "Mr. Clay, Mr. Clay," cries out two-fisted Uncle Toby, "Jackson's a-coming—Jackson's a-coming!" "Well, then," says Clay, "anti-tariff him in the *Journal.*" "I have, but he won't *stay* anti-tariffed."
>
> "Mr. Clay, Mr. Clay," bawls out Alderman Binns,

"the old farmer's a-coming, a-coming." "Well, then," says Harry, "coffin-hand-bill him." "I have," says Binns, "but he won't stay coffin-hand-billed."

"Mr. Clay, Mr. Clay," says John H. Pleasants, "the hero's coming, actually coming." "Well, then," says Mr. Adams (John Quincy), "Burr him, and traitor him." "I have, but he won't stay Burred or traitored!"

"Mr. Clay, Mr. Clay," says Charles Hammond, "Jackson is coming." "Well," says Clay, "prove him an adulterer and a negro-trader." "I have," says Charles, "but he won't stay an adulterer or a negro-trader."

"Mr. Clay, Mr. Clay," bawls out the full Adams slandering chorus, "we have Jackson a murderer, an adulterer, a traitor, an ignoramus, a fool, a crook-back, a pretender, and so forth, but he wont stay any of these names."

"He won't?" says Mr. Clay. "Why, then, I shan't *stay* at Washington, that's all!"

Antimasonry had become a political issue in New York. The associate editor had a deal of fun in treating this fantasy. His sprightliness drew much fire against the *Courier and Enquirer,* and he was all too often made a scapegoat for the paper's sins. Its strong antibank policy made it many enemies among New York business men, who sought to reach it by a stock control. This came about through the sale of an interest owned by Daniel E. Tylee. The associate editor was muzzled. He then devoted himself more to news-gathering than to editorial work, traveling about as a correspondent and rigging a relay service that brought the president's message from Washington to New York in fifteen hours!

Webb hauled down the Jackson flag on August 23,

1832. His flop caused a vast commotion and led to a congressional investigation, which revealed that the United States Bank had "accommodated" him to the extent of fifty-two thousand, nine hundred seventy-five dollars at one time or another. The inquiry revealed some interesting sidelights on the then state of metropolitan journalism. Webb testified that when he switched to the support of Biddle the Bank of New York, the Bank of the Manhattan Company and the National Bank called his loans. Also, the *Courier and Enquirer,* reckoned the most powerful paper of the day, had thirty-three hundred daily subscribers at ten dollars per annum, and twenty-three hundred weekly and semi-weekly readers at four dollars and a half a year. It had also two hundred and seventy-five advertising subscribers whose cards were carried, paper and card costing thirty dollars per year. Its daily income from advertising was sixty-five dollars. The total gross yearly income was sixty thousand, seven hundred fifty dollars; expenses thirty-five thousand dollars, profit twenty-five thousand, seven hundred fifty dollars. Of its outlay twenty-two thousand dollars was for print paper. Webb valued the property at one hundred fifty thousand dollars.

After Webb's shift Bennett was out of place on the *Courier and Enquirer.* He accordingly left the paper, and was ignominiously kicked in print by Webb for daring to differ with him.

October 29, 1832, the outcast editor began the publication of the New York *Globe,* proclaiming his purpose in this rather flamboyant fashion:

I publish this evening, at No. 20 William Street, the first number of a new daily journal called the New York *Globe,* price eight dollars a year. Early arrangements will be made to issue a weekly and a semi-weekly paper from the same office.

Since my withdrawal in August last from the *Courier and Enquirer*, I have been taking measures for the establishment of a new paper, but unavoidable obstacles have hitherto prevented its appearance. I am now in the field, sword in hand, with unfurled banner, resolved to aid the great cause of Jackson and Democracy—the Union of the States, and the rights of the States. My politics are well known. I was one of the first in this state to put the names of Jackson and Van Buren before the people in 1827—I fought through the great conflict in 1828, and again in June, 1829, I was the first to bring the name of our venerable President up for a re-election. I have always supported the principles and nominations of the Democratic Party, and shall continue in that course. Opposed to nullification, I adhere to Jefferson's doctrines of State Rights—equal legislation—economy in public expenditures—reduction of unneccessary taxes—and the advancement of human liberty and human happiness.

Up to the next election, politics will be the staple article of the *Globe;* but after that event I shall give it all the variety which makes a daily paper the welcome visitor of the tea-table or counting-room. And if industry, experience, and resolution are any warrant for success, I entertain no doubt that, in less than two years, I shall count, without affidavits, at least five thousand good subscribers to the New York *Globe*.

A word on the size of my paper. For years past the public has been cloyed with immense sheets—bunglingly made up—without concert of action or individuality of character—the reservoirs of crude thoughts from different persons who were continually knocking their heads against each other, without knocking any thing remarkably good out of them. I have avoided this inconvenience. I shall give my readers the cream of foreign and domestic events. My sheet is moderate in size, but neat and manageable, printed on fine paper and with beautiful type. When an overflow of patronage shall demand more room, as it soon will, I may enlarge a little, but I shall avoid, as I would a pestilence, those enormous sheets—the pine barrens of intelligence and taste, which have been undoubtedly sent into the world as a punishment for its growing wickedness.

In taking my position as the editor of a daily paper in this community, I am no new recruit—no undisciplined soldier. I have acted in this capacity for twelve years past, eight of which I have been associated with the *National Advocate,* the New York *Enquirer,* and latterly the *Courier and Enquirer,* all of this city. I have hitherto labored for the reputation and profit of others; I am now embarked on my own account—on my own responsibility. In coming before this community I do not feel therefore as a stranger thrown among new faces. Though personally unknown to many newspaper readers, I stand before them as an acquaintance—a friend—an intimate. I feel myself connected with New York by that captivating species of relationship—that delightful community of thought and sentiment which exists between an industrious and moral editor, and a numerous and encouraging body of readers. With these remarks I commit my bark to the breeze.

James Gordon Bennett.

New York, October 29, 1832.

In spite of this inspiring platform the *Globe* lived just one month. The poor weakling died from poverty and abuse. Its owner went down flying the Jackson flag. He fired a blast at Webb, showing that Biddle's boodle had more to do than principle in switching the *Courier and Enquirer,* and then began to scratch about anew for a living. He wrote for the New York *Mirror* and various periodicals, even descending to fiction in his search for pocket money. The field was lean, and with some small Democratic support, he invaded Nicholas Biddle's town and became editor of the Philadelphia *Pennsylvanian*. His going to Philadelphia was the outcome of an effort to join hands with Francis Preston Blair on the Washington *Globe*. Blair told him the paper was too small for two men of their size and suggested the Quaker City as offering a broader field. It proved painfully narrow.

From this distant vantage he bombarded Wall Street, and roused plenty of wrath in reply. It would appear that he told truths that have grown eternal about this great gambling center, but did not add to his metropolitan popularity. The *Pennsylvanian* lost money and in trying to raise twenty-five hundred dollars from Jesse Hoyt, Bennett was placed in an equivocal position, from which it was hard to emerge. His supporters found it easy to mistrust him when called to put up cash. He felt Hoyt's desertion keenly. "I am sorry," he wrote to that magnate, June 13, 1833, "to speak harshly of anybody, but really I think there is something of ingratitude in the way I have been treated. I want no favor that I cannot repay. I want no aid that is not perfectly safe."

In approaching Hoyt, Bennett was really feeling for Van Buren, a word from whom to the former would have brought relief. It did not come. Instead, the crafty "Matty Van of Kinderhook" dodged deftly in this fashion, writing to Hoyt: "If Mr. Bennett can not continue friendly to me on public grounds, and with perfect independence, I can only regret it, but I desire no other support. Whatever course he may pursue, as long as it is an honest one, I shall wish him well. He does not understand the relations between the editors he quarreled with and myself, or he would not complain of me for their acts. They are as independent of me in the management of their papers, as I wish him to be and remain."

His plea having brought him no response in his striving to make the paper hit some mark, Bennett became involved with Amos Kendall, Postmaster-General under President Jackson, who had come to Philadelphia on the latter's errand in his contest with the Bank of the United States. While opposing Nicholas Biddle, head of that much-hunted institution, Bennett had never been on bad terms with him. In the intense feeling of the day this moderation did not help his position and he fell down in expecting to please a political crowd who would not come to his aid. Kendall, when he wrote his autobiography handed out this slap to the editor:

He [Bennett] had been previously associated with Mordecai M. Noah and James Watson Webb in the management of the New York *Courier and Enquirer,* and when his associates, after obtaining accommodations to the extent of $52,000, went over to the Bank, he professed to remain loyal to the administration, and became editor of the *Pennsylvanian,* a leading Democratic newspaper in Philadelphia. By his profession of loyalty, he drew Mr. Kendall into a private correspondence with himself on the Bank question, and sought to obtain all the information he could in personal intercourse. [This during a visit by Kendall to Philadelphia]. But soon after Mr. Kendall's return to Washington, Bennett began to throw out in the *Pennsylvanian,* mysterious hints that a great conspiracy was on foot, of which he held the proofs. After attempting to work up the public curiosity in successive issues of his paper he came out with a charge that the conspiracy was against the Bank of the United States; that the chief conspirator was Amos Kendall; and finally he published Mr. Kendall's private letters as proofs of his allegations.

No notice was taken of the charges or the proofs, for, although the letters showed a determined hostility to the Bank and a strong desire for its destruction they showed also that the motives of the writer were patriotic and disinterested. While Mr. Kendall regarded the publication of these letters, without his consent, as conclusive testimony to the purity of his motives, yet the act was in itself so mean and dishonorable, that he never spoke to or recognized Mr. Bennett afterwards. What advantage, if any, the publication secured to Bennett himself, was never made known to the public. It doubtless had something to do with his secession from the *Pennsylvanian* whose patrons were generally Democrats, and his return to New York, where he established the New York *Herald,* and by his successful profligacy has done more to corrupt the American press and the public morals than all the other profligate editors in the United States.

Situated as he was in a hostile city, mistrusted and without backing, the venture soon came to an end. In 1834 Bennett was back in New York, out of a job, but more and more determined to establish a paper on lines that were to be his own. With a small amount of cash—five hundred dollars—he endeavored to induce Horace Greeley, then succeeding as a printer, to join him in getting out a daily. Greeley declined.

Recall that the adventurer was not young. He touched forty and had worked for fifteen years under hard and discouraging circumstances. Not only was he without substantial capital, but had two failures to his credit, besides being bitterly hated by the powerful James Watson Webb, then the overlord, or rather, bully, of New York journalism. He had made other enemies, financial, political, professional and personal, with his biting wit and ready pen; in short, he had become an ink-stained Ishmael, and was therefore free to do as he pleased, having neither obligations nor responsibility on his shoulders.

CHAPTER II

FOUNDING THE NEW YORK HERALD

Repulsed by Greeley, Bennett next went to Anderson and Smith, prosperous printers in Ann Street, who got out two evening dailies, the *Transcript* and the *Sun.* His five hundred dollars was sufficient to induce the partners to undertake the task. Therefore, on May 6, 1835, "James Gordon Bennett & Co." were able to issue the first number of the New York *Herald.* It was only a specimen copy, containing a prospectus covering the plans of its promoter:

James Gordon Bennett & Co. commence this morning the publication of the MORNING HERALD, a new daily paper, price $3 per year, or six cents per week, advertising at the ordinary rates. It is issued from the publishing office, No. 20 Wall Street, and also from the printing-office, No. 34 Ann Street, 3d story, at both of which places orders will be thankfully received.

The next number will be issued on Monday morning—this brief suspension necessarily taking place in order to give the publishers time and opportunity to arrange the routes of carriers, organize a general system of distribution for the city, and allow subscribers and patrons to furnish correctly their names and residences. It will then be resumed and regularly continued.

In the commencement of an enterprise of the present kind it is not necessary to say much. "We know," says the fair Ophelia, "what we are, but know not what we may be." Pledges and promises, in these enlightened times, are not exactly so current in the world as Safety Funds Notes, or even the U. S. Bank bills. We have had an experience of nearly fifteen years in conducting newspapers. On that score we can not surely fail in knowing at least how to build up a reputation and establishment of our own. In *débuts* of this kind many talk of principle—political principle—party principle, as a sort of steel-trap, to catch the public. We mean to be perfectly understood on this point, and therefore openly disclaim all steel-traps, all principle, as it is called—all party—all politics. Our only guide shall be good, sound, practical common sense, applicable to the business and bosoms of men engaged in every-day life. We shall support no party—be the organ of no faction or *coterie,* and care nothing for any election or any candidate from President down to a Constable.

We shall endeavor to record facts on every public and proper subject, stripped of verbiage and coloring, with comments when suitable, just, independent, fearless, and good tempered. If the *Herald* wants the mere expansion which many journals possess, we shall try to make it up in industry, good taste, brevity, variety, point, piquancy, and cheapness. It is equally intended for the great masses of the community—the merchant, mechanic, working people—the private family as well as the public hotel—the journeyman and his employer—the clerk and his principal. There are in this city at least 150,000 persons who glance over one or more newspapers every day. Only 42,000 daily sheets are issued to supply them. We have plenty of room, therefore, without jostling neighbors, rivals, or friends, to pick up at least *twenty or thirty thousand* for the *HERALD,* and leave something for others who come after us. By furnishing a daily morning paper at the low price of $3 a year, which may be taken for any shorter period (for a week) at the same rate, and making it at the same time equal to any of the high priced papers for intelligence, good taste, sagacity, and industry, there is not a person in the city, male or female, that may not be able to say, "Well, I have got a paper of my own which will tell me all about what's doing in the world. I'm busy, now,—but I'll put it in my pocket, and read it at my leisure."

With these few words as "grace before meat," we commit ourselves and our cause to the public, with perfect confidence in our own capacity to publish a paper that will seldom pall on the appetite, provided we receive moderate encouragement to unfold our resources and purposes in the columns of the *MORNING HERALD*.

Regular publication did not begin until the eleventh. The publication office was in a basement at No. 20 Wall Street, where the proprietor and editor did pretty much all of the work of writing, reporting, mailing and collecting. To fill the editorial column, cover the police courts, take account of the doings of Wall Street and get all the needed material into the forms, made a long day.

One substantial feature amid all the froth was the *Herald's* "money article," written by Bennett himself. The first appeared on May eleventh. On the twelfth a stock table was appended. It covered a list of thirty-two securities. On June 13, 1835, the money article with its accompanying table became a permanent feature and ever after continued to shed light on Wall Street. For three years Bennett not only wrote the article daily, but gathered the material. After that he took on assistance, but always supervised the copy. Of his early effort, he once wrote:

We went to Wall Street, saw for ourselves what was in progress there, and returned with our report sketched out on fragmentary fly-leaves of letters or other handy scraps of paper. We told the truth for we were in the interest of the public; and the truth of that locality was not complimentary in those days any more than it would be now (1869). War was made upon us right and left by the men whose little games were spoiled whenever the public came to know what they were at; and strangest of all things for a war originating in that quarter of it was a "moral" war. We lived through it however.

The little paper—a small folio—was so individualistic that it at once made headway. Anderson and Smith, however, lost the printing of the *Transcript* and the *Sun* by taking on a rival, the latter setting up a shop of its own. Like the *Sun*, the *Herald* sold for one cent and its revenues were thin. Anderson and Smith repented of their bargain, but Bennett's contract was of the kind that held. The uncomfortable relationship came to an end on August 12, 1835, when a great fire in Ann Street wiped out the printing office.

For eighteen days the *Herald* was out of business, but on the thirty-first of August, like the phœnix bird, it rose from its ashes and never again, under either father or son, failed to appear, gaining in strength and power with amazing robustness. "Company" was dropped and Bennett appeared as sole proprietor. In the revived paper there was a decided change in tone over its earlier numbers. These had been rather sedate, yet newsy. Dignity went to the winds after the fire. The sheet sparkled with "squibs and rockets" as a contemporaneous writer puts it. Bennett flayed the other papers and took special delight in picking on the *Sun*, which, with twenty thousand circulation, had the right of way. Benjamin H. Day, its owner, was deeply annoyed, but never returned the salutes. Webb, of course, came under the fusillade and replied with the heaviest guns in his battery. He and Bennett knew all about each other and both regaled the public with much that was not to the credit of either. That Bennett should reveal the secrets of other sanctums was regarded as treachery in the craft and added to his isolation. If he had a friend anywhere, none was visible to the naked eye. The *Herald's* circulation, however, kept on growing. He was turning on the light where little had shone before, and readers fast found it out. Slow-moving rivals were aghast at his impudence. He wrote up Wall Street swindles pitilessly and made no bones of using names.

The city then possessed fifteen other daily journals, viz: *New York Gazette and General Advertiser, Mercantile Advertiser and New York Advocate, New York Daily Advertiser, Morning Courier and New York Enquirer, New York Journal of Commerce, The New York Times, Business Reporter and Merchants' and Mechanics' Advertiser, New York Commercial Advertiser, The Evening Post, New York American, The Evening Star, The Sun, The Transcript, The Man* and *The Jeffersonian.*

To each of these the newcomer was anathema. That an old hack should show the springiness of a colt and proceed to outstrip them all was unbelievable and intolerable. Bennett did not care. Indeed, he gloried in obloquy. This he received in large quantities. His public was the lower half. The upper regarded him with loathing.

In chronicling his renewal of publication after the fire, Bennett observed:

We are again in the field, larger, livelier, better, prettier, saucier, and more independent than ever. The Ann Street conflagration consumed types, presses, manuscripts, paper, some bad poetry, subscription books—all the outward material appearance of the *Herald,* but its soul was saved—its spirit as exuberant as ever. From the past we augur well for the future. In the first six weeks of its existence, the *Herald* reached nearly the extraordinary circulation of seven thousand per day, and a corresponding amount of advertising patronage. We started then to reach a daily issue of twenty thousand in a period of six or nine months—*we restart now to rise to twenty-five thousand daily circulation before we stop.* This is no astronomical dream—no Herschel discovery in the moon. It can be done, and if industry, attention, resolution, and perseverance can accomplish the feat under the encouraging smiles of a kind public, the *Herald* shall do it. We are organizing on a better footing than formerly—have it entirely under our own control, and have arranged our carriers and routes in such a way that, as we think, a week will make us go like a piece of ingenious clock-work.

In other respects we trust we shall please the public. Avoiding the dirt of party politics, we shall yet freely and candidly express our opinion on every public question and public man. We mean also to procure intelligent correspondents in London, Paris and Washington, and measures are already adopted for that purpose. *In every species of news the Herald will be one of the earliest of the early.* Our Wall Street reports, which were so highly approved by every business man in the city, and copied extensively throughout the country, we shall enlarge and improve to a considerable extent. The former *Herald,* from its large circulation among business people down-town (being larger in that respect than any paper in the city,) had a very rapid increase of advertising patronage. We expect that the renovated *Herald* will far outstrip its predecessor. Our position at 202 Broadway is admirably central—more so than even in Wall Street. Several merchants and auctioneers are preparing to advertise in the *Herald.* They are beginning to find out that a brief advertisement in our sheet is seen and read by six times as many as it would be in the dull prosaics of the *Courier and Enquirer.*

On the whole, and to conclude, as Dogberry did not say, we bid our former kind friends and patrons a hearty, cheerful, and pleasant good morning; and we hope that while we give them a regular call to have a little chat over their coffee and muffins, we may often see them at 202 Broadway when they have any small thing to do, cheap and good, in the advertising line, or any hint or curious piece of information to communicate to the public, barring always discoveries in astronomy, which our friends of the *Sun* monopolize.

This last was a slap at the celebrated "Moon" hoax written by Richard Adams Locke and published in the *Sun.* Bennett had been particularly zealous in exposing what was really a literary masterpiece.

October 7, 1835, he was treated to his first assault when one "Doctor" Townsend whom he had been opposing attacked him in the street. Bennett invited his assailant to Weehawken to fight it out as a gentleman, but the matter went no further—beyond lurid accounts in the local sheets, including the *Herald.*

On October twelfth, he moved his office to 148 Nassau Street. The press-room was in the Theatre Alley. This brought the theater and the *Herald* closer together. He also began taking on help, observing thereon:

Heretofore I have done everything myself. I have written my own police reports, I have written my own Wall Street reports, I have written my own squibs, crackers and *jeu d'esprit,* I have been my own clerk and accountant, posted my own books, made out my own bills and generally attended to all business details in the office.

This did not mean that he was proposing to curtail his energies but intended instead to put more of them into the actual work of making the paper—which he vigorously proceeded to do.

By March 10, 1836, Bennett felt that his success was assured and uttered this exultant cry:

In a city of this kind there is no limit to enterprise, no bounds to the results of industry, capacity, and talent. I began the *Herald* last year without capital and without friends. Every body laughed and jeered at the idea of my succeeding. "Bennett, you are a fool"—"Bennett, you are a blockhead." By effort, economy, and determination I have got a firm footing, mastered all opposition, and begin this day a new movement in newspaper enterprise which will astonish some persons before I shall have completed it. The public are with me. They feel my independence—they acknowledge my honesty—and, better than all, they crowd in their advertisements. Without the aid of $52,725 from any bank, I am now in a position to carry rapidly all my own ideas of newspaper enterprise into effect. I never deal or dealt in stocks—never bought or sold a dollar's worth, although I have studied that science for many years. Hence my Wall Street reports are relied upon, because the public believe I have no private reason to deceive them.

The "$52,725," refers to James Watson Webb's borrowings from Nicholas Biddle's United States Bank.

The *Herald* now increased its size one-third, with

proper pride in its progress. Of its twenty wide columns, fourteen were filled with advertisements, procured by a magic that yet remains undisclosed. They were as a rule more interesting than the news stories.

The paper's great day came April 12, 1836, when it chronicled the murder of Ellen Jewett, a courtesan of extraordinary beauty, in a house kept by Rosina Townsend, in Thomas Street. She had been killed with a hatchet. Her last visitor was a young man named Richard P. Robinson, employed by Joseph Hoxie, a merchant. Robinson's cloak was found on the premises, indicating a hasty escape, but there was no evidence of any sort that he had committed the ghastly deed. Mr. Bennett visited the house and absolved Robinson, expressing the opinion that a woman, presumably jealous, had killed the girl. His rivals all pointed the accusing finger at Robinson, and more than intimated that Bennett's visit to the house was not the first of his calls at places of ill-repute; therefore it "came natural" to him. This thrust he sharply resented, declaring that he had never been inside such a place but once before, and that in Halifax, where the girls drove him out with the remark: "You are too ugly a rascal to come amongst us"—and accusing him of talking too much instead of enjoying their charms. He gave a good account of the murdered girl. She was Dorcas Dorrance of Augusta, Maine, who had lived in Boston as Helen Mar; coming to New York, she was a sensation, often walking in Wall Street, clad in green, holding a letter in her hand like a demure young miss on her way to the post-office. In taking the Robinson side Bennett was also accused of being in the pay of Hoxie, who came to the aid of his employee. Robinson, in the end, was acquitted for lack of evidence and vanished in Texas. The *Sun* went so far as to charge that Bennett had exacted thirteen thousand dollars to suppress the name of a rich man who was in the house the night of the murder. This, of course, was a falsehood.

The immediate effect of the case and controversy was to run the circulation of the *Herald* up from around five thousand per day to fifteen thousand, to the great satisfaction of its owner, who, in announcing the fact remarked: "We are rapidly taking the wind out of the big-bellied sails of the *Courier and Enquirer* and *Journal of Commerce.*" The two named were blanket sheets, the *Herald* despite its enlargement being still a small folio. In the midst of the boom, April 21, 1836, the paper moved from the basement at 148 Nassau Street to the surface in the Clinton Building at the corner of Nassau and Beekman Streets.

Two big signs graced its front. One read: "New York Herald," the other: "James Gordon Bennett." There was nothing modest about either the paper or its proprietor!

The young *Herald* printed no news in the modern sense and published no editorials. Bennett mixed the two in his own brisk way on the front page, either in lengthy text or short pungent paragraphs. This spiced the rather meager record of events revealed in the first year's files. When anything happened involving his brother journalists they received the full benefit of his style—not so much in malice, it would appear, as from the exuberance that comes to writers with full minds and liberty to print. For example, he devoted a column of the six at his disposal to accusing Gerard Hallock, of the *Journal of Commerce*, of being involved in a Connecticut real-estate promotion that did not promise well to investors, boldly proclaiming that he knew the facts himself and that his charges were not based on the testimony of others. Again he devoted two columns to a squabble between Henry William Herbert, famous afterward as "Frank Forester," the sporting writer, and one Tompkins, also a journalist. In concluding the narrative, Bennett rolled up his eyes and observed gravely: "We never engage in brawls." This could only mean that he never started one by personal action. He was in enough of them, as the record shows.

There existed in New York during the 'thirties and 'forties, a "set" of the most exclusive sort, to report whose doings afforded Bennett the keenest delight. The common people to whom he catered were miles below these aristocrats in the social scale, with small hope of ever rising to the exalted level on which Henry Brevoort, Luther Bradish, Philip Hone, Charles Augustus Davis, William B. Astor, William H. Aspinwall, G. G. Howland, S. S. Howland, William and Robert Bayard, J. Prescott Hall, George Curtis (father of George William Curtis),Francis Brockholst Cutting, Robert L. Cutting, Francis Cottenet, and a few more of their kind, maintained their chilly distance. Most of them were merchants. Trade had ceased to be plebeian. Lawyers had no special place, journalists none at all, though James Watson Webb was tolerated. The gentry read the *Courier and Enquirer*. William Leggett had made them chary of the *Evening Post*. Washington Irving was admitted to the circle and General George P. Morris, with his gifted associate, N. P. Willis, were regarded with mild esteem. William Cullen Bryant was a long way from being revered.

The little crowd regarded itself as sacrosanct, and when the *Herald* began its prying and its mocking reports of their doings, their indignation knew no bounds. Some choice samples of this feeling are found in the diary of Philip Hone, who, grown rich as an auctioneer of foreign cargoes, was for seven years mayor of the growing town and a social monitor. He spit like a scared cat at all innovations. Soon after the advent of the *Herald,* we find in his diary, under date of January 20, 1836, this notation:*

There is an ill-looking, squinting man called Bennett, formerly connected with Webb in the publication of his paper, who is now the editor of the *Herald,* one of the penny papers which are hawked about the streets by a gang of troublesome, ragged boys, and in which scandal is retailed to all who delight in it, at that moderate price. This man and Webb are now bitter enemies, and it was nuts for Bennett to be the organ of Mr. Lynch's late vituperative attack upon Webb, which Bennett introduced in his paper with evident marks of savage exultation. This did not suit Mr. Webb's fiery disposition, so he attacked Bennett in Wall Street yesterday, beat him, and knocked him down.

The Lynch in question was Henry Lynch, who had used the *Herald* as a medium for reflecting on Webb's touting specialties in the stock market, with a plain intimation that he was paid for rigging it. Bennett followed it up with a malicious editorial, in which he smacked his lips over the aspersions on Webb, who met

*From *The Diary of Philip Hone, 1828-1851.* Courtesy of Dodd, Mead and Company.

him the next day in Wall Street, and not only knocked him down, as Hone records, but beat him with a cane.

Bennett gave an account of the affair in the *Herald,* with an apology to his "kind readers" for the "want of my usual life to-day." It had been pretty well beaten out of him. He added, in an effort to make the most of the assault, that Webb, "by going up behind me, cut a slash in my head about one and a half inches in length, and through the integuments of the skull. The fellow, no doubt, wanted to let out the never-failing supply of good humor and wit, which has created such a reputation for the *Herald,* and appropriate the contents to supply the emptiness of his own thick skull. He did not succeed, however, in rifling me of my ideas. . . . He has not injured the skull. My ideas, in a few days, will flow as freshly as ever, and he will find it so to his cost."

"In the mean time," according to Hone, "Webb and Lynch maintain a relative position, something like that of France and the United States. They carry clubs, but do not strike. They can not adjust their pecuniary differences in an *honourable* manner, for each considers the other unworthy of his notice. None but men of acknowledged honour and good character are entitled to the privilege of having their brains blown out. If Lynch and Webb are both men of truth they are liars, and if neither is to be believed they are both honourable men."

The sneer at Mr. Bennett's "squinting" eyes was warranted. He did squint sorely, as the result of much misuse of his eyes during his days as reporter, correspondent and editor, when he strained his optical muscles by working under miserable artificial lighting.

Mr. Bennett, by the way, met the charge of being squint-eyed by thanking Heaven that he was not like many of his antagonists, "squint-hearted." At this period in his career he took pride in admitting the charge that he was much like John Wilkes, who had a similar defect. The resemblance extended to his purposes.

The difficulty with Webb began with the establishment of the *Herald*. The valiant Colonel was well aware of the quality of his former associate, and as the *Herald* was "personal" from the start, he knew he was in for it. Instead of going at the matter diplomatically, the Colonel met Bennett on the steps of the Astor House, on July 3, 1835, and warned him to take no liberties with the majestic name of Webb, making sundry threats as to what would follow if his demand was disregarded. The next day Bennett responded with a Declaration of Independence, stating that he would never again communicate with his old associate or regard him in any way, and would not "sacrifice the honest independence of the *Herald* to private solicitude or private friendship." Editorially, he declared, in continuing the controversy: "I shall never give up my rights. I will never give up my independence." He continued to assail Webb unmercifully as the crooked tout for Wall Street. In extenuation of his course toward Webb he wrote:

When I was associated with Mr. Noah, I was the first person who gave Webb the idea of uniting the *Courier* and *Enquirer*, and creating a newspaper that would take the lead of every other in the city. Not in possession of capital myself, and believing that his family connexions would supply the deficiency, he proceeded on the intimation I gave him, and purchased and united the two journals in question. I then became associated with him as an Editor, and he frequently solicited me to buy an interest. I soon found, however, that from his habits, education, temper, and talents, he was utterly unfit to have control of a newspaper, and that sooner or later he would disgrace the press and destroy his own reputation. Yet, having early imbibed a feeling favorable to the man, I continued for several years to treat his errors with great delicacy, but equal frankness. Possessing personal industry and indefatigability, with some talent, for which I am thankful to God Almighty, no one in the city can say aught against my private character. I can venture to say, that in all the relations of life, it is without a stain. The benefit of this indefatigability was entirely directed to advance the interests of Webb for nearly three years. To me he is principally indebted for the success and establishment of his paper. I can prove it by documents in my possession. Enjoying for many years a friendly correspondence with several of the most distinguished men in the country, among whom were Martin Van Buren, Vice-President, and Nicholas Biddle, President of the United States Bank, my endeavors during my connexion with Webb were to benefit his establishment as far as in my power, without compromising honor, reputation, and the decencies of life.

Naturally, this and much like it, did not soothe the doughty Colonel, and the war went bravely on. On May 9, 1836, Webb again assaulted Bennett. This is the latter's account of the affair:

As I was leisurely pursuing my business, yesterday, in Wall Street, collecting the information which is daily disseminated in the *Herald,* James Watson Webb came up to me, on the northern side of the street—said something which I could not hear distinctly, then pushed me down the stone steps, leading to one of the broker's offices, and commenced fighting with a species of brutal and demoniac desperation characteristic of a fury.

My damage is a scratch, about three quarters of an inch in length, on the third finger of the left hand, which I received from the iron railing I was forced against, and three buttons torn from my vest, which any tailor will reinstate for a sixpence. His loss is a rent from top to bottom of a very beautiful black coat, which cost the ruffian $40, and a blow in the face, which may have knocked down his throat some of his infernal teeth for anything I know. Balance in my favor $39.94.

As to intimidating me, or changing my course, the thing can not be done. Neither Webb nor any other man shall, or can, intimidate me. I tell the honest truth in my paper, and leave the consequences to God. Could I leave them in better hands? I may be attacked, I may be assailed, I may be killed, I may be murdered, but I never will succumb. I never will abandon the cause of truth, morals, and virtue.

Bennett's readers, though numerous, and growing, were too humble to come to his public support in the hostile situation created by his efforts to amuse, interest and inform them. The other papers, jealous of his success, united in howls of execration, to which he replied in kind, while the aristocratic element, which included the courts, regarded him with extreme reprehension. He was a vulgar disturbing personage, an enemy of the social order they had so strongly established, and no good came from him.

Quite conscious of this atmosphere, Bennett followed his story of Webb's assault with this comment concerning his antagonists:

Brute force, barbarian comment, and miserable trick and juggle are the only weapons they employ. The *Herald* is producing and will produce, as complete a revolution in the intellectual habit of daily life as steam-power is doing in the material. If a splendid fortune is the result to myself, that may be a matter of complacency, but is a matter of course. Like General Jackson, looking at the Presidency—"I neither seek, nor refuse it." If it comes, it comes, like an old boot, on the right leg, easily, quietly, smoothly, and perfectly satisfactory to all concerned.

These confessions of personal feeling were common with the hard-grained Scotchman, now past forty—and single. He excused himself for the latter failing, to his female readers, who made up the majority, in these terms: "Amid all these thronging ideas hurrying across the mind, crowds of feelings fresh from the heart, and projects of the fancy, stealing on the heads of each other, as if by enchantment, there is one drawback, there is one sin, there is one piece of wickedness of which I am guilty, and with which my conscience is weighed down night and day. I am a bachelor. I am unmarried, and, what is worse, I am so busy that I have no time to get a wife, although I am passionately fond of female society. For this great sin I have no apology to make. I can only throw myself, heart, soul, feelings, and all, upon the compassion—the heavenly compassion of my enchanting and beautiful female readers. I know well it is my duty to get married and obey the laws of God and nature, but formerly to me the female sex appeared all so beautiful, all so enchanting, all so fascinating, that I became entirely bewildered and confused, and now I am so much engaged in building up the *Herald*, and reforming the age, that actually I have scarcely the time to say, 'How do ye do?' "

The challenges of his contemporaries impelled him to make a sort of declaration of purpose. This was it:

> I mean to make the *Herald* the great organ of social life, the prime element of civilization, the channel through which native talent, native genius, and native power may bubble up daily, as the pure, sparkling liquid of the Congress fountain at Saratoga bubbles up from the center of the earth, till it meets the rosy lips of the fair. I shall mix together commerce and business, pure religion and morals, literature and poetry, the drama and dramatic purity, till the *Herald* shall outstrip everything in the conception of man. The age of trashy novels, of more trashy poems, of most trashy quarterly and weekly literature, is rapidly drawing to a close.
>
> This is the age of the Daily Press, inspired with the accumulated wisdom of past ages, enriched with the spoils of history, and looking forward to a millennium of a thousand years, and happiest and most splendid ever yet known in the space of eternity!

The *Herald* had now reached a point where its circulation was so large as to be a tax at one cent. It was accordingly doubled in price, August 17, 1836, without checking its growth a particle. Mr. Bennett proclaimed the move in this comprehensive table:

Daily circulation of the Herald	20,000
Receipts per day at one cent, 33 per cent off,	$133.34
Receipts per day at two cents, 25 per cent off,	$300.00
Difference in my favor per day	$166.66
Difference, clear, a week	$999.96

"With this sum," he commented, "I shall be enabled to carry into effect prodigious improvements, and to make the *Herald* the greatest, best and most profitable paper that ever appeared in this country."

He did all he promised. A weekly was also established, but that never throve. It could only summarize, and a *Herald* without spice was not inviting. To mar his complacency he now had to endure another physical assault, one that would appear to have been quite deserved. Thomas S. Hamblin, manager of the celebrated Bowery Theater, fell out with his wife and in the legal cases that resulted, the *Herald* took strong sides with the lady. This was going far enough, it would appear, but when the theater burned the *Herald* fought a proposition to accord the manager a public benefit. As a result the benefit failed to produce. Hamblin, a man of muscle, fired with an "undue sense of right," as Whistler once expressed the feeling, after a convivial party held at the quarters of Jared W. Bell, publisher of the *New Era,* decided to castigate the abusive editor. Accordingly, with a few companions, well lit up, he invaded the *Herald* office and began an affray that was ended by the arrival of the police. In the mêlée the cash drawer was robbed of three hundred dollars. Much turmoil followed in the press and consequent legal proceedings, which ended in Hamblin's conviction for assault. He was let off on the payment of costs.

Besides the occasional beatings at the hands of James Watson Webb, A. A. Clason, of Clason & Paine, 31 Wall Street, brokers, favored him with a horsewhipping. The whip broke at the first blow, and fell from his hand. Then Bennett picked up the

Cartoon in *Vanity Fair,* November 3, 1860

useless weapon and politely handed it to Clason, who made no further use of it. He had been angered by some pointed allusions to his firm in a news article.

It will be perceived that politics had no part in Bennett's program. He was intent upon social reform, not the least of which was breaking the strange bonds of prudery in which the country was at this time enthralled, plus the force of arms carried by individuals who walked about with chips labeled "honor," on their shoulders.

Civilization, [wrote the editor,] is yet defaced with traits of barbarism. We are only half civilized. In our most polished communities, solitary outrages spring up that are a disgrace to the age—more the inroads of the desert than the manners of a civilized country. We have plenty of laws, but they are powerless and weak. The radical defect is in our social system. Moral courage is unknown and brutal outrage encouraged. Virtue is driven from society, and vice impudently occupies the seats of honor and of power. This state of public opinion and of social manners must be reformed. Honor and reputation must only be associated with virtue, truth, order and cultivated mind. Now is the period to begin this great reform, and we are one of those cool, courageous spirits that will aid and assist it forward.

Such sentiments seem out of place in a scandalmonger, as he was openly regarded—and there was ample basis for the belief. But much must be allowed for what was rated scandal. It was not considered proper for newspapers to report certain obviously public affairs. One of the *Herald's* great offenses was printing the list of bankrupts, all too lengthy, in

1837. An error made by a reporter in naming one John Haggerty in a list of insolvents cost Bennett a fine of five hundred dollars, in September of that year. He paid the sum at once. But his cause was growing, and admirers among the expanding throng of *Herald* followers raised a like sum by subscription, and repaid the editor, with whom cash was as yet none too plentiful. He had corrected the error in the very next issue, but the court made an example of him in the alleged interest of accuracy. The real reason was resentment over the publication of matters coming under the law.

It was also considered outrageous to publish accounts of public dinners. The meticulous Hone made this entry in his diary, December 5, 1837:

A Mr. Price, sub-editor (as I am informed) of a scurrilous paper published in this city called the *Herald,* has addressed me a letter as chairman of the committee of arrangements for the Bell dinner, to know whether Charles King was authorized to forbid him to take notes of the speeches at the dinner, on which subject a correspondence has taken place between him and Mr. King. The gentleman is *bien enragé.* He says he bought his ticket like other people, and had a right like other people to take notes or anything else he pleased. King, who, I presume, thought he had no right to take anything but his dinner, would not allow him to proceed, and, being of the Hotspur breed, very probably showed him the door, and the man lost his ten dollars and his dinner in the bargain. For this he called King to account, and, his explanation not being altogether satisfactory, I was appealed to by the aggrieved party. In my reply I state that "the practice of reporting in the public prints the doings and the sayings of our convivial meetings without the consent, and frequently to the annoyance, of the parties who are thus unwillingly brought before the public, a practice so entirely repugnant to the feelings of our citizens, is happily confined as yet to so inconsiderable a portion of the press that it did not, I presume, occur to the committee to take any measures in advance to prevent it; but that I was of the opinion that Mr. King was authorized, by the express sentiments of the gentlemen forming the committee, to oppose the introduction of reporters for that object." This brought a rejoinder, and then the matter ended between Mr. Price and me; but the *Herald* will make two or three columns of the affair to dish up to his customers who like high-seasoned dishes.

April 23, 1838, the *Sirius* and *Great Western,* rival British vessels, came into New York harbor under steam—the greatest event in the history of world transportation. The arrival of the steamships was hailed by Bennett in these exalted terms:

The advantages will be incalculable; no more petty rivalries, or national antipathies; no odious misconstructions and paltry jealousies, but a mutual love and respect growing out of an accurate knowledge of one another's good qualities, and a generous emulation in the onward march of mind, genius, enterprise, and energy, towards the perfectibility of men, and the amelioration of our physical, social, moral, and commercial condition. Such are among the prominent features of the bright and exhilarating vision brought into birth by this most auspicious event, and by which the minds of our fellow citizens have been so excited. They are founded in fact, and have nothing Eutopian about them, and are as deducible from positive data, as any demonstration in the Novum Organum, or any solution in the Mecanique Celeste. In the popular style of encouragement, and in one very appropriate to the subject we most emphatically say, Go ahead!

Bennett thus saw in the coming of the steamships a new era in world relationship, and an end to the need of maintaining newspaper navies, since "the smallest newspaper can (now) have the news as soon as the largest."

He tried to stir New York investors into seizing the new form of enterprise by making it their own, but, content with supremacy by sail and contemptuous of steam, England was allowed to capture a lead which she has ever since maintained.

Determined to test out the new method of transit, and having for the first time enough money and leisure to afford visiting his native land, Bennett booked himself on the return voyage of the *Sirius*, for a well-earned vacation. He had written within the three previous years more than five thousand octavo pages of all sorts of matter ranging from editorials to fiction, and he felt the need of rest. Like the prudent Scotchman he was, he auctioned off most of his personal property before he left New York, and provided the *Herald* with a good bank-account against accidents to its owner. The ship sailed, May 1, 1837, for Falmouth. In spite of steam the trip covered eighteen days.

Bennett witnessed the coronation of Queen Victoria, made himself at home among the London journalists and, after a stay with his Scotch relatives, journeyed about Great Britain, and visited the Continent, returning September twentieth, on the *Royal William*, a new steamship that had joined the fast growing competition.

Back at home he put the fruits of his travels into

the *Herald*, through the establishment of six correspondents in Europe, besides men in Texas, Mexico, Canada and the larger cities of the United States. The celebrated Doctor Dionysius Lardner became for a time head of the Paris bureau. Early in 1839 Bennett made a tour through the South, both to get acquainted and improve his news service. This had to be a matter of mail and meant "letters" covering all sorts of things.

The outbreak of the Canadian rebellion, led by William Lyon Mackenzie in 1837, excited considerable sympathy in the United States. Bennett opposed this sentiment. When, in 1838, Mackenzie took refuge in the United States, he avenged himself by printing in a pamphlet defending his cause several letters written by the editor when in charge of the *Pennsylvanian*. Mackenzie's purpose was to "show up" the proprietor of the *Herald*. The blast was, however, without much effect, though it served to give his esteemed contemporaries another chance to throw bricks.

In fulfillment of his promise to make use of his increased revenues for improving the paper Bennett had, in 1837, organized a ship news service that was to become and remain the pillar of its prosperity. Smart sailing craft were secured, which cruised beyond Montauk Point to pick up incoming tidings from Europe, and give the arrival of vessels. The Sandy Hook pilots were also enlisted, with results that threw all rivals into the shade. The Long Island railroad had been completed and messengers were always awaiting news from the sea at the far end of Paumanok, whence they hurried to New York by rail.

Three sharp sailboats, the *Teaser*, the *Tom Boxer* and the *Celeste* composed the *Herald's* fleet. Proof-slips were sent to other newspapers throughout the country by express mail. These reciprocated in kind, to the *Herald's* great advantage, thus beginning what was finally to develop into the Associated Press. The steamships shortened the time across the Atlantic and ran on schedules, vastly increasing the freshness and quality of news from overseas. They produced rivalry and cut out the Montauk terminal, making Sandy Hook the center. Then it was that faster light craft became engaged to pick up mail and intelligence at Quarantine and hurry it up to the city. The *Herald* had the smartest boat, as usual, the *Fanny Elssler*, named after the liveliest dancer of the day. One of Bennett's "brags" is worth repeating:

> The way in which we walk into the whole combined Press of New York, in newspaper enterprise and energy, is, as they say in the West, "a caution." We will here describe our last effort—that of the arrival of the *British Queen*, as performed by our beautiful boat, the *Fanny Elssler*, on Saturday morning.
>
> On Friday night last, at 12, Commodore Martin, our high admiral, was quietly asleep on a delicious hard board, in the log cabin or boat-house of Dr. Doane, at the Quarantine Ground, Staten Island. On each side of him were his men, also in the same state of tranquility. At the wharf, under the window, lay our beautiful new boat, called the *Fanny Elssler*—cool and quiet, yet trembling on the top of the moonlit waves like a bird ready to shoot into the eternal blue of the heavens at a moment.
>
> They were waiting for the arrival of the *British Queen*, momentarily expected.
>
> On a sudden, at half past 12, the voice of a big gun

was heard booming up the harbor like the voice of distant thunder. The cry was raised outside the log cabin, "The *Queen* is coming," "The *Queen* is coming." Martin—half asleep, half dreaming—was on his feet in an instant; rubbing his eyes and clapping his hat on his head, he looked down the harbor towards the Narrows. A big bright blue light went up to heaven and almost dazzled the brilliant moon. "Rouse, boys, rouse! The *Queen* is coming; there's her blue light."

In another moment, Martin, with his two men, were in the *Fanny Elssler*—sail set, oars splashing, and dashing over the bright wave down to the Narrows. The moonlight was most brilliant, and the shores of Staten and Long Islands were almost as bright as day. As the lovely *Fanny* skimmed like a swan over the silvery wave, another boat, clumsy and heavy, like a tub, came sneaking and swearing after her. It was the news-boat of the Wall Street Press, called the *Dot-and-go-one*.

The beautiful *Fanny* kept her watery way, and in ten minutes' time was, as a certain prince now is, under the lee of the magnificent *British Queen*.

"Steam ship ahoy!" cried Martin.

"Ay, ay," responded the gallant Captain Roberts.

"The *Fanny Elssler*," roared Martin.

"The what?"

"The *Herald*," responded Martin.

"Oh—stop her," cried Captain Roberts to his engineer. "Throw him a line."

Martin clinched the line, and in an instant was on the deck of the *Queen*.

"Martin, is that you?" said Captain Roberts. "How in the devil do you always beat?"

"By working harder than my competitors—the way you beat, captain. Where's your private bag?"

"Here are your papers," replied the captain.

By this time the news-boat of the Wall Street Press, *Dot-and-go-one*, came alongside, after a great deal of puffing and blowing. In a few minutes the steamer was at the Quarantine Ground. Here she stopped for the physician. Martin, with the private bag for the consignees, jumped aboard the *Fanny Elssler,* and started for the city, *Dot-and-go-one* having started a little ahead; but it was no go.

"Rouse up, *Fanny,*" cried Martin, coaxing his boat—"courage, *Fanny*—stir up, my angel of a skiff!"

In a few minutes *Fanny,* skimming over the bright blue waters, and seeming to feel the words of her commander, passed *Dot-and-go-one* almost without an effort, and with a sort of gentle smile on the figure-head which adorns her prow.

Martin whistled and gayly cheered his lovely skiff—"Skim along, *Fanny*—skim along, my lovely angel! Don't you see the big bright moon and the seven stars looking down upon you, and betting a thousand acres of the blue heaven that you will beat? Skim along, *Fanny*—skim along, love!"

Fanny did skim along. She shot past the Wall Street tub, and reached Whitehall at half past two o'clock on Saturday morning.

Martin jumped ashore, rushed up Broadway, down to 21 Ann Street, and found the lights burning brightly at the *Herald* office. In five minutes all the editors writers, printers, pressmen were in motion. The immense daily edition of the *Herald* was about one fourth worked off when the news arrived. The press was stopped—the announcement made: this was the second edition. In two hours it was stopped again, and three columns of news put in and sent by the various mails: this was the third edition. In another two hours six columns were put in: this was the fourth edition—also sent by the mails. By this means we sent the news all over the country—New England, Canada, the South and West, one day in advance of every other paper in New York.

This is the way in which we are producing a revolution in the New York Press. The *Fanny Elssler* is

Whitehall at sunrise any morning, or to the Park this
a beauty of a skiff. If you want to see her, go to
evening.

In January, 1839, returning from his southern trip, the editor stayed some time in Washington, where he interviewed his quondam idol, President Van Buren, and wrote fifty-six letters to the *Herald*. In the summer Van Buren made a tour of the North. Bennett followed suit and the *Herald* teemed with his stories. He paused longest at Saratoga, to produce the following amiable comment from Philip Hone, who was also a visitor at a time when President Van Buren was enjoying his vacation at the Spa:

The President takes the head of one of the tables and the modest Bennett of the *Herald,* the other. The President cannot help this, to be sure, and the juxtaposition is somewhat awkward. Bennett will make a great thing of this with those who are not aware that any person may take this seat who has impudence enough, and that it would require a pretty smart rifle to carry a ball from one end of the table to another. I wish the President would leave his seat and give the *Herald* man all the honors of the table.

Bennett declined to wilt under the shadow of social scorn. Besides the President, General Winfield Scott and Henry Clay were amid the throng of notables. During the two weeks of his stay, the editor wrote fourteen short and amusing letters from the Spa, giving in none of them any clue to his political purposes, which the politicians were keen to learn. He next toured New England and the letters flowed from his pen, adding zest to the *Herald's* columns.

The United States Bank and the banks of Philadelphia had suspended specie payments in August, 1839. Bennett went after them, being familiar with the queer town, which has never changed its habits, and brought on his head a shower of attacks, to which were added those of his neighbors in New York.

In addition to intruding into the sacred precincts of finance, the best society and the courts, the *Herald* made the first use of illustrations in the daily press. There were no fast methods of pictorial reproductions. The camera had not been invented and pictures had to be hand drawn and wood engraved. The earliest example was a diagram of the burned district after the great fire of 1835. In the same year a picture of the Merchants Exchange, later the Custom House, and now the National City Bank, on Wall Street, was published. Bennett invented the "war map" by reproducing the geography of Grand Island in the Niagara River during the Canadian revolt of 1837. The paper also gave depictions of scenes at the polls and in Wall Street in 1838.

The sublime social event of the era was the great costume ball given by Mr. and Mrs. Henry Brevoort, the leaders of the aristocracy. It could hardly keep out of the newspapers, and such progress had the *Herald* made that the Brevoorts actually connived at having the event described in its columns. Let Philip Hone reveal both the glory and melancholy of the event. He writes, February 25, 1840:

There is little dependence upon newspapers in a record of facts, any more than in their political dogmas or confessions of faith. If they do not lie from dishonest motives, their avidity to have something new and in advance of others leads them to take up everything that comes to hand without proper examination, adopting frequently the slightly grounded impressions of their informers for grave truths, setting upon them the stamp of authenticity, and sending them upon the wings of the wind to fill the ears and eyes of the extensive American family of the *gullibles*.

The great affair which has occupied the minds of the people of all stations, ranks, and employments, from the fashionable belle who prepared for conquest, to the humble *artiste* who made honestly a few welcome dollars in providing the weapons; from the liberal-minded gentleman who could discover no crime in an innocent and refined amusement of this kind, to the newspaper reformer, striving to sow the seeds of discontentment in an unruly population,—this long anticipated affair came off last evening, and I believe the expectations of all were realized. The mansion of our entertainers, Mr. and Mrs. Brevoort, is better calculated for such a display than any other in the city, and everything which host and hostess could do in preparing and arranging, in receiving their guests, and making them feel a full warrant and assurance of welcome, was done to the topmost round of elegant hospitality. Mrs. B., in particular, by her kind and courteous deportment, threw a charm over the splendid pageant which would have been incomplete without it.

My family contributed a large number of actors in the gay scene. I went as Cardinal Wolsey, in a grand robe of new scarlet merino, with an exceedingly well-contrived cap of the same material; a cape of real ermine, which I borrowed from Mrs. Thomas W. Ludlow, gold chain and cross, scarlet stockings, etc.; Mary and Catherine, as Night and Day; Margaret, Annot Lyle in the "Legend of Montrose;" John, as Washington Irving's royal poet; Schermerhorn, as Gessler, the Austrian governor who helped to make

William Tell immortal; Robert, a highlander; and our sweet neighbour, Eliza Russell, as Lalla Rookh.

We had a great preparatory gathering of friends to see our dresses and those of several others, who took us "in their way up." I am not quite sure whether the pleasantest part of such an affair does not consist in "the note of preparation," the contriving and fixing, exulting and doubting, boasting and fretting, and fussing and scolding, which are played off in advance of the great occasion; and perhaps, after all is over, the greatest doubt is *"si le jeu vaut la chandelle."* And if ever that question is tested, it must be by this experiment, for never before has New York witnessed a fancy ball so splendidly gotten up, in better taste, or more successfully carried through. We went at ten o'clock, at which time the numerous apartments, brilliantly lighted, were tolerably well filled with characters. The notice on the cards of invitation, "*Costume à la rigueur,*" had virtually closed the door to all others, and with the exception of some eight or ten gentlemen who, in plain dress, with a red ribbon at the button-hole, officiated as managers, every one appeared as some one else; the dresses being generally new, some of them superbly ornamented with gold, silver, and jewelry; others marked by classical elegance, or appropriately designating distinguished characters of ancient and modern history and the drama; and others again most familiarly grotesque and ridiculous. The *coup d'œil* dazzled the eyes and bewildered the imagination.

Soon after our party arrived the five rooms on the first floor (including the library) were completely filled. I should think there were about five hundred ladies and gentlemen; many a beautiful "point device," which had cost the fair or gallant wearer infinite pains in the selection and adaptation, was doomed to pass unnoticed in the crowd; and many who went there hoping each to be the star of the evening, found themselves eclipsed by some superior luminary, or

Cartoon in *Vanity Fair*, December 15, 1860

at best forming a unit in the milky way. Some surprise was expressed at seeing in the crowd a man in the habit of a knight in armour,—a Mr. Attree, reporter and one of the editors of an infamous penny paper called the *Herald*. Bennett, the principal editor, called upon Mr. Brevoort to obtain permission for this person to be present to report in his paper an account of the ball. He consented, as I believe I should have done under the same circumstances, as by doing so a sort of obligation was imposed upon him to refrain from abusing the house, the people of the house, and their guests, which would have been done in case of a denial. But this is a hard alternative; to submit to this kind of surveillance is getting to be intolerable, and nothing but the force of public opinion will correct the insolence, which, it is to be feared, will never be applied as long as Mr. Charles A. Davis and other gentlemen make this Mr. Attree "hail fellow, well met," as they did on this occasion. Whether the notice they took of him, and that which they extend to Bennett when he shows his ugly face in Wall street, may be considered approbatory of the daily slanders and unblushing impudence of the paper they conduct, or is intended to purchase their forbearance toward themselves, the effect is equally mischievous. It affords them countenance and encouragement, and they find that the more personalities they have in their papers, the more papers they sell.

"Attree" was William H. Attree, who, from being a compositor in the Connor type foundry, had become a police reporter on the *Transcript* some years before, at the wage of three dollars per week. He had got up in the world of reporting from that low station to wearing a tin suit at the Brevoort ball!

As the first American editor who refused to be a statesman or a party hack, Bennett was, of course, both a novelty and an offense. The function of the newspaper had been partisan; news was secondary. Party support was the vital necessity for its existence, the sole excuse for its being. That any one should stoop to sell news and gossip was considered bemeaning, if not rascally. The shrewd Scotchman had, however, sensed a public need. When one looks back at the files, when the importance of the items have faded, it is as difficult to discern what all the row was about as it is to find in the New York *World* of 1883-1888 the reasons that called anathema down upon the head of Joseph Pulitzer when he came bounding into New York from the breezy West.

Printed in fine type, without special display or headline, the items could only have offended from the liberty they took in telling what was going on. When Bennett wrote mockingly of social functions, to amuse his readers, and slyly to make fun of caste, he cut deeply. The reaction was that people thought he was angered because he was not invited. People then felt their importance was enhanced by exclusiveness, where now they bask in publicity and support numerous press agents and clipping bureaus in their desire to know how far the trumpet has sent their fame—an extraordinary change that leaves one uncertain as to its merits beyond the unquestioned extinguishment of aristocracy by publicity.

One of the queerest kick-ups of the period developed when the *Herald* began printing religious news in 1839, covering the proceedings of church conferences and like uplifting affairs. Instead of welcoming the publicity, the clergy and the religious press treated it as sacrilege. Pastors denounced the infamous proceedings from their pulpits, and a pretty howdy-do resulted. Unabashed, the *Herald* continued to return good for evil and later began the custom of reporting popular sermons. This practise led to the establishment of a paid classification of religious notices that grew into a profitable feature, so much so that for many years it served as a real church directory.

Bennett kept his good humor as a stock in trade and was a laughing Ishmael. That rich monetary reward came to him was, of course, highly satisfactory. He knew what it was to be poor until pass forty, and so luxury made no appeal. That became the specialty of his son. Plus his good humor he had a mind so well balanced that it would tip either way and still preserve its equilibrium. Most men playing with great power are apt to misuse it and be struck down by the recoil. Bennett never suffered this to happen. If he was called unprincipled his answer was that he was not following principles but events, as he was there to report, not to reshape or divert. The *Herald* did not thunder. Indeed, it had policy like quicksilver that picked up solids and liquified them as it flowed brightly on. He could be serious enough upon occasion, but not at the expense of being consistent. Yet he was not one to act on expediency any more than on impulse. He wanted to interest his public and did a good deal to inform them. With all its silly writing the *Herald* had pages of the dullest facts in its columns, like the news of ships and stocks. Economic questions required large space; nor were art and letters neglected. The thing he played fast and loose with was the news of the day. Here he showed the temperament of a chattering blue-jay to the last. He loved to splash passers-by but the water was not muddied with seriousness; the drops sparkled that fell. If the *Herald* reveled in scandal so did its public. It never printed anything worse than some human being did. This is not said defensively, but descriptively. Bennett aimed to make the *Herald* a mirror, but crinkled the mercury on the back of the glass.

The editor accepted his place as outcast with the utmost composure. Indeed, his attitude was something like that of an Indian pariah, interviewed by Charles Godfrey Leland, who expected to find the low caste personage depressed by his lack of social position. On the contrary he was quite cheerful, and, being asked the reason therefor, said he represented the protest against too much piety and goodness in the world. This was just about the position taken by James Gordon Bennett.

CHAPTER III

THE MORAL WAR

In five years, by defiance of convention, writing down to the level of common thought, the *Herald* had outstripped all its rivals and put half a dozen of the weaker ones under its feet. It had outraged every feeling possessed by the elect and shocked the prudish beyond measure. It had printed all the news that was fit to print, and a great deal besides. Prudery and the press, therefore, in May, 1840, united in a combined attack on the *Herald*, extraordinary in its violence and more unseemly in method than anything the *Herald* had ever employed.

Judged by the tyrannical social standards of the day, Bennett had been a great offender. This was a deliberate policy. The editor was a man of sense and spirit, kept apart from his fellows by his occupation. He saw human foibles with clear eyes and undertook a venturesome enterprise, that of knocking nonsense out of the human mind. He saw creeping over the country a reign of formality and custom far more despotic than anything that could be devised politically. Against this he set his lance. He knew that Eastern countries like India and China had been reduced to subjugation by caste and formalism, and had observed the severe effects of the latter on Scotland.

To the present-day reader it may seem absurd that

a young woman should swoon at the word "pants," but the affected damsels of that period could and did. Bennett began his crusade to bring "pants," "legs" and "arms," to say nothing of more hidden items of the human structure, into plain speech. He did it with elaborate mockery of such extreme sensibility, which now seems silly, but was then of sufficient import as to bring blushes and burning ears where downright unconsciousness did not follow. Indeed, it was the era of smelling salts, prettily bottled, which every female carried to restore her nerves when they failed at the mention of a forbidden word by some unheeding vulgarian.

To restore sanity of speech the *Herald* improved upon the cult of the period. It turned arms and legs into "branches" of the divinely created body. "Linen" had become the synonym for shirts, and "inexpressibles" for trousers, while as for petticoats, these chaste coverings could not be mentioned at all.

The editor rubbed in offending words: "Petticoats—petticoats—petticoats—petticoats—there—you fastidious fools, vent your mawkishness on that."

This they proceeded to do. The newspapers of New York, regardless of party or principles, arrayed themselves for a combined assault designed to demolish the impertinent intruder. The prudish and "society" joined hands and the crusade found followers among press and people in Boston, Philadelphia and Baltimore, with small dogs barking in between. Park Benjamin first opened fire in the New York *Evening Signal* of which he was editor. The *Courier and Enquirer* followed with ponderous broadsides. The *Evening Star*, edited by Mordecai M. Noah sent up rockets. David Hale, the pious publisher of the *Journal of Commerce,* echoed James Watson Webb. The *Express, Sun, News* and *Mercury* rat-tatted with adjectives. Bennett, instead of sending solid shot in response, rattled peas in a bladder. He "joshed" his antagonists in a style that can be afforded by victors and laughed his antagonists into dismay.

Had the assault been confined to the columns of rival newspapers the situation could soon have become comic. It went much further, however, and developed into a personal campaign against the editor. Committees were organized to boycott both the *Herald* and its owner. The word had not yet been invented, but the practise was not new. Bodies of self-constituted vigilantes went about the city making demands on advertisers to forsake the *Herald's* columns or suffer in consequence. Men of standing in church and trade united in the effort to efface the effulgent journal. The city was in turmoil and the excitement spread over the eastern part of the nation. Philip Hone took deep delight in the outbreak, recording on June 2, 1840:

The career of the infamous editor of the *Herald* seems at last to have met with a check, which his unblushing impudence will find some difficulty in recovering from. Some of his late remarks have been so profane and scandalous as to have drawn out the editors from the contemptuous silence which they have hitherto observed toward the scoundrel. In one of his late attacks upon the editors of the *Evening Signal* and another paper, in alluding to some personal deformity in each of them, he uses the shocking expression that they are "cursed by the Almighty."

The evil has reached a pitch of enormity which renders further forbearance criminal, and a simultaneous attack is made upon the libellous paper, its editor, and those who, from fear or a fellow-feeling, support it. The *Evening Star* has several excellent articles on this loathsome subject. Bennett is absolutely excoriated by the *Signal,* and all the other papers, without regard to party, have joined the righteous crusade. This is the only thing to be done; the punishment of the law adds to the fellow's notoriety, and personal chastisement is pollution to him who undertakes it. Write him down, make respectable people withdraw their support from the vile sheet, so that it shall be considered disgraceful to read it, and the serpent will be rendered harmless; and this effect is likely to be produced by the united efforts of the respectable part of the public press.

An exposé of the inside crookedness of the Philadelphia banks which had suspended payment, made early in 1840, added the power of the Pennsylvania press to the anti-Bennett fusillade. He was charged with hostility to the city and the state because of his failure to succeed with the *Pennsylvanian.* His answer was that he was hostile only to dishonesty and fraud whether generated in New York or Philadelphia, and was always "first to sound the alarm of bank mismanagement" for which "watchfulness and industry in the cause of public morals we have received a support and a patronage unparalleled in the annals of the New York press."

On June third, at the end of the first month of the "war," Mr. Bennett summed up the results in this fashion:

THE FORCE IN THE FIELD

It may be interesting to many of our readers to know the exact circulation of the press, as compared with our own, which the Wall Street Holy Allies bring into the field to put down the *Herald.* We shall here state them from undoubted data in our possession:

The Holy Allies		The Herald	
Name	*Circulation*		*Circulation*
Evening Star.........	2,200		
Evening Signal.......	600		
American	700	Daily, Weekly,	
Courier and Enquirer.	4,200	and Extra...	51,000
Journal of Commerce.	3,100		
Express	2,800		
Sun	21,000		
News	450		
Mercury	1,500		51,000
			36,550
Aggregate circulation	36,550		
Herald circulation over the allies			14,450

In the midst of the campaign against him, Mr. Bennett decided to change his single state to one of matrimony. Quite characteristically, and with a taste that could well be criticized, he took his readers into his confidence. Canny Scot as he was, he had a high bump of self-appreciation and took much space to talk about himself. The announcement of his coming marriage was made a spread-head in the *Herald* of June 1, 1840, in this flamboyant style:

To the Readers of the Herald—Declaration of Love—Caught at Last—Going to be Married—New Movement in Civilization.

I am going to be married in a few days. The weather

is so beautiful; times are getting so good; the prospects of political and moral reform so auspicious, that I can not resist the divine instinct of honest nature any longer; so I am going to be married to one of the most splendid women in intellect, in heart, in soul, in property, in person, in manner, that I have yet seen in the course of my interesting pilgrimage through human life.

. . . I can not stop in my career. I must fulfill that awful destiny which the Almighty Father has written against my name, in the broad letters of light, against the wall of heaven. I must give the world a pattern of happy wedded life, with all the charities that spring from a nuptial love. In a few days I shall be married according to the holy rites of the most holy Christian church, to one of the most remarkable, accomplished, and beautiful young women of the age. She possesses a fortune. I sought and found a fortune—a large fortune. She has no Stonington shares or Manhattan stock, but in purity and uprightness she is worth half a million of pure coin. Can any swindling bank show as much? In good sense and elegance another half a million; in soul, mind and beauty, millions on millions, equal to the whole specie of all the rotten banks in the world. Happily, the patronage of the *Herald* is nearly twenty-five thousand dollars per annum, almost equal to a President's salary. But property in the world's goods was never my object. Fame, public good, usefulness in my day and generation; the religious associates of female excellence; the progress of true industry—these have been my dreams by night, and my desires by day.

In the new and holy condition into which I am about to enter, and to enter with the same reverential feelings as I would heaven itself, I anticipate some signal changes in my feelings, in my views, in my purposes, in my pursuits. What they may be I know not—time alone can tell. My ardent desire has been through life to reach the highest order of human excellence by the shortest possible cut. Associated, night and day, in sickness and in health, in war and in peace, with a woman of this highest order of excellence, must produce some curious results in my heart and feelings, and these results the future will develop in due time in the columns of the *Herald.*

Meantime, I return my heartfelt thanks for the enthusiastic patronage of the public, both of Europe and of America. The holy estate of wedlock will only increase my desire to be still more useful. God Almighty bless you all.

JAMES GORDON BENNETT.

To this statement was appended a postscript giving notice to his editorial foes that he would have no time to attend to them "until after marriage and the honeymoon." The event took place on June sixth, and was announced in the *Herald* in the following form, on the eighth:

MARRIED

On Saturday afternoon, the sixth instant, by the Reverent Doctor Power, at St. Peter's Catholic Church, in Barclay Street, James Gordon Bennett, the proprietor and editor of the New York *Herald,* to Henrietta Agnes Crean. What may be the effect of this event on the great newspaper contest now waging in New York, time alone can show.

The lady who chose to share his fast rising fortune was Miss Henrietta Agnes Crean, whom he met at an evening party. It was a case of love at first sight. According to a chronicle of the day, Miss Crean was "the daughter of highly respectable parents, formerly of the West of Ireland, descending from the Warrens of Dublin on one side and the Crean-Lynch family on the other. She had come to the United States in the year 1838 with her mother, sister and brother, and soon distinguished herself by her accomplishments, particularly as a composer of music."

The same authority describes her qualities of mind and heart as of "no ordinary character," while as a writer she displayed "perceptive power worthy of admiration," with a highly creditable taste in art and music. She was also a linguist, speaking "several modern languages" with fluency, and credited with an "impulsive generosity of heart," that was "ever ready to assist the needy" or "aid the struggling student in literature, art, or science."

Instead of waiving hostilities during the honeymoon, the "poison" press kept up a rapid fire. When the bridal pair returned from their tour and repaired to the Astor House, a concerted effort was made to have Charles Stetson, the landlord, exclude them from his hostelry, then the most fashionable in New York. Some of the sheets actually printed the statement that they had been refused accommodations. This was totally untrue and Stetson compelled the papers to print corrections.

The full fury of the moral war now broke. Surely dictionaries were never so thumbed before to extract abusive missiles. Frederic Hudson, in his *History of Journalism in the United States,* amuses himself with tabulating some of the severer sort. Park Benjamin, in his *Signal,* is credited with the following magnificent efforts at objurgation:

"Scoundrel pen," "Obscene vagabond," "Infamous blasphemer," "Loathsome and leprous slanderer and

Courtesy of James Melvin Lee, Department of Journalism, New York University

James Gordon Bennett, the Elder

From a painting

libeller," "Wretch," "Profligate adventurer," "Nuisance," "Venomous reptile," "Accursed sting," "Notorious bane and curse," "Filthy sheet," "Pestilential scoundrel," "Vagabond," "Habitual scoffer," "Witless balderdash," "Instinct of brutes," "Mass of trash," "Ghoul-like propensity," "Murdered reputation," "Fiendish lies," "Venal wretch," "Instrument of mischief," "Cursed," "Daring infidel," "Monstrous lies," "Infamous Scotchman," "Foreign vagabond," "Polluted wretch," "Habitual liar," "Licentious," "Prince of darkness," "Infamous journal," "Veteran blackguard," "Contemptible libeller," "Lying slang and abuse," "Scurrilous," "Caitiff," "Monster," "Foul jaws," "Black-hearted," "Dirt," "Ass," "Gallows," "Rogue," "Ribaldry."

Mordecai M. Noah showered malediction in the *Star*, such as: "Rascal," "Rogue," "Cheat," "Licentious," "Infamous," "Lies," "Vile," "Nuisance," "Outrage," "Common bandit," "Dungeon," "Scaffold," "Prowling," "Pollution," "Demoralize," "Contaminate," "Slander," "Libel," "Vicious," "Depraved appetite," "Drummed out," "Not live an hour," "False," "Inquisition," "Torture," "Villain," "Turkey-buzzard," "Falsehood," "Humbug."

James Watson Webb's best specimens were these: "Unprincipled conductor," "Grossly slanderous," "Vulgur attacks," "Pollute our sheet," "Wretch," "Blasphemy," "Obscenity," "Cell at Sing Sing," "Personally offensive," "Fulsome praise," "Disgusting attacks," "Dastardly assaults," "Reckless depravity," "Unprincipled adventurer," "Moral pestilence," "Infamous," "Lowest species of scurrility," "Disgusting obscenity," "Revolting blasphemy," "Slanderous abuse," "Moral leprosy," "Insidious poison," "Gloat," "Disreputable sheet," "Disgusting organ," "Worthless sheet," "Horror and disgust," "Ribald vehicle," "Vile sheet."

The boycotters went about the city persistently, requiring clubs and hotels to cast out the *Herald*. Some did, only soon to repent. The manager of Gilpin's Exchange and Reading Room, a popular mercantile resort, was ordered to remove the paper from his files and did so. Immediately, a sufficient number of patrons protested to bring it back. Edward K. Collins, founder of the ill-fated Collins line, a great merchant, was waited on by one of the committees and told to keep his announcements out of the *Herald*. He called to a clerk in their presence and asked how many advertisements were running in the journal. "Three," was the reply. "Insert three more," was his order. The committee retired. John Boyd, another figure in the commercial world, told a committee that he got along well by minding his own business and advised imitation on their part.

A concerted attempt was also made to force theaters out of the *Herald's* columns. These numbered Niblo's Garden, the Park, Olympic, Chatham, Franklin and Bowery. Their managers were told that further use of the *Herald* would lead to exclusion from the columns of the combined press. Hamblin, of the Bowery, who hated Bennett, was the only one to obey. The *Journal of Commerce* did some theatrical printing and threatened Manager Thorne of the Chatham with a refusal to continue getting out posters and hand-bills. Thorne found another printer and kissed the *Journal of Commerce* good-by. All phases of social and business life, transportation and hotels were involved in the controversy, in the midst of which Bennett kept his temper and the *Herald* throve amazingly.

In the course of the attacks Bennett was accused of having been a pedlar in the streets of Glasgow, where it must take peculiar talents for one to thrive in that precarious occupation. He answered the accusation rather nobly in these terms:

I am, and have been, a pedlar—and part of my name is Gordon. This I admit. From my youth up I have been a pedlar, not of tapes and laces, but of thoughts, feelings, lofty principles, and intellectual truths. I am now a wholesale dealer in the same line of business, and people generally believe I have quite a run, and, what is better, no dread of suspension. I was educated and intended for a religious sect, but the Almighty, in his wisdom, meant me for truth and mankind, and I will fulfil my destiny in spite of all the opposition made to me either in the old or new hemisphere.

Yes, I have been a pedlar, and am still a pedlar of the thoughts, and feelings, and high imaginings of the past and present ages. I peddle my wares as Homer did his—as Shakespeare did his—as every great intellectual and mighty pedlar of the past did—and when I shall have finished my peddling in this world, I trust I shall be permitted to peddle in a better and happier region for ever and ever.

I have been a wayward, self-dependent, resolute, self-thinking being, from my earliest days. Yet there were implanted in my burning soul those lofty principles of morals, honor, philosophy, and religion, that the contumely of the world can not shake, or all the editors or bankers in Christendom intimidate. I feel myself, in this land, to be engaged in a great cause—the cause of truth, public faith and science, against falsehood, fraud, and ignorance. I would not abandon it even to reach the glittering coronet of the extinct title of the Duke of Gordon. I am a firm believer in the remarkable effects of blood and race in men, women, and horses, but I am also an equal votary in the faith of talent, in the blood of genius, in the race of lofty intellect and original mind. To be a friend of the human race, to support the cause of the oppressed against the oppressor, to put down the vulgar aristocracy of fraudulent paper wealth by the noble aristocracy of talent, genius, and civil liberty itself, will confer a more lasting glory on my name than to entwine my brow with the glittering bauble of a ducal coronet, even were it within my reach.

His opinion of his antagonists was curtly expressed in this paragraph: "These blockheads are determined to make me the greatest man of the age. Newspaper abuse made Mr. Van Buren chief magistrate of this republic—and newspaper abuse will make me the chief editor of this country. Well—be it so, I can't help it."

The blockheads did not make him the greatest editor in the country, but they did aid in making the *Herald* the most successful newspaper from the standpoint of circulation and earning power. Among the sins ascribed to Bennett were atheism and disrespect for religion. To these charges he replied with spirit:

Atheism is an absurdity. An atheist never existed. Materialism is an equal absurdity as contradistinguished from mentalism. Really and truly we know nothing of mind or matter. We only know our sensations, our thoughts, our feelings, our ideas, which are all, more or less, synonymous words. From these beautiful raw materials of our existence we infer—mind, matter, God, heaven, and eternity. The whole circle of human knowledge and happiness is merely inference from these mysterious sensations, which,—like an invisible but incomprehensible frame-work, spread over man a web of intelligence. Common sense—the constant series of our mysterious sensations, is the foundation of all philosophy, all religion, all literature, all poetry, all human happiness.

Replying further to the accusations of impiety he observed:

When I was quite a youth, perplexed with the violent controversies between the Catholics and Protestants, I used to go to the banks of a stream, and pour my regrets into its gentle ripples, that I had not lived in the dark ages, when there was only one opinion and one religion to believe.

Religion—true religion—consists not in eating and drinking—not in high salaries—not in hanging around the apron strings of rich old women—not in presuming to judge the opinions of others beyond what their acts will justify. Neither does true religion—nor real Christianity consist in believing the dogmas of any church—or the *ipse dixit* of any man. The Bible is before me. Have I not a right to read that book—to draw out from it religious opinions—and to create a belief and a church of my own?

I had not reached the age of eighteen, before the light of nature—the intelligence of the age—the progress of truth and knowledge had broken to pieces all the ridiculous superstitions of the church of Rome, without affecting a single moral principle which I had received in the course of my early instruction. With the sacred document in my hand, and all history spread out before me, I would not submit to bigotry, either Catholic or Protestant, even at that early age. I went to the sources of true religion, and drank of the pure stream, uncontaminated by priest or prelates, parson or minister; and as long as we have these sacred volumes in full circulation here below, defiance may alike be set to the bigots of Catholicity or of Protestantism. We care for neither. We are independent of all. Like Luther—like Paul, we go on our own hook.

He made use of the charges to write an exposition of his views of the Bible, which is refreshing to read even in days of pro-evolution:

The first book I recollect anything of was the Scriptures. In the school in which I was taught to read, the Scriptures were the principal book. The history of the patriarchs, of the prophets, of the apostles, of the martyrs, of the Son of Man himself—is as familiar to me as the expression of my mother's face, and the light of my mother's eye. My imagination, my fancy, my taste, my morals were formed on the perusal of the Scriptures. The literature of the Greek and Roman classics—that even of England and of Scotland, was a study subsequent to that of the Scriptures. In the day, and in the country in which I was a boy, the Scriptures were the text book—the reading book—the Vade Mecum—the companion of Saturday night and of Sunday all day. I was educated a Catholic, in the midst of a Protestant community—yet both Catholic and Protestant breathed the moral atmosphere of the Scriptures. My parents, my schoolmaster, my associates—all venerated the book of heaven alike. My literary and moral tastes are all founded on the striking passages in the Scriptures; and I do verily believe, that to this early habit of reading the Bible at school, am I indebted for that force, brevity, spirit, and peculiarity which makes the style of the *Herald* as popular with the uncontaminated masses of a community who are yet imbued with the spirit and literature of the Bible.

Effort was made to stir up Catholic antagonism to-

curred in assisting the building of railways. The bonds had been marketed abroad, where the *Herald* had already become the chief source of information concerning America. As it was especially strong on financial news, the "Wall Street journals," as they were termed, denounced this prediction as the result of bribes from the London Stock Exchange and the Paris Bourse to prevent the further sale of American securities abroad. Bennett printed the accusation in his issue of November twenty-sixth. It is enough to say that the states named did repudiate their obligations.

Bennett's clarity of vision in politics and finance, being hampered neither by partisanship nor personal interest, gave him a commanding position as an interpreter of conditions. The death of President Harrison after a single month in office brought John Tyler into his chair. The *Herald* predicted that this would be fraught with evil consequences to the Whigs, a prophecy that came all too true. As Horace Greeley was a master of political facts, so James Gordon Bennett was a great charter of political and trade currents. The man was almost uncanny in his sensibility in these matters.

Unlike Greeley, however, Bennett did not quarrel with conditions. He saw in the coming of Tyler the beginning of the end with the Whig party, but he did not clash with Tyler on that account. Indeed, Tyler's policies suited him perfectly. He refused to revive the United States Bank, and in other things pleased the *Herald* admirably. The sudden shift in administrative policy—Tyler being much more of a southerner than a Whig—roused great public interest in Washington affairs, so much so that Bennett decided to establish what was the first Washington bureau, as he had himself, in a way, been the first Washington correspondent. To this end he put Robert Sutton, a very capable man, in charge and gave him a staff of men to nose about for news. Thus *Herald* reporters became much in evidence at the Capitol, so much so that Senator Samuel L. Southard, of New Jersey, President *pro tem* of the Senate, excluded them from its floor under an old rule that but two men from each local paper could have that privilege. The rule was made to protect the lazy Washington sheets from competition and Bennett riddled it with a biting attack, to this effect:

> It is caused by the selfish and malignant influence of the Washington newspapers, in order to maintain a monopoly of Washington news, and to rob the public treasury, under the color of public printing, in order to gratify their extravagant habits of life. According to Mr. Clay's statement, we find that during the Congress of 1838, the following amount was paid out of the public treasury, for printing, to the three Washington prints:—Washington *Globe,* Blair & Rives, ninety thousand dollars—*National Intelligencer,* Gales and Seaton [no amount given], *Madisonian,* Thomas Allen, three hundred and thirty thousand dollars.
>
> There is this enormous amount of the public money thrown away upon these prints—and for what? It is necessary, as they say, in order to remunerate them for reporting the debates of Congress. We propose, and will give, a daily report and circulation of these debates, better and more comprehensive, without asking a cent of the public treasury.

Furthermore, the enterprising editor made a frank

appeal to Senator Henry Clay of Kentucky, in these terms:

New York, June 5, 1841.

Hon. Henry Clay.

Sir: The peculiar circumstances of the case will be my apology for troubling you with the present note.

I have organized, at an expense of nearly two hundred dollars per week, a *corps* of reporters, to give daily reports of the debates in both Houses of Congress. In the House there is no difficulty, but in the Senate there is a rule, I am told, excluding from the reporters' seats all not connected with the Washington press. Now I conceive this exclusion to be hostile to the public interests. I can and will give daily reports of the Senate, without asking any of the printing, or indirect remuneration of that body, but I am met with a rule that certainly is illiberal and injurious both to private enterprise and public advantage.

I address myself to you as one of the most liberal and enlightened members of your body, for the purpose of requesting that a motion may be made for the repeal of the rule in question. No individual in this land will sooner see the propriety and public advantage of such motion than yourself.

I am, sir, with great respect,

James Gordon Bennett.

Clay answered rather lamely that he would try to secure "accommodations" for the *Herald's* men, pleading quite untruthfully that the rule was in force because of limited room. The question was referred to a committee which did not report, and for long the *Herald's* Washington staff had to cover the Senate as best it could. Other out-of-town sheets, it might be said, were not excluded and it was this favoritism that aroused the *Herald's* owner. He had to await the coming of the telegraph to get full value out of his enterprise, but fast couriers did pretty well and the *Herald* was always ahead in the Capital. Moreover, the *Herald* soon established an "inside" relationship that was of great value in news-getting. Tyler had to seek friends outside his party and found one in Bennett, so much so in fact, that Philip Hone, stout Whig, wrote on September 20, 1841:

> The New York *Herald* is now understood to be the champion of President Tyler, and, if report speaks true, its correspondent in Washington (a person named Parmly) is his confidential adviser, enjoys in the most enlarged degree the run of the presidential kitchen, and is favored with copies of his messages and other public acts before they have been submitted to his cabinet ministers. For these high privileges and distinguished favors he, of course, evinces his gratitude, and does his share of the dirty jobs about the palace, by abusing in the most gross and vulgar language, the members of the late cabinet, and Mr. Ewing, the late Secretary of the Treasury, having been the most prominent among the abdicators, comes in for the largest share of this reptile's venom. A long article is published in the *Herald,* filled with the grossest vituperation against this gentleman, against whom the tongue of slander has never until now been raised.

Plus this advantage the *Herald* reported the speeches of Clay, Webster and Calhoun in full, enlarging to give them space.

The triumphant *Herald* was not merciful to its persecutors in the "war," when any of them got in the way. The result was now and then an indictment for libel. Philip Hone reports the outcome of one of these episodes in his diary, under date of February 14, 1842:

> This impudent disturber of the public peace, whose infamous paper, the *Herald*, is more scurrilous, and of course more generally read, than any other, has been tried in the Court of Oyer and Terminer, and convicted on two indictments for a libel on the Judges Noah and Lynch, of the Court of Sessions; he was sentenced this morning to pay a fine of $250 on one, and $100 on the other. This will do him more good than harm; he will make money by it; the vitiated appetite for slander which pervades the mass of the people will be whetted by the notoriety which this trial will give him, for dearly do the people love the scandal of which themselves are not the subject! The court consisted of Hon. William Kent, president, and two Loco-foco Aldermen, Purdy and Lee; the two latter, "birds of a feather," overruled the judge in making up the sentence, of which he took care to inform Bennett in the address which he made to him in announcing it, telling him plainly that if he had had his way he would have sent him to the penitentiary, and intimating that whenever he gets a chance he may expect it at his hands, on the commission of another such offence.

It is proper to state that Major Mordecai M. Noah, who had been both employer and opponent of Bennett, and had become a judge, cheerfully consented to the quashing of a couple of indictments, admitting that he had provoked the reprisal upon which they were based. In one case brought by Noah, his former associate was fined three hundred dollars, largely on the theory that the greater the truth, the greater the libel.

Another libel action of great public import failed of its purpose. Bennett was prosecuted under the bankruptcy act for publishing the schedules of Anthony Dey, whose family name is perpetuated in Dey Street. The prosecuting attorney, Mr. Whiting, framed his plea for conviction in a glowing tribute to the *Herald's* power and progress, pointing out the pride Mr. Bennett took in the fact that his newspaper "was circulated in every land and clime the sun shone upon. If you go to England, you find it there; in France it is almost the only paper that can be found in file; it penetrates through the snows and dreary wilds of Russia; you may see it upon the summits of the Alps; if you travel in India you will find it; upon the Seven Hills of Rome; upon the time honored and classic soil, and beneath the balmy skies of Italy, there you may read the *Herald.* Cross over the Bosphorus—go into Asia—and, in short, wherever the English language is spoken or translated there does the New York *Herald* circulate."

This was rather piling it up, but from his own eulogy, he argued that so much potency ought to be curbed that its power might not become perilous. He held that great caution and discretion should be exercised by the editor of such a medium, making it quite plain that such had not been the case.

Bennett's retort was that he had offended less against good morals, good taste and the laws of society than any paper in the city. Such errors as had occurred were unintentional and were always corrected as soon as detected. The jury agreed with him, and he was acquitted. The bankruptcy law was changed and schedules of the unlucky became public property.

Discussing the case against himself and his policy of promptly acknowledging error, in contrast with the conduct of his contemporaries, who usually stood by their sins, he wrote, February 1, 1843:

> . . . Our rivals . . . hated us for our successful enterprise. It was not our conduct, as they alleged, which they wished to amend—it was to destroy us and our establishment so that they might occupy our position. Hence the terrible falsehoods just invented and published by the rival newspapers—hence the attacks not only upon our journal, but on our character, on the very females of our family—on the wife of one's own bosom. Never, perhaps, was there such an instance in human nature, of such a conspiracy to destroy a man and his family, as there has existed in certain cliques in New York for the last few years against us and the *Herald*. They attempted to drive us from our very apartments in the Astor House, by gross and false insinuations against characters in private life, as pure, as spotless, as honorable, as accomplished as any in this or any other country.

Thus he summed up accurately the motive behind the moral war. In the face of it all the circulation of the *Herald* rose until it equaled that of the great London *Times,* while it became and long remained the chief source of American perspective for European editors.

In 1842 a quarrel between sundry New York editors and James Fenimore Cooper brought on a series of libel suits by the novelist, who had managed to stir up the bile of James Watson Webb, Horace Greeley, Thurlow Weed and William L. Stone, the last then a young editor of the *Journal of Commerce.* Cooper's fight against the press became state-wide. He won suit after suit. Bennett saw no excuse for the assaults and stood stoutly by Cooper.

He was able in June of that year to have considerable fun at the expense of James Watson Webb, who earned a prison sentence for fighting a duel with Thomas F. Marshall, of Kentucky, on the twenty-fourth. The editor placed an order for cigars with a tobacconist, to be sent to the imprisoned Colonel. The dealer took the trouble to verify the order. "Send the best," answered Bennett. Webb declined the weeds, quite to the amazement of the donor who could not understand Webb's "insulting a box containing one hundred of the very best cigars," besides rejecting them with a threat "to kick them into the street instead of smoking them."

"If he will apologize like a reinstated gentleman," Bennett continued on his comment, "for his conduct, and smoke one of those cigars, as the Indian does the calumet, as an emblem of peace, we will go to Delaware and settle his business quietly, or throw a wet blanket over the length and breadth of the state that will bury it thick in a fog till the day of Judgment comes—on the 23rd of April 1843, according to Prophet Miller."

In the duel Webb had received a flesh wound in the leg, and after indictment in New York was sentenced to two years in Sing Sing. A petition for his pardon was circulated, Bennett being one of the first signers. Governor William H. Seward granted the plea, so the doughty Colonel never wore strips. In gratitude he named his next born son William Seward Webb.

As editor of the only non-partisan paper in an extremely partisan age, Mr. Bennett readily became the target of charges that he was a mercenary. He retorted that there was no distinction between the Whigs and the Democrats, the then ruling parties. The difference was a mere shadow, fictitious and artificial—a passion and prejudice, behind which there was no principle, heightened and exaggerated by partisans who made politics a trade, to delude the people into their support—which was all too true. His reason for supporting Tyler was that he had risen above party:

To attempt to show that Mr. Tyler's administration has placed itself upon the old Jeffersonian platform, or that it eschews the leaven of federalism is a trick of rogues to impose upon honest men. Mr. Tyler's administration is elevated above the Jeffersonian platform—far above all party—far above all moth-eaten prejudices. From his first accession to power, we have watched its operation, and supported its policy, because it is adapted to the spirit of the age—because it has broken loose from all party—because it has taken a high, moral, independent position, above all party, all faction, and thrown itself upon the intellect, morals, intelligence, justice, and patriotism of the whole nation for its support. We have also approved of all the vetoes of the President, not because a bank is unconstitutional, for we firmly believe it is—but because the horrible morals of the financiers of the present day have unfitted the country for any bank—or any currency other than gold or silver. Within the last few years nearly one hundred and fifty banks, including the United States Bank, have broken to pieces, and property amounting to a hundred and fifty millions of dollars, or more, has evaporated under the management of the bankers and financiers of the age. On this ground alone the veto power is justified.

It was this attitude toward getting rich quickly that gave the *Herald* its standing abroad. Even in the 'forties the British were badly burned. They held much stock in the United States Bank. No wonder then, the *Foreign Quarterly Review* said of the *Herald,* in its hour of trial during the moral war:

> The New York *Herald* has been one of the most powerful instruments in the United States in exposing frauds, bubbles and stock-gambling machinery, which our fund-mongers had organized in America for robbing the land and labor in that country, as they have robbed since the days of Walpole. For correctness of detail, research, industry, sound political economy, and decided talent, the New York *Herald* might challenge comparison with any daily paper in Europe. Its money articles have not yet been equalled on this side of the water; but it is the bold, and able, and honest exposure of the corrupt paper system which those money articles contain, and not the wit, levity, and colloquial humor of the *Herald,* which has excited the indignant reprobation of our money changers.

It is rather curious that Horace Greeley, whose honesty was never questioned, advocated paper money, and that James Gordon Bennett, whose honesty was always aspersed, should have been a firm believer in sound money! He was an unpopular truth-teller in a wildcat age. The *Herald's* financial articles, it may be recalled, were the products of his own pen, and were the first that really told the truth unsparingly to appear in American newspapers. The fact that the editor knew how to develop information to advantage brought great quantities to his desk. He never betrayed a source, and as a result, his files were full of material upon which he could draw in support of his position. Men came to the *Herald* knowing they would

BADGERING HIM.

J. G. B——TT.—Bow! Wow! Come out, Mr. Lincoln!

not be betrayed; others because they knew they would be paid. So it was that the paper never lacked for exclusive news or ammunition with which to return a fire. Withal, it was intensely American, and mercilessly anti-foreign, fighting against English influences in trade, finance and politics. Remember, we were still regarded as children—and pretty bad ones—by the "mother" country. Not until the border treaties were settled to our advantage under the skilled hands of Webster, were we half-respected or really accorded rights. There was much showing of teeth in the period when these matters were under discussion; all of which the *Herald* liberally encouraged. Yet the editor did not hesitate to lay the lash on the shoulders of Pennsylvania when its press and politicians went out of bounds on the Oregon question, and howled "fifty-four forty or fight" until they were purple. "With boundless riches, and great means of wealth," he wrote, "that state has given the disgraceful example of repudiating her honest debts, and delaying the payment of interest under the plea of paltry excuses. No man or set of men in the community can have the true feeling of patriotism, or should be allowed to lick John Bull, unless they have honesty enough to pay their debts and rid their consciences of such burden. It is impossible for Philadelphia to get up a patriotic meeting, and convince England and the world that they can whip John Bull until they pay their debts. Church burners, rioters, repudiators are not the stuff of which true patriotism can be formed, or brave men manufactured."

Here again he spoke as one with authority. Pennsylvania, following the panic of 1837, had defaulted interest on her bonds, sold mainly abroad by Nicholas Biddle, head of the United States Bank. That rank repudiation was in the air is quite plain. Europe was enraged. One American banker was mobbed on the Exchange in Amsterdam and narrowly escaped with his life. The family savings of William Wordsworth were wiped out, by what the poet termed "the perfidy of Pennsylvania's repudiators." Sydney Smith's losses took all the humor out of him for the moment. He wrote the London *Globe* under date of May 8, 1843:

Had this refusal been the result of war, of civil discord, of unwise application of means in the first years of self-government, of a poor state struggling with the barrenness of nature, every friend of America would have been content to wait for better times. But the fraud has been committed in a period of profound peace, by the richest state in the Union, after a wise investment of the funds in roads and canals, of which the repudiators are every day enjoying the advantages. A great nation, after trampling under foot all earthly tyranny, has been guilty of a fraud as enormous as ever disgraced the worst king of the most degraded nation in Europe.

It is worth while noting that Pennsylvania was soon shamed into paying up. The *Herald's* share in bringing this about added to its prestige abroad. Incidentally it may be added that in the course of our career as a nation seventeen states have attempted to evade their responsibilities and eight are still in full default.

Besides the moral war and the Hard Cider Campaign, the 'forties developed a series of amazing news stories, to which the *Herald* gave the highest expression that audacity and enterprise could employ. Special occasions were emphasized with pictures. When a "Boz Ball" was given in honor of Charles Dickens, at the Park Theater, in 1843, the enterprising editor gave his readers twelve illustrations of the event. A pictorial page showing General Andrew Jackson's funeral cortège was printed in June, 1845. Envious contemporaries made much fun of the rather coarse cuts, and the Albany *Evening Journal,* of which Thurlow Weed was editor, alleged that the Jackson pictures had already done duty as depicting Queen Victoria's coronation, the funeral of President William Henry Harrison and the celebration held in honor of the opening of the Croton aqueduct. Bennett repelled this infamous insinuation with a certificate from Thomas W. Strong, wood engraver, to the effect that the Jackson cuts were fresh made in his own shop.

CHAPTER IV

MORMONS AND CATHOLICS

The new cult called Mormonism founded by Joseph Smith, the Prophet, migrating from Ohio, to Missouri, had been driven out of the latter state after a conflict that amounted to civil war. The Mormons, led by Smith, settled in Nauvoo, in Illinois, on the Mississippi River and soon had a thriving city as their capital with nearly twenty thousand people within its borders. Smith organized a military brigade called the Nauvoo Legion, made himself lieutenant-general and gave it a liberal supply of major- and brigadier-generals. The community soon became a center of disturbances. The Saints, as they dubbed themselves, grew fast in numbers and were a balance of political power in the state, swinging from Democratic to Whig as proved most profitable, while the Prophet prophesied and did a number of other things that attracted wide attention. To all their doings Bennett gave great space. They were interesting as well as disturbing and deserved it all. Smith had a keen eye for publicity and welcomed correspondents from the East. He appreciated all the *Herald* did. One of the first institutions founded at Nauvoo was a full-fledged university. This honored the editor of the *Herald* in 1842 with the degree of LL. D. In addition he was given "the freedom of the city." This was not the end of his glory.

Quarreling with Major-General James C. Bennett, Commander of the Nauvoo Legion, Smith deposed him and put in the next in rank, General James Arlington Bennett. Evidently not wanting to reduce the number of Bennetts at his disposal, Smith, August 21, 1842, appointed James Gordon Bennett a brigadier-general and aide-de-camp. The gentleman so honored did not decline but commented on the receipt of an order from Major-General James Arlington Bennett, by which he was told to report for duty, thus merrily:

Blood and 'ouns, I'll go. It never shall be said that the blood of the Bennetts did not rise to the top. Who knows but I may get one of their glorious bullets in the calf? [Alluding to a bullet inserted therein on the person of James Watson Webb by Tom Marshall, of Kentucky, in their duel.] What would Colonel Webb say if I disobeyed a military mandate? In the meantime I highly approve of my superior in command, ascertaining first the constitutionality of the measure by direct application to Governor Carlin to see if there be any necessity of a veto. [The Legion was then enrolled as part of the Illinois Militia, and notice of the appointment had been sent for approval to his Excellency.] But still I must prepare. I have no uniform. Egad, I must advertise for proposals. So here goes:

"Wanted to Purchase—a full suit of uniform for an officer of the rank of Brigadier-General in the Nauvoo Legion; also a fine horse, thirteen hands high, a sword, etc., including a good old Bible and Prayer-Book. Nothing like being provided with all sorts of ammunitions."

It will be perceived that Joseph Smith was an even better advertiser than James Gordon Bennett. Governor Carlin took the appointment seriously. The result was chronicled in the *Herald* of August 13, 1842, in these terms:

Rising in the World

"Since you will buckle Fortune on my back,
To bear her burden whe'er I will or no,
I must have patience to endure the load."

We are rising very rapidly in this sinful world. A short time ago, the Corporation of Nauvoo, Illinois, conferred upon us a freedom of the city. How far this freedom extends we know not, but we suppose it embraces a vast number of DELICIOUS PRIVILEGES, *according to the Mormon Creed.* The next step was to raise us to the dignity of LL. D., a regular Doctor of Laws, by the University of Nauvoo, *an honor which we highly prize,* and which is as good, and perhaps better, than that conferred on General Jackson by the University of Harvard, or that on his Excellency, Edward Everett, by the University of Cambridge, in England. But this is not all. Yesterday,—blessed be the day!—we received by a special messenger from Illinois, the intelligence that that state had gone entirely for the Mormons and locofocos, in the elections; and also an enclosure which contained the parchment, *conferring a high military rank upon us,* of which document the following is a true copy—the original being in our salamander safe, with the titles of the *Herald* building:—

"Thomas Carlin, Governor of the State of Illinois, to all to whom these Presents shall come, Greetings:

"Know ye, That James Gordon Bennett having been duly elected to the office of Aid-de-Camp (with the rank and title of Brigadier-General) to the Major-General of the Nauvoo Legion of the Militia of the State of Illinois, *I, Thomas Carlin,* Governor of said State, for and on behalf of the People of said State, do commission him Aid-de-Camp to said Major-General, with rank and title as aforesaid, to take rank from the twenty eighth day of May, 1842. He is, therefore, carefully and diligently to discharge the duties of said office, by doing and performing all manner of things thereunto belonging; and I do strictly require all officers and soldiers under his command to be obedient to his orders; and he is to obey such orders and directions as he shall receive from time to time from his Commander-in-Chief, or his superior officer.

"In testimony whereof, I have hereunto set my hand, and caused the Great Seal of State to be hereunto affixed. Done at Springfield, this second day of June, in the year of our Lord one thousand eight hundred and forty-two, and the Independence of the United States the sixty-sixth.

"By the Governor, Tho. Carlin

"Lyman Trumbull, *Secretary of State.*"

There's honor—there's distinction—there's salt and greens for a modest, simple, calm, patient, industrious editor. We now take legitimate rank, far above Colonel Webb, Major Noah, Colonel Stone, General George P. Morris, or all the military editors around and about the country. We are only inferior in rank—and that but half a step—to good old General Jackson—he being Major-General and LL. D.—we being Brigadier and LL. D. also.

In an hour after the arrival of this precious document, but before I received it, I found myself two inches taller, three inches more in circumference, and so wolfish about the head and shoulders that I could have fought a duel with Marshall, provided he had given me the same terms on the "bandanna Handkerchief plan" that he generously gave to Colonel Webb. It was no doubt caused by the military title approximating to its owner. "God tempers the wind to the shorn lamb"—the devil heats the fire to suit the sinner, and I must bear the honors that are thickening around me.

It will be seen, therefore, that I am *Aid-de-Camp,* with the rank of Brigadier-General, to the Major-General of the famous Nauvoo Legion. *This Major-General is no less a man than the* Prophet Joe Smith, *who is very busy establishing an* original religious empire *in the west, that may swallow up all the other different sects and* cliques, as the rod of Moses, turned into a serpent, swallowed up, without salt, the rods of Jannes and Jambres, and the other magicians of Egypt. Heavens! how we apples swim, as the sprat said to the whale, Mount Etna bawling out at the same time, "Let's have another segar." Wonders will never cease. Hereafter, I am James Gordon Bennett, Freeman of the Holy City of Nauvoo, LL. D. of the University of Nauvoo, and Aid-de-Camp to the Major-General, and Brigadier General to the Nauvoo Legion, with the fair prospect of being a prophet soon, and a saint in Heaven hereafter.

Though thus placed on flourishing terms with the Mormons, the editor was not so fortunate in his relations with his mother church. Before 1840 the number of Catholics in the country had been negligible. The building of railroads and the resulting expansion of industry stimulated immigration with their demand for labor. Poverty in Ireland pushed out enormous numbers of natives from that green isle. Their flocking produced a new situation in what had been a land of undisturbed Protestantism. Concentrating as they did in New York City, they developed at once that aggressiveness which has continued to be a characteristic of the race and religion, under the lead of a militant prelate, Archbishop John Hughes. He was a builder and a fighter on behalf of both the newcomers and his church.

Hughes established a weekly newspaper, the *Metropolitan Record,* in which he urged his cause and castigated its opponents. Both parties bid for the support of the newcomers. The Whigs were new as an organization, and kept in power. William H. Seward was their leader in New York and governor of the state for a second time in 1842, when Hughes demanded a share of the public revenues for the support of parochial schools. He recommended an allowance in his annual message to the legislature. To this the *Herald* took exception and turned against Hughes, who had made a speech urging the Catholics of New York to form a political party and so effect purposes in the church interest. Bennett observed in the *Herald*:

The whole thing, from beginning to end, is only a preposterous insult to the common sense of an intelligent community. To all minds of intelligence it will, after the election is over, reduce Bishop Hughes to the lowest state of degradation and contempt. He has shown himself to be utterly deficient in honesty, or in common sense. There is no alternative on which to hang his crosier. If he meant seriously, in a Protestant country, to succeed in his project, he took the very method that would for ever put a barrier between his church and the claim on the School Fund. One of the first principles of American freedom is to keep separate and distinct the institutions of Church and State. No element of liberty is more deeply imbued in the American mind than this is. How, then, in such a happy, and free, and positive condition of public opinion, could Bishop Hughes expect that if the Church of Rome had a favor to ask of a Protestant country, the best method to acquire it was to trample this holy principle under foot, and organize his church into a political club. If Bishop Hughes did not see this view, his mind must be blinded to all facts—to all truths—save the dogmas and drivellings of the Catholic church in the last stage of decrepitude. But Bishop Hughes did see this, and therefore he becomes liable to the charge of dishonesty in his conduct and opinions—of a ridiculous attempt to commit a detestable fraud upon the understanding of the intelligent Catholics of this country.

As noted earlier Bennett was intensely American in all his attitudes, which was a large factor in the paper's influence abroad. He was believed to reflect the country as a whole more than any other journalist. This was true. He wanted to sell the *Herald* to as many people as possible. The constituency, therefore, being American, he made the most he could of it.

The Archbishop was nothing if not militant and knowing Bennett's Catholic origin, presumed upon it in dealing with him, thereby making a serious mistake. Although born and married within the church, Bennett did not like its mastery and said so plainly. One who knew him well asserted that his feeling against the church as an organization grew out of the death of his brother Cosmo, who was so enervated by the asceticism he was compelled to exercise as part of his training to be a priest that he died in early youth; the editor felt that his brother had been killed by the restrictions enforced to conquer his spirit and would have no hierarchical domination.

As the Know-Nothing sentiment grew, the Archbishop became more virulent, thundering against Bennett in press and pulpit—rival editors being foolish enough to print his fulminations. He also, in effect, excommunicated the aggressive editor—all of which helped the *Herald*. Undauntedly the editor continued his crusade, and went so far as to demand the separation of the Catholic Church in America from the rule of Rome. He wanted an American church free from the overlordship of the hierarchy and argued at length.

It must not be thought that the editor allowed the Archbishop to go unscathed. He summed up the result of the prelate's activities in this form:

The conduct of the Bishop in 1841 gave the Irish a preponderance in 1842, which created in its turn a reaction in the American mind in 1843, resulting in the organization of the Native American party last Spring, and whose operations we have all seen. But all these movements, here as well as in Philadelphia, can be traced with the accuracy of mathematical calculation, back to Bishop Hughes's first entrance into Carroll Hall as a political agitator, and the motives which impelled the Bishop then can be guessed at now with a good deal of certainty. He was the first dignitary of the Catholic Church, in this free and happy land, that ever attempted such a movement, and we trust that he may be the last of the same faith that may ever thus disgrace his holy calling. In all these movements he has most wofully mistaken his duties. He has most wofully mistaken his position in this city, in this country, and in this age. He has forgotten that he is living in a land of freedom and universal toleration, in a republic of intelligent men, and in the nineteenth century.

Coming fresh from the seclusion of his cloister, he imagined when he became a Bishop, that he was living in the fourth or fourteenth century. His policy would, indeed, have been in keeping with the spirit of those dark ages. It is precisely similar to that conduct by which the priesthood destroyed the Roman Empire—decided who should wear the purple, and finally delivered that old heroic nation into the hands of the Northern barbarians. It is precisely similar to that interference of the hierarchy in political affairs which overwhelmed the Italian republics of the Middle Ages with irreparable ruin. It is precisely similar to that conduct which lighted up the fires in Smithfield and the Grass-market. It is precisely similar to that course of policy which whitened the valleys of Piedmont with the bones of thousands slaughtered in civil war. It is precisely similar to that policy which has torn and distracted unhappy Spain. It is, in fact, the same accursed interference of ecclesiastics with the affairs of State, which has, in all ages, brought such disgrace on Christianity, and crushed the liberties of mankind. Need we say that it is utterly at variance with the precepts of Christ and the spirit of his religion? No. We all know that it is in open and blasphemous defiance of the principles of Him who came to proclaim universal peace and good will, as they were developed in his sermons on the mountains of Judea and on the shores of Galilee.

So it was that the *Herald*, perceiving the petrifaction of the old parties, encouraged the Native Americans, who grew into sufficient strength to decimate the Democrats, destroy the Whigs and become the Republican party.

In 1843 Bennett made another visit to Europe, accompanied by his wife and infant son, the second James Gordon Bennett. He sailed this time on June twenty-sixth, in a packet-ship, the *Garrick,* which accomplished the passage in twenty-two pleasant days. The Irish Repeal question was up before Parliament and the great Daniel O'Connell a central figure in the fight. The *Herald's* Dublin correspondence and its editorial policy had been against the measure, to such an extent as to interfere with the collection of contributions to the cause in America. The Hughes row also supervened. Bennett had announced his purpose to visit Dublin and O'Connell bottled up some spare wrath against his coming. The editor arrived in Dublin on August sixth, and, desiring to hear O'Connell, visited the Corn Exchange, where the great orator was holding forth, with results that he himself has best described in the following letter to the London *Times*:

To the Editor of The London Times.

Sir:—On my return to London, after a tour of three weeks over Ireland and Scotland, I embrace the first opportunity of asking permission to reply to a very gross and unjustifiable attack made upon me on the 7th and 8th instant, by Mr. O'Connell, in the Corn Exchange, Dublin, while as a mere traveler, I was quietly pursuing my journey through that city. This attack appeared in your Journal of the 9th and 10th instant, in the shape of a correspondence from Dublin, and has been circulated very extensively in the newspapers throughout the United Kingdom.

In visiting Ireland, which I then did for the first time, I had received a number of introductory letters from a highly respectable Irish gentleman in London to a number of his friends in Dublin. Among these letters was one to Mr. O'Connell. I reached Dublin on the 6th instant, and having only a very short time to devote to that city, I procured a carriage on the same afternoon, and called in person upon the gentlemen to whom my letters were addressed. Among others, I drove to Mr. O'Connell's residence, Merrion Square, and left my letter, together with my card, writing on it "Gresham's Hotel," where I stopped. During a course of nearly twenty years as an editor in the United States, eight years of which I have been proprietor of the New York *Herald,* I have always entertained and expressed a high and liberal opinion of Mr. O'Connell, and a warm sympathy for the Irish people. There was nothing, therefore, in our relations to make the introduction to him improper.

Next day (Monday, August 7th) I went around Dublin, in company with a gentleman of that city, for the purpose of viewing the public buildings, institutions, and other sights. About two o'clock we had finished our tour; but on our return to the hotel, I remarked, "I must see the Corn Exchange, and if possible hear

O'Connell; it will not do to return to New York without having seen that sight."

We accordingly drove to the Corn Exchange. After paying a shilling admittance fee at the door, I attempted to get in, but it was so small and so crowded that it was found impossible. As a last effort, my name and residence were given at the private entrance. Several persons cried out, "Make way for the American gentleman;"—"Why the divil don't you make way?"—and I was handed in with as much attention to one Tom Steele as if I had been the bearer of a large amount of "rent" from New York to swell the funds of the association in Dublin. As soon as my name was mentioned to O'Connell, and while I was standing near the table, and quietly looking over the singular scene, I was assailed by Mr. O'Connell in those discourteous, inhospitable, and brutal terms, in which he was reported in your Dublin correspondence. The suddenness and abruptness of the outrage seemed not only to astonish his own auditors, but even to astonish himself, for he hurried over the scene and proceeded in his business at once. After taking a look around the assembly, I retired very quietly.

Next day, Mr. O'Connell, being well aware of the gross breach of ordinary decorum he had committed, endeavored to justify himself by making an additional attack upon my public and private character—an attack equally unfounded, untrue, and malevolent. Having violated all decorum on the first day, he endeavored to justify that violation by deepening it into barbarity, falsehood, and outrage. Mr. O'Connell offered as a passive apology a statement made by a Mr. Silk Buckingham, to the effect that I had endeavored to extort money from the latter when he visited the United States a few years ago. This charge, and all such charges, I pronounce utterly untrue. Mr. Buckingham came to the United States on a money speculation, travelling through the country, delivering lectures for pay on Oriental literature and customs.

He sent his advertisements and self-laudatory notices (puffs, we call them) to the newspapers, and among others to mine. The clerk who attends to this branch of my business told his agent that his puffs were also advertisements, and must be paid for as usual. I never had any intercourse with Buckingham—never saw him—never heard him lecture; yet out of these simple facts Buckingham has manufactured the falsehoods he has published in his work, and Daniel O'Connell, in the extremity of some secret revenge, endorses his falsehoods in the Dublin Corn Exchange, and endeavors to assail the character of a man who feels himself to stand at least on as high a level of honor, morals, worth, and public spirit, as he does.

The real motives which actuated Mr. O'Connell in making so unprovoked an attack upon me, have hitherto been concealed from the public eye. I will now disclose them, and they will be found sufficient to account for his conduct. I contributed to stop the "rent" that was expected from America. This will be apparent in giving a brief sketch of the rise, progress and extinction of the Irish Repeal agitation in the United States, and of the position the New York *Herald* assumed in that business.

The Repeal agitation began in New York several weeks before I left that city, which was on the 26th of June last. They then held their meetings nightly, for ten days or more, at a large building in Broadway, called Washington Hall. Immediately on the commencement of the agitation I was called upon by several of its leaders and promoters to ascertain my views on the subject, and whether I would support the movement. They were anxious to procure the aid of the *Herald*, because from its extensive circulation, and its superior corps of reporters, it would do the cause more good than any other paper. I thanked them for their good opinions, replying that I had for many years been friendly to the Irish people, who were a generous and a high-spirited race—that I had always supported their rights in the United States, and sympathized with their distresses in their native land; but that the repeal of the Irish Union was a very questionable and impracticable measure—that it could not remove social evils in Ireland—and that there was as much impropriety in Americans endeavoring to promote the dismemberment of the British empire while we had treaties of amity in existence, as there was in certain fanatics in England, and even in Mr. O'Connell himself, in endeavoring to encourage an agitation against the Southern States, which might lead to a dismemberment of our own Union. They acknowledged the justice of the view, but apologized for Mr. O'Connell's abuse of the Southern States by attributing it to his ignorance of American opinion and constitutions, and especially to his ignorance of the character of his own countrymen when they come to the United States.

They told me further, that many of them had the same view of the absurdity and impracticability of a repeal of the Legislative Union as I had, but they assured me that the great movement of Repeal in Ireland, with its affiliated movements in the United States, was only the beginning of a grand revolutionary drama, that soon would be able to subvert the monarchies and aristocracies of England, France, and all Western Europe, and establish republics throughout all those countries. On hearing this remarkable disclosure, I had nothing further to say about the technicalities of Repeal. I assured them that I would send my reporters to their meetings, and report their proceedings fully and accurately. I did so; and in these reports will be found an open avowal, by their speakers and leaders, of the real meaning of the Repeal agitation, both in Ireland and the United States. At these meetings large sums were collected to be transmitted to Ireland; but among the native American population there was great doubt felt of the propriety of interfering with the internal affairs of

Ireland, many probably thinking that the honest debts to foreign bond-holders should be first liquidated, before money should be generously sent to Dublin to create a revolution, or supply the wants of Daniel O'Connell and his men.

In the midst of these feelings and views, while Repeal in New York was raging very high, and spreading rapidly all over the country, while the "rent" was coming in from all quarters, some of the papers began the publication of Mr. O'Connell's famous speeches in the Corn Exchange abusing and calumniating the Southern States, and avowing his purpose was to begin an agitation against them as soon as he should have finished his Irish business. These violent speeches I republished in the New York *Herald*, and that gave them a very extensive circulation. I wished the peace and commercial intercourse of the two countries preserved and invigorated, not violated and weakened. These speeches were published, however, without any disrespectful remarks towards O'Connell. I still considered him to be a man of as much purity of motive as of great talent and tact—although subsequent experience has, in my estimation, somewhat diminished both.

The consequence of these publications, disclosing his attacks on the Southern States, and the promulgation of the whole truth, was to nip the Repeal agitation in the bud. Several meetings held in the neighborhood of New York turned out to be failures—little money was collected. In Philadelphia a Repeal meeting ended in a row, and little "rent." In Baltimore, Charleston, and other Southern cities, where Repeal associations had been formed, and large sums of money just ready to be transmitted to Ireland to draw a smile from the "Liberator," as it was counted out in the Corn Exchange—in all these cities the association distributed the "rent" for charitable purposes at home, and dissolved their existence forthwith.

In this way as the proprietor of a largely circulating journal, and for simply publishing "the truth, the whole truth, and nothing but the truth," was I one of the instruments in putting an end to the transmission of hundreds of thousands of dollars from the pockets of the poor and honest Irish and American people to the coffers of the Dublin Repeal Association, which no doubt is within the reach of the patriotic, pure, and loyal hands of Daniel O'Connell and his adherents.

Of all these facts no doubt Mr. O'Connell had received private intimation, and certainly they were quite sufficient to account for his gross breach of hospitality when I visited the Corn Exchange as one of the curious sights of Dublin. I received, however, during that visit the worth of the shilling I paid at the door—perhaps to a greater extent than I had by paying a sixpence at the Zoological Gardens in the Phœnix Park to see the wild beasts there. In both cases the tigers growled, and showed their teeth—but in the former case I learned to distinguish between a selfish and hypocritical patriot, and a generous, oppressed, and high-spirited people. For the distresses and social evils of the gallant people of Ireland, I have, as an American, a sympathy less expansive than Mr. O'Connell's, but equally as sincere—a hand that may not dive as deep into their pockets, but may be as liberal in its contributions to alleviate their real evils. I would not extort money from a distressed people under the shallow cry of patriotism, merely to supply my own necessities and extravagance. I would not try to extort money from my countrymen in a foreign land under the mask of beginning a great revolution, and when that attempt had failed by my own folly and ignorance, then abuse the people of that country, and insult a quiet traveller on his way, whose object was truth, kindness, and correct information.

I am,

Sir,

Your most obedient servant,

James Gordon Bennett, of New York.

Long's Hotel, New Bond Street, August 28, 1843.

The *Times* correspondent gave this short version of the affair:

> The proceedings were here interrupted for a moment by the introduction of Mr. James Gordon Bennett, whose card Tom Steele handed to Mr. O'Connell, intimating that its owner (who then stood beside Mr. O'Connell) was the proprietor of the New York *Herald.*
>
> MR. O'CONNELL—*I wish he would stay where he came from*; it is a much fitter place for him than this. We don't want him here (Mr. Bennett, a gentleman about fifty years of age, suddenly retreated, as he entered, across the table). He is one of the conductors of one of the vilest gazettes ever published by infamous publishers. (Laughter, and a partial disposition to hisses, which was suppressed by the Chair and persons around it.)

Much use was made of this unpleasant episode by Bennett's American foes in and out of journalism. The hostile Hone made this exultant notation in his diary:

> September 2—Bennett, the editor of the *Herald,* is on a tour through Great Britain, whence he furnishes lies and scandal for the infamous paper which has contributed so much to corrupt the morals and degrade the taste of the people of New York. If the following article, which is published to-day in the *Courier and Enquirer,* be correct (and it is too circumstantial to admit of its being doubted), it will require all of his impudence to get over the effects of it. Such a rebuff, from such a quarter must have been unexpected as it was mortifying. "The rejected of O'Connell" is not an enviable title. The occurrence took place at a great repeal meeting held at Dublin, on the 7th of August, at which the "great repealer"

was, of course, the most prominent actor. The statement relating to Mr. Bennett is as follows: "A gentleman, who had for some time been sitting beside Mr. O'Connell, here addressed Mr. Steele, and, handing him his card, requested an introduction to Mr. O'Connell. Mr. Steele accordingly presented the card, and intimated that Mr. James Gordon Bennett, of New York, was present. Mr. O'Connell replied: "He is a person with whom I can have nothing to do. He is the editor of the New York *Herald,* one of the most infamous gazettes ever printed, and I shall have nothing to say to him." This was a reception that Mr. Bennett did not count upon, and he forthwith proceeded to take his departure. The room being very full, his movement was much retarded; but, by the aid of the chairman, he struggled out amid the groans of the meeting.

CHAPTER V

FULL-TIDE SUCCESS

In 1840, the Cunarders began making Boston their first port of call. Bennett was moved by this to consider starting a newspaper in Boston, to make the most of the new facilities, but wisely gave up the project and organized rapid connections with New York instead. By August, 1841, the paper was so thoroughly established and so certain a money-maker that Bennett was enabled to buy a corner twenty-one by seventy-five at Fulton and Nassau Streets to accomodate his publishing plant. This was enlarged ten years later by the addition of fifty feet on Fulton Street. Here the *Herald* was to remain until it moved to Broadway.

Bennett mildly surprised the town, October 26, 1842, by offering his whole establishment for sale at an upset price of two hundred thousand dollars. His ostensible reason was to undertake a daily in London "for the purpose of defending, explaining and exhibiting to Europe the institutions, laws, morals, resources, movements and tendencies of the United States, which are now subject—from imperfect knowledge and strong prejudices—to misrepresentations and falsehoods of all kinds from all quarters."

This was an obvious bit of self-advertising and there were no bidders. He withdrew the offer on November second, being rather disappointed at the small stir made by the proposition.

If he had but known it some one would have made a rare bargain by taking up the offer. The *Herald* was on the full tide of success. The rocks were passed, its position and profits assured and there was soon to come a development that was to revolutionize the American daily press. This was the invention of the telegraph by Samuel F. B. Morse. Bennett was one of the first to grasp the importance of the new device to his profession. "What has become of space?" he asked in the *Herald* on June 4, 1844, after "What God hath wrought" had been successfully flashed from Washington to Baltimore.—"The magnetic telegraph at Washington has totally annihilated what there was left of (space) by steam and locomotives and steamships. We give a certified copy of ten minutes conversation between Mr. Silas Wright at Washington and Colonel Young in Baltimore in relation to the nomination of Mr. Wright. This shows what can be done."

It did indeed. Soon the network of wires began to spread across the land. New York was connected with Washington via Philadelphia, Wilmington and Baltimore. For a time there was a gap between the last two towns that had to be covered by rail. The amazing instrument of transmission, the Morse "key," was placed on exhibition at 563 Broadway, where the *Herald* urged its readers to go and view the marvel. By May 23, 1846, the *Herald* was able to get Mexican War news from Washington via the new method. A speech made by Henry Clay at Lexington, Kentucky, was sent by courier eighty miles to Cincinnati, and thence to the *Herald* by wire in time to appear in full on the morning of the next day. It cost five hundred

Cartoon of Mr. Bennett in *Vanity Fair,* April 27, 1861

dollars. Albany and Buffalo were united in 1846, but New York and Albany were not joined until June 22, 1847. Boston and New York, however, had effected junction on July 18, 1846, which did away with cruising for news from ocean steamers off New York, Boston becoming the news landing place for the time being. The bold pioneers who strung wires were F. O. J. Smith, of Portland, Maine, Henry O'Reilly, and Ezra Cornell, founder of the university that bears his name. The lines were not built connectedly. Bennett used such as existed lavishly, as far as he could. It soon became plain that the new method was expensive as well as expeditious and the tendency of one paper to "plug" the slow wire, to the disadvantage of another, added an impulse toward getting together on bulky matters that led later to forming the Associated Press. In 1848 the *Herald,* the *Journal of Commerce,* the *Tribune,* the *Courier and Enquirer, Sun* and *Express,* all of New York, quit cutting one another's throats. They combined at first on harbor news, and then went farther abroad. When the *Times* came into being in 1851, it was taken in. Gerard Hallock, of the *Journal of Commerce,* became president. He long and peacefully steered the organization.

The Texas-Mexico situation became of interest in 1844 and Bennett gave the matter careful attention, quickly extending the *Herald's* news service by establishing a courier system between New York and New Orleans, the center of news-getting from the troublesome Texans. This went into operation in January, 1845, with an exchange between the *Herald* and the *Crescent City* of New Orleans, an enterprising daily.

The "express," as it was called, beat the United States mails from one to four days, to the great wrath of Postmaster-General Wicliffe, who caused the arrest of Mr. O'Callaghan, one of the *Crescent City's* owners, for violating the postal laws which forbid the moving of mail by private means. This blocked the enterprise. Soon the Mexican War broke out in the spring of 1846 and nimbler news transport was required than that furnished by the Post Office Department. Bennett therefore reestablished his "express" in conjunction with the Philadelphia *Ledger* and the Baltimore *Sun.* This was continued during the war, often requiring the daily dispatch of special messengers. The success of the method caused its extension to other fields. The *Herald* proclaimed, on April 10, 1847, that four "expresses" from various parts of the country, bearing important information, had reached the office within twenty-four hours.

The next day it announced the fall of Vera Cruz and the capture of the great castle of San Juan D.Ulua:

"Our special and extraordinary express, which we had arranged for some time past on the Southern line between Philadelphia and New Orleans, arrived at Philadelphia yesterday morning at eight o'clock, when the news which it brought was transmitted to our office by telegraph." The "news" was the two events noted. This enterprise landed the important information in New York so that it could be published on Saturday. The regular service by mail did not get along till Monday. The publication, however, was not exclusive, as the *Herald* took care of the *Journal of Commerce,* the *Sun* and *Tribune,* who were also able to announce along with the *Herald* the successful assault on the City of Mexico and its defenses which was published on October 21, 1847. "Our readers will be pleased," observed the *Herald* on that date, "to see in this morning's *Herald* the long looked for intelligence from the City of Mexico. It reached New Orleans on the 13th inst., and was brought by the special overland express for the New York *Herald* and other papers. Owing to its importance, however, our messenger was instructed to bring the intelligence to the government at Washington and it will at once have general circulation throughout the country. This we thought due the public."

The extension of the telegraph soon put couriers, special railway engines and carrier pigeons out of business and news-getting became commonplace.

Strange as it may seem, the *Herald* was the only New York paper to send a correspondent to report the Mexican War. Two New Orleans journals, the *Picayune* and *Delta* alone of the rest of the American press, indulged in the enterprise. The others were content to get their news from the War Department at Washington. Instead of establishing his own attitude toward the war, Bennett accepted that of those who urged it. "The multitude cry aloud for war," he remarked editorially as early as August, 1845. In excuse he accurately described the American people in general as "restless, fidgety, discontented, anxious for excitement." This statement comes pretty near to being a good description of himself.

When the *Herald* was twelve years old, in 1847, it was the greatest advertising medium in the United States. Its contemporaries carried lifeless announcements, dull cards, published by the year and musty in their inefficiency. The *Herald* did the people's business. Up to the year noted it had suffered no advertisement to "run" or to be charged for more than two weeks. January 1, 1848, a new rule went into effect. No announcement would be accepted for more than one insertion. It had to be paid for cash down. Thereafter the *Herald* kept no books and its advertising columns took on the aspect of news. All cuts and "display" disappeared at the same time. Each advertiser was compelled to dress in the same garb as his neighbor. If he wished large type it had to be built up of agate letters in what were known as logotypes. This style was affected until nearly the end of the century, when competition forced the use of outline letters and later standard forms of typographical emphasis. There is no question, however, but the rule as invented and enforced by Bennett became a powerful factor in the paper's prosperity, and added to its value as a conveyor of news. With everybody treated alike the public felt a sense of fairness not to be found in any journal. Besides this, all paid the same rate. There were no discounts or special prices for large space—one of the modern injustices cultivated by all American newspapers, by which small advertisers are sacrificed to big ones who are thus made monopolists by the paper's aid.

This restriction on advertisers was successfully evaded by Robert Bonner, who, when Bennett refused him "display," resorted to repetition of the small lineage to which he was limited. In this way he carried his point, paying the *Herald* two thousand dollars for a single announcement. This forced the paper to print a quadruple sheet for its accommodation.

Not the least item in the *Herald's* success was its personal column, which, strangely enough, was later to become one cause of its ruin. But that in its place. These little "liners," full of mystery and suggestion, were closely read. That the column was used much as a means for making assignations is also true. The date-makers added zest to the classification. To-day the "agony" column of the London *Times* is the most interesting feature, as it was the *Herald's* in its prime.

In January, 1862, the *Times* overhauled the *Herald* for the suggestive character of some of its "personal" advertisements, but went no further than to dub it a "spicy" paper. To this comment, *Vanity Fair,* the clever comic paper of the day, added: "On consideration of the matter we conclude that the spice of the *Herald* must consist chiefly of cloves, because the cloven foot is seen sticking out very often, and the proprietor boasts that he lives in clover!" This jest has a flavor of Artemus Ward, then the new editor of *Vanity Fair.*

Bennett spent the winter and spring of 1847 in Paris. He was presented at the court of Louis Philippe, and like a thrifty Scotchman made no permanent investment in regalia, paying instead thirty francs a night rental for the use of a court dress, sword and chapeau. According to his biographer, Isaac C. Pray: "It was suggested, as he held a commission as a Major-General in the Mormon Army, that he should appear in the costume suited to his distinguished rank, but as he had never consulted his tailor on the subject, he was not prepared as military Americans traveling in Europe usually are, with the glittering pageantry of war."

His letters show a wide range of interest—from Lola Montez, then beguiling the King of Bavaria, to theaters, art, and the trembling thrones that were uncertainly awaiting the outcome of 1848. He also studied the press of London and Paris and gave the result at length in the columns of the *Herald;* he journeyed to Scotland in June and spent August and September in London and Liverpool investigating financial conditions, for which he always had a keen eye. He returned to America on the steamship *Cambria,* reaching Boston on October nineteenth. The *Herald* had grown in his absence and required new machinery to keep pace with it. This he made it his immediate business to procure.

The new year was full of action. Europe boiled over with revolutions, and in America the Whigs unhorsed the Democrats.

Thanks to superior sources of information, the *Herald* printed the certain ousting of Louis Philippe nearly a week before the news came that it had occurred. Another "scoop" was printing the treaty with Mexico. This cost Nugent, the *Herald's* Washington correspondent, some days in jail on order of the Senate. The editor went to the Capitol and rescued his diligent reporter. The enemies of the administration made much of the *Herald's* close relations with Secretary of State Buchanan in connection with this incident.

Following his policy of standing in with the administration, Bennett, who had supported Zachary Taylor in the belief that he would be elected, wrote him:

New York Herald Office, Nov. 17, 1848.

General Taylor, Dear Sir:-

Allow me to congratulate you on the result of the recent election.

Perhaps you may remember the Cataract Hotel, at Niagara Falls, in the summer of 1840, when I met with you, soon after your return from Florida. That casual intercourse was the basis of my recent course.

When we received in New York, an account of your dangerous position and subsequent brilliant affairs on the Rio Grande, in April and May, 1846, I remembered the acquaintance at Niagara, and then took the course in my journal which it has since followed.

You are now elevated to the high honor of President of the United States by the spontaneous outburst of the popular will. I joined in the movement simply from a conviction of your patriotism and capacity, but I want nothing, personally, of any administration but wisdom in its management, and the public good for its leading purpose. As an independent journalist and an early friend of your election, I can offer you a warm support when you may be right, with a respectful dissent when I am convinced you may be wrong. The highest human intellect is weak and erring before Heaven, yet I have every hope that your administration of this great Republic will be as wise, patriotic, and successful as that of the Father of his Country.

I am, sir, with great respect, your obedient servant,

James G. Bennett.

Unfortunately this kindly wish was not to come true. After a few months in office that promised well, President Taylor died and was succeeded by the Vice-President, Millard Fillmore of New York. The chief exploit of his administration was the expedition to Japan, to which enterprise the *Herald* gave its heartiest support.

The extraordinary expansion of American enterprise upon land and sea that followed the discovery of gold by James Wilson Marshall, the Mormon foreman of Captain John A. Sutter's ranch on the north fork of the American River, January 18, 1848, owed much of its initial impetus to the *Herald*. Some flakes of the precious metal from California came into the hands of Thomas D. Larkin, United States naval agent at Monterey, who was a *Herald* correspondent, and he contrived to get a pinch or two to Bennett, in New York. The editor had heard much of gold discoveries in the east that turned out to be mere traces, and so refused to be moved by the few glittering particles. Larkin had made a rather casual mention of the discovery in his letter accompanying the sample. Later letters showed more enthusiasm—so much so, indeed, that Bennett got out the despised sample and sent it to an assayer. It stood the test, as the following certifies:

New York, Dec. 8, 1848.

Mr. Bennett:

Sir:—I have assayed the portion of gold dust, or metal from California, which you sent me, and the result shows that it is fully equal to any found in our Southern gold mines.

I return you 10¾ grains out of the 12 which I have tested, the value of which is 45 cents. It is 21½ carats fine—within half a carat of the quality of English sovereigns or American eagles, and is almost ready to go to the mint.

The finest gold metal we get is from Africa, which is 22½ to 23 carats fine. In Virginia we have mines where the quality of the gold is much inferior, some of it is as low as 19 carats, and in Georgia the mines produce it nearly 22 carats fine.

The gold of California which I have now assayed is fully equal to that of any, and much superior to some produced from the mines in our Southern States.

Yours respectfully,
JOHN WARWICK,
Smelter and Refiner, 17 John Street.

Upon the publication of this assay the East took fire. Within a few days a company of adventurers chartered the bark *John Benson,* and sailed from New York to Chagres. Sixty of them reached the land of gold, and at least one, Jem Grant, who ran a *Herald* barber shop in Ann Street, became an alderman in San Francisco and a reputed millionaire. The tidings of treasure trove electrified the earth. An extraordinary rush followed from all quarters of the world, with New York as the chief starting point. Lines of transit were opened across Panama and Nicaragua, in the first instance developing into a railway, and in the second to steamer lines on Nicaraguan lakes and rivers. Taking the lead in exploiting the discovery the *Herald* gained great favor in the land of gold. Every steamer took out heavy consignments of copies—running to ten thousand and fifteen thousand a day, which were eagerly bought by the argonauts on arrival at San Francisco.

In the course of a trip to the Pacific coast in 1859, Horace Greeley fell in love with Colorado and broadly proclaimed its potentials in agriculture and mining. Gold had been discovered, and Mr. Greeley boomed the fact. Henry Villard, then a young and adventurous newspaper writer, representing the Cincinnati *Commercial,* kept him company to the mines, as did Albert D. Richardson, another celebrated correspondent, then attached to the Boston *Journal*. The three united in a statement supporting the splendor of the gold "prospects." For this Greeley was ridiculed and abused, especially by Bennett in the *Herald*, who held that the rival journalist had been fooled and was fooling others. It was the sort of petty performance all too common in American journalism. Mr. Greeley happened to be right and Colorado has never forgotten his valorous services on her behalf. Thus both from super-skepticism and scorn for Horace Greeley, Bennett failed to make the killing out of the mineral discoveries in Colorado which had attended his ready acceptance of California as an El Dorado.

The last assault on Bennett's person occurred November 9, 1850. He was walking on Broadway, near White Street, with Mrs. Bennett, when John Graham, who had been defeated as the Tammany Hall candidate for district attorney a few days before, came up with his brothers, DeWitt and Charles K. Graham. They carried cowhides and were accompanied by a guard of heelers. Bennett was knocked down and badly beaten with the whips. Mrs. Bennett had to stand by and watch in helpless agony. Bennett described the affair in an editorial the next day:

Yesterday morning about ten o'clock, the ninth inst., I was walking down Broadway with my wife. On reaching the corner of Broadway and White Street I was assaulted by a gang of rowdies and ruffians headed by John Graham, late candidate for District Attorney, and his brother DeWitt Graham—an employee in the Custom House under Hugh Maxwell—and also Charles K. Graham, another brother, with a

GREAT EXPECTATIONS.

GREAT EXPECTATIONS.—CHARLES DICKENS' BEST BOOK.—GREAT EXPECTATIONS.—TWO ILLUSTRATED EDITIONS, IN DUODECIMO AND OCTAVO FORM.—CHARLES DICKENS' NEW BOOK.—AUTHOR'S COPYRIGHTED EDITIONS.—DICKENS' MASTER-PIECE.—GREAT EXPECTATIONS.—GREAT EXPECTATIONS.—GREAT EXPECTATIONS.—GREAT EXPECTATIONS.—DUODECIMO ILLUSTRATED EDITION.—Two editions, with thirty-four illustrations, by McLenan, in cloth, either in duodecimo or octavo form, for $1.50 each, as well as a cheap edition in paper cover, price 50 cents. Is published and for sale this day by

T. B. PETERSON & BROS., No. 306 Chestnut-street, Philadelphia.

Copies sent per mail anywhere, free of postage on receipt of price.

VOL. 4. NO. 87.

VANITY FAIR

Saturday,

AUG. 24,

1861.

PUBLISHED EVERY SATURDAY, AT 100 NASSAU STREET, NEW-YORK.

PRICE THREE DOLLARS PER ANNUM—SINGLE COPIES SIX CENTS.

"THE REPUBLICAN QUEEN" VISITS LONG BRANCH.

See N. Y. Herald, Aug. 7.

GALLANT FEAT OF SIR JAMES GORDON, WALTER RALEIGH, BENNETT.

Bennett Cartoon in *Vanity Fair*, August 24, 1861

concerns was a liberal crop of libel suits. Bennett hired the best legal talent he could secure and fought all cases to a finish, to the discouragement of prosecutors. In one instance, however, the promoters of an opera season sued the *Herald* for adverse criticism that affected them disastrously and won ten thousand dollars damages in 1855. Bennett carried it on from one court to another, securing several reversals but in the end was mulcted six thousand dollars.

The *Herald* sustained the Compromise of 1850 against "the fanatical abolitionists" and "the ultra southerners," appealing to all Union-loving citizens to regard both as menacing to its safety. It was pretty severe on the abolitionists led by Greeley, Weed and Seward. The Massachusetts opponents of the fugitive slave law were "incendiaries, rebels and traitors," whose "opposition to the law is not freedom but anarchy." It called upon President Fillmore to enforce the act, pointing out that a fugitive slave had been peacefully given up in New York and bought back by philanthropists. With the conduct of the law it found no fault. Both North and South had given up much in the Compromise, and the *Herald* pleaded that both sections suppress their radicals else disunion would become inevitable. At the time the paper certainly represented the sentiment of its community. The editor's first anxiety was to save the Union. In this respect he was in entire accord with Abraham Lincoln, when the problem reached his hands. Yet for its sane attitude the *Herald* somehow earned an odium it could never shake off. Read to-day, its editorials are reasonable and sound. Events proved their correctness. Bennett represented the general interest, not a "cause." At the end of Millard Fillmore's administration Bennett saw no hope for the Whigs. Free Soil and Know-Nothingism had done their work. Besides, General Winfield Scott, the Whig nominee, was a joke. Bennett accordingly put the power of the *Herald* behind Franklin Pierce, of New Hampshire, an old acquaintance, in the belief that Democratic success alone could save the Union from disruption. Pierce was elected. Bennett's shifting of sides was much resented, and there were charges that he had done so in the expectancy of securing the French mission as his reward. It was not true. Pierce did not even write him directly in giving thanks, but requested a third party to convey this much of a message: "I have not been insensible to the vast influence of the *Herald* throughout the late canvass. Will you assure Mr. B. when you write him that I appreciate both the motive and the ability, and at the same time present to him my sincere acknowledgments."

After the election of Pierce in 1852, Bennett thought abolitionism was dying and vented his scorn on Horace Greeley and his "nigger worshipers," as he pleasantly dubbed the friends of African freedom. In all this he was wrong; indeed he was often mistaken in the direction of popular currents.

The energy Bennett put behind the news-gathering forces of the *Herald* has never been beaten. "Exclusively in the *Herald*" became almost a trade-mark. The other papers, try as they might, seldom or never beat it in the news hunt. What they got they usually stole from the *Herald's* columns. No night editor ever slept until he had conned the contents of every edition of the *Herald*.

One of these news-stealing exploits was rather elaborate in its way. The Collins Line steamer *Arctic* went down in the Atlantic, September 28, 1854, with many souls, as the result of a collision on the preceding day. She was returning from Liverpool and was so long overdue that the worst was feared, when, on October tenth, rumor solidified into a firm belief that she was lost. This reached the office of the New York *Times*, where, unable to confirm or deny, a paragraph embracing the belief was inserted and the night city editor started for home at three A. M. Dozing on the horse car he overheard a disjointed conversation anent the *Arctic*, and caught a hint that a rescued person had reached port and found his way to the *Herald*. Threading out that the tale bearer had sold his great story to the *Herald*, he retraced his steps to the *Times* office and, stopping its presses, sent a scout to the *Herald* shop. He found it all alight, with every door locked. Hanging about, he was able to buy a copy as the delivery began under guard. In it was the two-column narrative of the survivor, George H. Burns, who had dictated his account of the disaster and received a rich reward. It was cut up into four-line "takes" and put into type within an hour. The *Herald*, meanwhile, held back its city edition, only to be outfooted by the managers of the *Times*, who ran their presses until two o'clock in the afternoon, supplying the demand, and quite blanketing their over-cautious contemporary. The scout got fifty dollars for his enterprise, and the night city editor had five dollars added to his weekly pay for his share in the exploit. The *Times* tried to excuse itself on the ground that the "exhausted Burns" had relied on the *Herald* to tell his tale to everybody and had been deceived in trusting to the "honor" of the *Herald.*

Professional success did not lead Bennett to muffle the blowing of his own personal horn. In 1854 James Parton, a young Englishman with a bent for biography wrote one of Horace Greeley that achieved great popularity. Not to be outdone, Bennett contrived with Isaac C. Pray, a New York journalist, to produce *James Gordon Bennett and His Times.* It was a good deal of an apology. Though interesting, it did not become as good a seller as the Greeley book.

The American habit of giving testimonials was occasionally used to gratify the vanity of the *Herald's* proprietor. Frederic Hudson thus describes one incident: "On the 1st of January, 1855, a large, mysterious-looking box was sent to the St. Nicholas Hotel for Mr. Bennett. He looked at it attentively for a few moments and declined receiving it, saying, 'That looks like another infernal machine on a large scale.' He could not decipher the signature of the note accompanying the handsome box. But the hotel keeper assured him it was all right by bringing down one of the firm of Ball, Black and Co., from whose establishment it came. It was then opened and found to contain a splendid service of silver plate, consisting of ten pieces, each with an appropriate inscription. This is the chief one:

Presented
to
James Gordon Bennett
as a
Testimonial

To the Editor of the Truly National Newspaper of the American Republic; the firm and unwavering Supporter of the Constitution; the Opponent of the Spoils System of Government; the Ready and Effective Advocate of the Rights of the People.

New York City, January 1855.

On the milk pitcher—the inscription should have been engraved on the hot-water pitcher—were the words:

Presented to
James Gordon Bennett
the most abused
Editor in America.

Mr. Hudson does not reveal the source of the gift and there was a suspicion that the editor sent it to himself.

Whether Bennett made gifts to himself to attract attention or whether others made them to shine in the acquired publicity themselves, the practise was so much in vogue that *Vanity Fair* found in it ample occasion for mirth. Here is one of its skits burlesquing the notion with the *Herald* as a foil:

A TESTIMONIAL TO THE "HERALD."

Actuated by a sentiment of gratitude for past favors, as well as by a pretty sharp look out, perhaps, for more of the same sort in prospect, the charming Waiter Girls of the Broadway Concert Saloons have been giving expression to their esteem for that excellent patron of theirs, the *New York Herald.* At a meeting held, about a fortnight since, by those attractive demigoddesses, at Vestal Hall, in Diana Street, a committee was appointed for the purpose of drawing up resolutions of thanks to the Senior Editor of the *Herald,* for the course dictated by him to that truly Christian journal with regard to the subterrene Cecilian and Terpsichorean establishments of this City. Two of the young ladies, who are noted for their proficiency in draughting off lager beer, were appointed to draught off the resolutions, which they did in true tapster style "with a head on." In addition to the thanks, which were ordered to be engrossed upon a tambourine, the committee decided upon presenting the venerable Senior Man of the *Herald* with a medal, commemorative of the exertions made by him in favor of Terpsichore and Tod. This medal, with an engraving of which we have the pleasure of presenting our readers, is appropriately made of brass, cast from the trimmings of the brass mounted pistol with which Gil. Snickerfoot shot Redash Cole in the Temple of Everlasting Felicity on lower Broadway. The design speaks for itself. It is extremely chaste, as might have been expected from the character of the fair quarter from which it came, and is the combined production of the young man who plays the piano in the above-named place of amusement and the young woman who dances the Highland Fling. The venerable recipient of the medal was so touched by the expressions of the fair donoresses that he immediately suspended it from his neck, with a garter presented to him by the young lady in spangles who dances the Schottische, after which they all supped together, and had a very merry evening of it until late on the following afternoon.

Prize-fighting was not a plutocratic profession in these old *Herald* days. The "pugs" fought with bare knuckles in lonely barns for small sums and in constant fear of raiding by officers of the law. There were no million-dollar purses paid out of the proceeds of a two million, five hundred thousand dollar "box." The manly art was backward in everything except skill and endurance. Against these were to be credited brutality

Presentation of a Medal by the Pretty Waiter Girls to the old Man of the Herald.

Cartoon in *Vanity Fair*, February 29, 1862

and popular disapproval. Indeed, when John C. Heenan, "The Benicia Boy," champion of America, defeated Tom Sayers in an open ring in England, where they were less squeamish, *Harper's Weekly,* which was run by three sedate Methodist brothers, labeled a picture, drawn by Thomas Nast at the ringside, "Brutal and Disgusting Prize Fight," to get away with the odium.

Cock-fighting was another surreptitious sport. It, too, was carried on by its votaries and admirers in hidden lofts and country stables. The reporter of the pastime had to be always on the alert to keep track of "mills" and "mains." "Tad" McAlpin, the *Herald's* veteran in these lines, seldom failed to score. To get an "exclusive" on one of the events was to make a mark in journalism. Though still retaining its popularity in Latin-America, the cock-fight no longer secures space in North American newspapers. Fancy this appearing in a modern newspaper, as it came from Troy, New York, to the *Herald*:

> This long anticipated cock-fight—the Athenian amusement, the boasted pleasure of China, India and the Philippine Islands, and the favorite subject of Aristophanes, the Greek—between Albany and Troy cocks, came off in this city this evening in the cock loft of Paul Cavanaugh's saloon, in Congress Street. The *élite* of American sportsmen, from John Morrissey down, were present, and the whole scene was mostly characteristic of American liberal life, unrestrained by the police.

So the tale went on for a column and a half filled with technical phrases, "minute and disgusting" details, as a critic of the day described them, and much "slang and vulgarity." Indeed, however much an Aristophanes might have enjoyed the fight, the report was hardly up to his classic taste. It was not written for him, however, but for the lop-eared crowd. New York sent Morrissey, a prize-fighter, to Congress, and for years the state allowed him to run a splendid gambling "hell" in Saratoga. Bennett knew his times and did not try to improve them. To size up events with a popular appeal and make them interesting to the kind of minds they fed was his mission as a news-seller. For this he was abused, yet Charles A. Dana did the same thing in the *Sun* at a little later day without inviting criticism. To Dana anything interesting was "news," and he made it respectable.

CHAPTER VI

BENNETT AND BARNUM

The high-powered modern press agent has nothing on P. T. Barnum of gorgeous memory. For two decades and a half he vied with Bennett in the great art of attracting attention, sometimes in harmony, but often out of tune. Recognizing the *Herald* as the popular medium for a twenty-five-cent show, Barnum made free use of its columns when he could. Bennett did not mind a puff if it was interesting, but he collected for it by gibing Barnum mercilessly whenever the chance occurred, which was pretty often. Barnum's manner of approach is well indicated by the following found among Bennett's papers:

Museum—March 27/50

Mr. Bennett—I hope that you will find the subject and the style of the article left this morning of such a nature (as well as those which will follow it) as will make it worth your while to let them appear in the *Weekly Herald*. Of course I can not press this, but if found of sufficient interest for your weekly and if you have the room to spare it will be a favor for which I shall feel much obliged.

Truly yours,
P. T. Barnum.

Another article on same subject (of almost ½ column) will be ready about Monday next.—P. T. B.

Again:

American Museum
May 15/50

Mr. Barnum's comps to Mr. Bennett and begs to say that if the enclosed "Review" should happen to be just the thing for the *Herald* he would like to have it appear, but if it is not apropos, or in any manner interferes with more valuable matter, let it be consigned to the flames.

Barnum's greatest triumph was in bringing Jenny Lind, the Swedish songstress, to America for a series of concerts in 1850. His publicity campaign was a masterpiece of planning and execution. The *Herald* and newspapers generally were fed up by the newly fledged impresario who resorted to the ingenious plan of selling first-night tickets by auction. In New York John N. Genin, a hatter, paid two hundred and twenty-five dollars for the first ticket, gaining much free advertising thereby. In Boston Ossian E. Dodge, an entertainer, gave six hundred and twenty-five dollars for No. 1. In Providence, Philadelphia and Baltimore equally extravagant prices were paid for introducing the lady to America. Barnum gave the *Herald* the lead in his press notices, even sending Mr. Bennett a copy of his letter engaging rooms for the lady at the Irving House, addressed to Landlord Howard. It read:

New York, April 16, 1850.

D. D. Howard, Esq.,
Dear Sir:—

The apartments in the Irving House which you had the kindness to show me to-day as in your opinion calculated to please and accommodate Jenny Lind, Julius Benedict, Esq., Signor Belletti, and their suite I consider elegant and commodious in the extreme and hasten to inform you that I will engage the same for that distinguished party and wish them to be held in reserve for them on and from the tenth day of September next.

Respectfully
Your obt sevt
P. T. Barnum.

This copy was accompanied by the following ingenuous note:

Museum, Tuesday Evening.

Mr. Bennett,
Dear Sir:
I engaged apartments at the Irving today for Jenny Lind & suite and the above is a copy of the letter sent to Mr. Howard by myself. I have also today put up the large amount of money required by Jenny Lind to be lodged in the hands of Baring Brothers and send it by tomorrow's steamer. If any of the above is found of public interest sufficient to get in tomorrow's *Herald* I shall feel much obliged as I wish to send it in print across the Atlantic tomorrow.

Truly yours,
P. T. Barnum.

The *Herald* badgered Barnum a bit on Jenny Lind's coming, objecting to the ballooning of the price of seats, and demanding three-dollar admissions. The day after the first concert, which was given on October 24, 1850, Miss Lind wrote to Barnum urging lower rates. He at once conceded three-dollar, four-dollar and five-dollar seats according to location. This was a victory for Bennett, who modestly acclaimed the fact. The Boston *Chronotype* had printed a tale to the effect that John McClenahan, a *Herald* reporter, had attempted to blackmail the songstress. It was untrue and Barnum hastened to make an affidavit to that effect. This the *Herald* printed, commenting complacently:

We shall say nothing further about Barnum. Let the sinner have a chance to repent. . . . Barnum, we have frequently admitted, has some good points about him. There is some genuine good in his composition. He is like the mother mountain of gold in California, with two and one-half per cent of gold dust to a mountain of primitive rock. As for ourselves we deserve a charity concert, the funds to be devoted to the benefit of the poor for the work we have accomplished in reforming Barnum—a reform going beyond his own temperance humbug.

The *Herald's* critique of the first concert was more than kind, even if it did poke fun at her manager, and during Miss Lind's stay in New York the paper was certainly most considerate. Nevertheless, it did not fail to keep its eye on Barnum while he was on the road.

"After permitting one favorable notice in his paper," Barnum writes in his autobiography, rather unfairly, "Bennett had turned around as usual and abused Jenny Lind and bitterly attacked me. There was an estrangement, no new thing between the editor and myself. The *Herald,* in its desire to excite attention, has a habit of attacking public men and I had not escaped. I was always glad to get such notices, for they served as inexpensive advertisements to my Museum, and brought custom to me free of charge."

This comment was written apropos of an encounter

with Bennett on the steamer *Falcon* of the Havana-New Orleans Line, on which Barnum and the Jenny Lind party were bound for the latter port. So were Mr. and Mrs. Bennett. Barnum had a ticket-taker by the name of Henry Bennett, who bitterly resented the *Herald's* attacks upon his employer. He had announced a firm purpose in New York of horsewhipping the editor and had been persuaded not to by Barnum, who may be allowed to continue the story thus:

When Editor Bennett came on board the "Falcon," he had in his arms a small pet monkey belonging to his wife, and the animal was placed in a safe place on the forward deck. When Henry Bennett saw the editor he said to a bystander:

"I would willingly be drowned if I could see that old scoundrel go to the bottom of the sea."

Several of our party overheard the remark and I turned laughingly to Bennett and said: "Nonsense; he can't harm any one, and there is an old proverb about the impossibility of drowning those who are born to another fate."

That very night, however, as I stood near the cabin door, conversing with my treasurer and other members of my company, Henry Bennett came up to me with a wild air, and hoarsely whispered:

"Old Bennett has gone forward alone in the dark—and I am going to throw him overboard!"

We were all startled, for we knew the man and he seemed terribly in earnest. Knowing how most effectively to address him at such times, I exclaimed:

"Ridiculous! You would not do such a thing."

"I swear I will," was his savage reply. I expostulated with him, and several of our party joined me.

"Nobody will know it," muttered the maniac, "and I will be doing the world a favor."

I endeavored to awaken him to a sense of the crime

he contemplated, assuring him that it could not possibly benefit any one, and that from the fact of the existing relations between the editor and myself, I should be the first to be accused of his murder. I implored him to go to his stateroom, and he finally did so, accompanied by some of the gentlemen of our party. I took pains to see that he was carefully watched that night, and, indeed, for several days, till he became calm again. He was a large, athletic man, quite able to pick up his namesake and drop him overboard. The matter was too serious for a joke, and we made little mention of it, but more than one of my party said then, and has often said since, what I really believe to be true, that "James Gordon Bennett would have been drowned that night had it not been for P. T. Barnum."

Mr. Barnum did not confide the episode to Bennett, nor does he say that they sought each other socially during the voyage. Arriving at New Orleans, the process of bidding for concert tickets was resumed and coincidentally there appeared in the *Herald* a broad charge that the ingenious Mr. Barnum was behind the bidding. To this he sent an indignant challenge to the *Herald,* on these terms:

New Orleans, March 4, 1851.

Mr. James Gordon Bennett,
Editor and proprietor of the New York Herald.
Sir:

I will pay a reward of Five Thousand Dollars to any person who shall prove by respectable witnesses that I was ever directly or indirectly in the remotest degree interested with any person in bidding for or purchasing tickets at auction for the Concerts of Mlle. Jenny Lind as stated in your paper of the 21st of February. I assert positively that this was never the case, but that in the disposition of tickets on all occasions either at public or private sale, I have invariably given directions that the strictest fairness and impartiality should be maintained with the public, and this has always been done.

P. T. Barnum.

The Bennett trip to Havana was taken shortly after the assault by John Graham and his brothers, related in an earlier chapter, and was much needed as refreshment after the injuries to body and nerves then received.

This visit followed an attempt by Lopez to land at Cardenas with a filibustering expedition in the spring of 1850. It came to nothing, but put Cuba much in the news, and a doctrine of "manifest destiny" had been evolved in the southern part of the United States that advocated the annexation of the island. Mr. Bennett had a good time in spite of the friction. He arrived about the first of December, 1850, and dined with the Governor-General at the palace. On December seventh a "grand ball" was given by the Signor Conde de Penalver, at which the editor and his wife were prominent guests. The Havana papers treated them with distinguished consideration. "We had the pleasure of admiring Mrs. Bennett of New York, so remarkable for her judgment, and whose manifest talents attracted the greatest interest," said the official journal. "She was attired with perfect taste, and her exquisite dress was observed with the deepest attention. She was accompanied by Mr. Bennett."

Soon after, Lopez landed again accompanied by a number of adventurous Americans. He was captured and shot, as were some of our countrymen. Mr. Bennett had concluded as the result of his observations that Cuba was not ready for liberty and vigorously opposed the doctrine of manifest destiny, while Mrs. Bennett, then in Europe, made a personal appeal to the Court at Madrid and secured the release of a number of the Americans who had been sent to prison.

The *Herald* continued to make sport of the showman and his entertainments. New York, envious of London's Crystal Palace, attempted a similar enterprise on the ground now called Bryant Park, facing Sixth Avenue, between Fortieth and Forty-second Streets. The management failed to make expenses and unloaded on Barnum and Horace Greeley, who undertook to speed up the exhibition. Naturally neither appealed to Bennett. His attacks were hurtful and Barnum ventured to plead for a truce:

Office of the Association for the Exhibition of the Industry of all Nations, 218 Broadway, New York.
April 28, 1854.
Mr. James Gordon Bennett—
Dear Sir:

I send you this letter as a Flag of Truce and not for publication.

I doubt whether you really entertain any enmity against me from the fact that you have frequently told Mr. Cromwell that you did not—but having been in the habit of making me a kind of target for the last 18 years, this habit has become a kind of "second nature" to you, and thus do we find "Mermaid," "Joice Heth," "Woolly Horse," &c., stereotyped, as it were, and it has sometimes struck me that your readers would think you were dosing them ad nauseum.

Well, I think your experience in this instance has convinced you that I am not to be killed by newspaper bullets. So far from it, I rather liked your attacks and squibs when you did not attempt to impeach my integrity.

But now comes the question: Don't you think it is time to let me drop? I mean as a target for your ridicule. I decidedly think it is and respectfully request you to do so. For myself personally I don't care two straws for all the newspaper squibs that could be written in a century. But I am now engaged in managing a public enterprise which I hope and believe will be made highly conducive to the interests and reputation of this city and the country at large.

Second, I have a family growing up around me—am myself not quite as young as I once was, and all things considered, I have to request that you will hereafter not speak of myself or my actions in a spirit of ridicule or abuse except I, or they, really deserve it.

If in addition to desisting from such a course, you should (for a wonder) begin to speak of me and my efforts with some little degree of respect and encouragement, (selecting some other butt for your sarcasm for the next 18 years) I really think you will consult your own interests as well as oblige

Truly yours,
P. T. Barnum

However effective this might have been in tempering the wind it was not of long endurance. The Crystal Palace burned to the ground and so cut short its problems. The Civil War next broke out, but did not wholly do away with pleasantries about Joice Heth and the Woolly Horse, for among the Bennett papers appears a Barnum note dated January 25, 1864, reading: "Your article today is calculated to do me serious injury and as it is not by any means borne out by the facts, I ask as an act of justice you publish the enclosed communication."

Soon a new cause for trouble developed between the pair, one that was severely to try the strength of both.

July 13, 1865, Barnum's American Museum at Broadway and Ann Street was destroyed by fire. The ground was a leasehold with eleven years to run. Bennett had long desired to place the *Herald* establishment on Broadway. The day after the fire he approached Barnum on the subject of purchasing his lease, having in view the acquisition of the property on which the lease was a lien. The shrewd showman had secured an appraisal of two hundred and seventy-five thousand dollars as the value of his contract. When Bennett asked his price he replied: "Please go or send immediately to Homer Morgan's office and you will learn that Mr. Morgan has the lease for sale at two hundred and twenty-five thousand dollars. This is fifty thousand dollars less than the estimated value, but to you I deduct twenty-five thousand dollars from my already reduced price, so you may have the lease for two hundred thousand dollars."

A few days later Bennett handed Barnum a check on the Chemical Bank for two hundred thousand dollars. He had previously agreed with the owner to take the fee at five hundred thousand dollars—one hundred thousand dollars down, plus a mortgage for four hundred thousand dollars.

According to Barnum:

> When, therefore, Mr. Bennett saw it stated in the newspaper that the sum which he had paid for a piece of land measuring only fifty-six by one hundred feet was more than was ever before paid in any city in the world for a tract of that size, he discovered the serious oversight he had made; and the owner of the property

NO DRAFTIN' IN BALDINSVILLE.

THE FIRST OF A SERIES OF ORIGINAL LETTERS ON THE WAR, WRITTEN EXPRESSLY FOR VANITY FAIR, BY ARTEMUS WARD, WILL APPEAR IN OUR NEXT NUMBER.

THEY WILL BE CONTINUED WEEKLY.

VOL. 6. VANITY FAIR NO. 142.

Saturday, SEPT. 13, 1862.

PUBLISHED EVERY SATURDAY, AT 116 NASSAU STREET, N.Y.

PRICE TWO DOLLARS PER ANNUM—SINGLE COPIES SIX CENTS.

PHINEAS TAYLOR BARNUM:

Blowing, with all his might, for his "Happy Family," the confiding Public.

Cartoon in *Vanity Fair*, September 13, 1862

was immediately informed that Bennett would not take it. But Bennett had already signed a bond to the owner, agreeing to pay $100,000 cash, and to mortgage the premises for the remaining $400,000.

Supposing by this step he had shaken off the owner of the fee, Bennett was not long in seeing that as he was not to own the land he would have no possible use for the lease, for which he paid the $200,000; and accordingly his next step was to shake me off also, and get back the money he had paid me.

In this endeavor Mr. Bennett's attorney invited Mr. Barnum to call at his office. The showman did so quite unsuspectingly. Here is what followed:

"Mr. Barnum," said the lawyer, "I have sent for you to say that Mr. Bennett has concluded not to purchase the museum lots, and therefore you had better take back the lease, and return the $200,000 paid for it."

"Are you in earnest?" Barnum asked.

"Certainly, quite so," he replied.

"Really," smiled Barnum, "I am sorry I can't accommodate Mr. Bennett; I have not got the little sum about me; in fact, I have spent the money."

"It will be better for you to take back the lease," observed the lawyer gravely.

"Nonsense," answered Barnum. "I shall do nothing of the sort, I don't make child's bargains. The lease was cheap enough, but I have other business to attend to, and shall have nothing to do with it."

The next day Barnum's advertisement—he was playing his museum company at the Winter Garden—was omitted from the *Herald*. He called at the *Herald* office and found the owner absent, so he took the matter up with Frederic Hudson, the managing editor, remarking:

"My advertisement is left out of the *Herald;* is there a screw loose?"

"I believe there is," was the reply.

"What is the matter?"

"You must ask the Emperor," said Mr. Hudson, meaning of course Bennett.

The "Emperor" would not be in until Monday. Barnum decided not to see him, but instead called a meeting of the local theatrical managers for noon the following day, where, after stating his case, it was moved to pull all their advertisements out of the *Herald,* unless it relented on Barnum. Messrs, Lester Wallack, Wheatly and Stuart were appointed a committee to carry the dictum to the editor. According to Barnum:

The moment Bennett saw them, he evidently suspected the object of their mission, for he at once commenced to speak to Mr. Wallack in a patronizing manner; told him how long he had known and how much he respected his late father, who was "a true English gentleman of the old school," with much more in the same strain. Mr. Wallack replied to Bennett that the three managers were appointed a committee to wait upon him to ascertain if he insisted upon excluding from his columns the Museum advertisements,—not on account of any objection to the contents of the advertisements, or to the Museum itself, but simply because he had a private business disagreement with the proprietor—intimating that such a proceeding, for such a reason, and no other, might lead to a rupture of business relations with other managers. In reply, Mr. Bennett had something to say about the fox that had suffered tailwise from a trap, and thereupon advised all other foxes to cut their tails off; and he pointed the fable by setting forth the impolicy of drawing down upon the Association the vengeance of the *Herald*. The committee, however coolly insisted upon a direct answer to their question.

Bennett then answered: "I will not publish Barnum's advertisement; I do business as I please, and in my own way."

"So do we," replied one of the committee, which thereupon departed. The next day the Association unanimously resolved to cut out the *Herald's* columns and to withdraw their printing from its job office, in all a loss of from seventy-five thousand dollars to one hundred thousand dollars a year. The warfare became bitter at once. The *Herald* expanded its notices of the cheap shows outside of the Association and abused the performances given by its members. These retorted by putting a line: "This establishment does not advertise in the New York *Herald*" over their announcements in the other papers. Mr. Barnum asserts that the public took sides against the *Herald* and thronged the playhouses. The boycott with its incidental heating of the *Herald's* columns lasted two years. Before the end of this time Mr. Bennett had been sued under his contract by the seller of the land and settled the day before the case came to trial. Peace was made with the Association, who found it paid, after all, to use the *Herald*. Barnum had formed a partnership with Van Amburgh which was the beginning of the "Greatest Show on Earth," and did not follow his associates. Soon (March 2, 1868) the museum, then located farther up-town, burned, and Barnum made his further way under canvas. He thought Bennett would have got the worst of it even had he taken back the lease as under its terms he would have been compelled to build a new museum. Both sides had overestimated their powers in the contest. The theaters lost, especially in out-of-town patronage, which the *Herald* had always supplied through its wide circulation and the fact that it was most read by guests at the hotels. Barnum once estimated that the price paid for the plot—seven hundred thousand dollars—would have covered it with gold dollars.

Upon this costly site Bennett built a structure of marble and iron, fireproof throughout, in which the *Herald* made its home until it moved up-town in 1894. Outwardly it was white and attractive. Within, the iron stairways and dark finish made it gloomy to the eye. There was no elevator; men climbed to their work on the metal stairs. It was, however, the most modern and costly newspaper building in New York. In 1895 James Gordon Bennett the younger sold the corner to Henry O. Havemeyer for one million dollars—no great advance from the price paid in 1865, including as it did an expensive structure. This the purchaser pulled down and erected the sky-scraping Colonial Building in its stead.

The *Herald's* columns abounded in puffery as well as slams. Bennett was liberal in praises of men he liked or procured patronage from. Indeed the puffs printed would in modern days be regarded as shameless unless pleasantly disguised as news by some ingenious press-agent. Here is a fine example, taken from the issue of June 18, 1842:

The Kremelin Dining Saloon, 111 Broadway. We stopt at those lovely rooms yesterday about soup time, and such Turtle Soup we never drank. It was not drink—it was eating. It was really balm for the body. We enquired of our host whether he was always so full? He said, no—we are never so full as when you come here. We wonder why the visits of other distinguished editors should not attract as well as ourselves. Even the Col. (Webb) won't draw. We will be there to dine tomorrow at 4 o'clock, and dine with our old friend in the Game room.

How the writer must have smacked his rather wide lips! Note also his listing himself as an attraction along with calipash and calipee! Yet did not Londoners in the eighteenth century gather at the Mitre Inn where Doctor Samuel Johnson dined, to see that great man feed?

CHAPTER VII

BENNETT AND BUCHANAN

BENNETT'S early experience in political journalism had taught him to be wary of parties and politicians, and he never tied the *Herald* columns tightly to any cause. He could be friendly and helpful, but not devoted, and he reserved always the right to switch without notice. He preferred to be a chronicler pure and simple, and to sit on the side-lines and throw stones to stir up the animals when they became sluggish. His one definite purpose was to tell all that was worth telling about everybody and everything.

This policy did not by any means take him apart from public life. He never put his heart in the crux of any cause to have it broken as Horace Greeley did, nor would he imperil his paper by causing it to stand or fall on one policy or another but took the world as he found it and made the most of it. If the *Herald* was normally superficial and seldom serious, it was due to this studied system. Its power grew from its overwhelming lead on the news.

Naturally, an editor, so delightfully situated, perfectly independent through the profits of his paper, was in an enviable position. He was sought by political leaders, usually without avail. His chief use for a statesman was to get tips from him that would serve the *Herald*. If he turned quickly it was because he thought events had earned the shift. Widely acquainted through his service in Washington, he could open almost any door. One of these was that of James Buchanan, James K. Polk's Secretary of State, Franklin Pierce's Minister to Great Britain, and President of the United States, from March 4, 1857, to the same date in 1861.

In 1846, when preparing for a trip to Europe, Bennett had called upon the Secretary of State for credentials. To his request the latter replied:

Washington, 30 May 1846.

My dear Sir:

I have received your favor and it will afford me pleasure to comply with your request. You shall, also, have the courier's passport for the steamer of the 16th June. Please to remind me of this a few days before your departure.

With my best respects to Mrs. Bennett, I remain,

Yours very respectfully,

JAMES BUCHANAN.

James G. Bennett, Esq.

Several letters of introduction followed, the first reading:

Washington, 9 June, 1846.

My dear Sir:

It affords me pleasure to introduce to you the bearer hereof, James G. Bennett, Esquire, of New York. In company with his lady, whom I desire specially to commend to your kind attention, he proposes to visit the Hague.

In my personal intercourse with Mr. Bennett I have ever found him to be a gentleman and his reputation as a public journalist must be well known to you.

May I bespeak for himself and his lady those kind attentions which you so well know how to bestow, and which, proceeding from the Representation of three countries in a foreign land, will prove so acceptable.

From your friend,
Very respectfully,
JAMES BUCHANAN.

Auguste Davezac, Esquire.

A second note read:

My dear Sir:

This letter will be delivered to you by James G. Bennett, Esquire, of New York, to whom I have given a courier's passport as bearer of Dispatches to Mr. M'Lane. He will be accompanied by Mrs. Bennett.

During their stay in Liverpool, may I bespeak for them your kind attention. It will gratify me to learn that you have afforded them every facility which you so well know how to bestow.

I refer you to Mr. Bennett for the news. He is as capable of giving it to you as any gentleman within my knowledge.

From your friend,
Very respectfully,
JAMES BUCHANAN.

General Robert Armstrong.

During the months preceding the securing of these credentials, Bennett had spent some time in Washington, writing letters to the *Herald* and picking up inside facts for guidance. He departed for England on June sixteenth, and as a "bearer of dispatches" pried open hitherto closed doors in London. For his dispatches carried reassurances to England concerning the Oregon boundary dispute that had bred so much bluster, and following their delivery, on July seventeenth, a formal settlement of the vexed question was arrived at. Bennett basked in the good will surrounding the circumstance, which, removing the peril of war with England, left the United States free to go ahead and fight Mexico. In addition to this, Pennsylvania had voted to pay her suspended debts, and an era of "good feeling" set in. The editor was warmly welcomed, even in society. He wrote complacently to the *Herald* for the information of his New York enemies:

Of all the soirées which we have attended since our arrival in London, one of the most agreeable was a *récherché* night we spent at Lady Morgan's elegant residence in one of the beautiful squares near Hyde Park. Lady Morgan, better known in the United States as the once beautiful Miss Owenson, the famous authoress, moves in the highest circles of fashion and literature, and is one of the most delightful persons we ever met. The evening of her days is poetry and grace, brought down from heaven to human life.

We have seen a great deal of the structure, forms, shapes, and appearances of the upper and fashionable circles here, and a general and vivid description of such a state of society I have never yet seen written. It can be done so as to be pleasing, without any personality. To-morrow we proceed to the Rhine, and shall visit Baden-Baden, Southern Germany, Vienna, Switzerland, etc.,—after that return to Paris, and think of St. Petersburgh, and also of Italy. We have received numerous letters in London and elsewhere, to persons of the highest rank on the continent.

Being made a bearer of dispatches indicates a pretty close connection with "Old Buck," as people called the statesman. This was not maintained; a misunderstanding arose that cleared itself up when Bennett found it again to his purpose to back Buchanan.

William L. Marcy became Secretary of State under Franklin Pierce, and had ambitions to succeed him in the presidency. The fact that he supported Pierce did not influence Bennett into forgetting the way Marcy had double-crossed him twenty years before. He had camped on his trail, indeed, through the double decade, and, after the establishment of the *Herald,* was able to pay the gentleman with compound interest. Richard Schell, an eminent Tammany leader in New York (this was before the days of the Boss), sought to reconcile the two. Marcy was in the city and Schell called on Bennett with an invitation to get together with the Secretary. He curtly declined: "I have no desire to see Mr. Marcy. I am already acquainted with him. I helped to make him governor of this state; I do not intend in any way to make him president of the United States. That's his present object."

To defeat Marcy became his great objective. Thus it was that he put his support behind Buchanan, who won the nomination, and was elected with much help from the *Herald.* Bennett had encouraged the elements that came together in the Republican party and nominated John C. Frémont. But they were going farther and faster than he cared to travel. Radical in its opinion of men and things, the *Herald* was not much given to overthrowing institutions.

Buchanan was glad to resume relationships, as this letter, written October 20, 1856, from Buchanan's home at Wheatland, Pennsylvania, shows:

My dear Sir:

I have this moment received, when about to leave home for Philadelphia, a letter from our mutual friend, Mr. W. which has afforded me great satisfaction. I rejoice that our former friendly relations are about to be restored. I can assure you I am truly sorry they were ever interrupted; and this not only for my own sake but that of the country. The *New York Herald,* exercising the influence which signal ability and past triumphs always commands, can contribute much to frustrate the sectional party which now so seriously endangers the union and to restore the ancient friendly relations between the North and the South.

Mr. W. refers to something about a letter from Mr. Dillon, which I do not exactly comprehend. I never received a letter from that gentleman for you; but I did receive the one from him about you which gratified me so much. The truth is that when I parted from you in Paris I had neither the purpose nor the desire again to become a candidate for the Presidency. A ground swell, however, in this State among a noble people who had sustained me for more than thirty years, forced me reluctantly into the field.

I confess I had calculated, with the most perfect confidence, you would be as you had been, my friend. It has been throughout between us a comedy of errors in which I have been the sufferer. But let bye-gones be bye-gones; and when we again get together I feel that we shall never separate.

Yours very respectfully,
James Buchanan.

James Gordon Bennett, Esquire.

P. S. It is too late for our mail. I shall have to take this with me and post it in Philadelphia, where I go for only two days.

Some further lines in the P. S. are illegible, but they indicate an unsuccessful effort on Buchanan's part to enlist Bennett on his side. "W" refers to the "Chevalier" Wikoff, of whom more anon.

Bennett replied:

I have received with great pleasure your kind letter—your very kind letter. I reciprocate most warmly the desire you so kindly express that we may soon meet not to separate by any comedy of errors—however, my dear sir, I am not altogether to blame for recent separations.

Following Buchanan's inauguration, Mrs. Bennett evidently sent him a note of congratulation. This reply was found among the family papers:

Washington, 14 April 1857

My dear Madam:

Many thanks for your kind congratulations! These ought ere this to have been responded to, though your letter lingered long on the way; but since the inauguration my time has been so incessantly occupied that I have been impelled to neglect, though I can never forget valued friends like yourself. Let me assure that I cordially reciprocate all your kindness and rejoice in the prospect of welcoming you to this country. Since "the auld lang syne" I am gratified to know that you have ever been my friend. I regret very much that I had not the pleasure of meeting you in Paris, though I earnestly desired it. Your son paid us a visit some weeks ago. He appears to be a fine, promising boy. I beg his pardon, there are no longer any boys in the United States—they are all young gentlemen.

I am glad to learn that Mr. Bennett has promised you "to stick by my administration through thick and thin." Thus far he has given it a powerful support with occasional aberrations, for which I am always prepared and do not complain. He is an independent man and will do just what he pleases—though I know there is an undercurrent of good will towards me in his nature and he is disposed to treat me fairly. The *Herald* in his hands is a powerful instrument and it would be vain for me to deny that I desire its music should be encouraging and not hostile. Mr. B. makes his mark when he strikes and his blows fall so fast and heavy it is difficult to sustain them. I learn he proposes to visit Washington early in May, and shall be glad to see him because, when together, we always get along well. It is my desire as well as my interest to be on the best of terms with him.

Justice is a kind providence. I hope that my administration may equal your friendly wishes. I shall do my best with all honest purpose and leave results to Heaven.

Again expressing the hope that I may ere long welcome you to Washington, I remain in haste and with warm regard

Very respectfully
Your friend,
JAMES BUCHANAN.

Mrs. James Gordon Bennett.

P. S. Your letter did not reach me until some time after the 4th March, though dated on the 4th January.

Buchanan went so far as to entrust Bennett with advance copies of his messages as this note shows:

Private and confidential
Washington, 7 Dec. 57

My dear Sir:

I inclose you one of my messages and know I can implicitly trust to your honor that this copy will not be used for printing before 12 o'clock tomorrow. You will have an opportunity of perusing it and forming your own opinion of it in advance. Another copy for the *Herald* is in the bundle of papers to be delivered to Mr. Schell. With many thanks for your very kind and very efficient support, I remain,

In haste, very respectfully,
Your friend,
James Buchanan.

James Gordon Bennett, Esquire.

To Mrs. Bennett the President wrote again, two years later:

Washington, 1 April, 1859

My dear Madam:

Miss [Harriet] Lane and myself have deeply sympathized with you in the loss of your darling son. This mournful event has often been the subject of our conversation. We have contrasted the gaiety, the brilliance and the talent of the happy mother on her late visit to Washington, with the grief and the gloom which must now make the heart sad. Alas for the vanity of all things mortal! Your best consolation in such a calamity is to be found in the words of our compassionate Saviour: "Suffer little children to come unto me, for of such is the Kingdom of Heaven."

Reflecting that it might be gratifying to you to know how much and how sincerely I have sympathized with you in the hour of your affliction my pen proceeds at once to record the sentiments of my heart.

With my kind respects to Mr. Bennett, I remain, with warm regard,

Sincerely your friend,
James Buchanan.

Mrs. James Gordon Bennett.

When Buchanan's honesty was questioned by the Covode resolution, providing for a Congressional investigation in 1860, as the clouds of secession were growing, the pestered President wrote appealing to Bennett:

Private and Confidential
Washington, 18 June 1860

My dear Sir:

I thought I never should have occasion to appeal to you on any public subject, and I know if I did I could not swerve you from your independent course. I therefore now only ask you as a personal friend, to take the trouble of examining yourself the proceedings of the Covode Committee and the reports of the majority and minority and then to do me what you may deem to be strict justice. That committee were engaged in secret conclave for nearly three months in examining every man *ex parte* who from disappointment or personal malignity would cast a shade upon the character of the executive. If this dragooning can exist the Presidential office would be unworthy of the acceptance of a gentleman. In performing my duties I have endeavored to be not only pure, but unsuspected. I have never had any concern in awarding contracts, but have left these to be given by the heads of the appropriate Departments. I have ever detested all jobs and no man at any period of my life has ever approached me on such a subject. The testimony of Wendall contains nothing but falsehoods, whether for or against me for he has sworn all round.

I shall send a message to the House in a few days on the violation of the Constitution involved in the vote of censure in the appointment and proceedings of the Covode Committee. I am glad to perceive from the *Herald* that you agree with me on the Constitutional question. I shall endeavor to send you a copy in advance.

With my kindest regards to Mrs. Bennett, I remain,

Very respectfully your friend,

James Buchanan.

James Gordon Bennett, Esq.

Bennett, with clear prescience, sensed that in the course of the National Democratic party lay the safety of the country. Should the party split, or so conduct itself as to make possible the triumph of the expanding Republicans, secession was certain. That he believed the party would divide is plain from the policy adopted by the *Herald,* as the new year of 1860 ushered in the critical period. To its editor the only way out was the renomination of James Buchanan, about whose "Constitutional" attitude there could be no question. As early as February second, the *Herald* said editorially:

> The man for Charleston is Mr. Buchanan. His Administration has been so firmly and wisely conducted as to win the applause of the whole country. . . The conservative Union men of the great Central States will demand a man whose election will allay the foolish slavery agitation, restore confidence between the North and the South, insure the permanence of our institutions and promote the material prosperity of the republic. Mr. Buchanan is this man. He will call out the full strength of his own party and the independent reserve vote. Mr. Buchanan, then, should receive the Charleston nomination by all means.

There was no reasonable way, however, of reaching such a result. Douglas had gone too far in his popular sovereignty course to be headed off, and Buchanan had no hold on his party—North or South. The times were in a flux and had to flow.

The *Herald* stood by President Buchanan to the last. When one by one the southern members of the Cabinet dropped out, the *Herald* commented: "We can regard as comparatively trifling matters the bankrupt condi-

Cartoon in *Vanity Fair,* October 20, 1860

tion in which Secretary Cobb left the Treasury, the enormous lobby jobs and speculations charged to the account of the late Secretary Floyd, the untold embezzlements occurring in the Department of the Interior under Secretary Thompson" in return for giving over their places to union men. It also pictured Buchanan "relieved of these gentlemen going out of office with credit and with many enemies coming to his vindication."

For days "The Revolution" was a standing line over the first column of the first page, where were gathered all the sensational items that proclaimed the growing secession. The editor saw war coming, but strove to head it off. Lincoln's inaugural address was "a very carefully drawn and elaborately finished state paper." Yet it contained a contradiction which the sharp-eyed editor made the most of. The Confederacy proclaimed it a declaration of war. Beyond all its contemporaries the *Herald* printed the news from the South. Its correspondents at Charleston and Montgomery did their work well. While nothing could exceed the saneness and clarity of the *Herald's* editorial page, it did not coddle the South, though much accused of so doing. Bennett knew the leaders and their motives. Jefferson Davis, he described as "a restless, subtle, scheming southern radical."

A week after his retirement from office, Buchanan closed the correspondence with the following:

Wheatland, 11 March 1861

My dear Sir:

Will you be kind enough to direct the *Herald* to be sent to me to Lancaster. I have been quite lost without it.

I am once more settled at this my quiet home and one of my first impulses is to return you my cordial and grateful thanks for the able and powerful support which you have given me almost universally throughout my stormy and turbulent administration.

Under Heaven's blessing the administration has been eminently successful in its foreign and domestic policy, unless we may except the sad events which have recently occurred. These no human wisdom could have prevented. Whether I have done all I could, consistently with my duty, to give them a wise and peaceful direction towards the preservation or reconstruction of the Union, will be for the public and posterity to judge. I feel conscious that I have done my duty in this respect and that I shall at last receive justice.

With my very kindest regards to Mrs. Bennett, I remain,

Sincerely and respectfully
Your friend,
JAMES BUCHANAN.

James Gordon Bennett. Esq.

Bennett had clearly discerned that Buchanan's perplexity during the last months of his régime was no greater than that of any other American. No one knew what to do except to hope for the best. Buchanan was not inferior to any statesman of his time in dealing with nations other than his own. In the Oregon dispute, which was ended with the dispatches carried by Bennett, he did his country masterly service. James G. Blaine, in his *Twenty Years of Congress,* describes Buchanan's correspondence with Pakenham, the British Minister in Washington, as "conspicuously able," strengthening him at home and giving him "an enviable reputation" in Europe, while "his political management of the question was especially adroit."

Alas, no one could be sufficiently adroit in 1860-61!

CHAPTER VIII

Bennett and Lincoln

Probably no man ever came nearer being the Perfect American than Abraham Lincoln. This does not mean one of the haloed sort, but a human being in whom were blended most of our native characteristics. He had humor, keenness, sentiment, laziness, adventure, guile and courage. He was the first president who was not an aristocrat. Andrew Jackson, whom Bennett esteemed above other men, was of the military caste, even though his birth was lowly. Not the least of Lincoln's offenses to the socially superior South was that in him an ungainly rail-splitter and cross-roads lawyer had come to the White House. With these views Bennett could have no sympathy. His objection to Lincoln was his party and the certainty that it would split the Union. He governed himself accordingly. Caring nothing about politics for their own sake, he was not intimately informed about the new man. "From day to day" was his motto. He was therefore free to act as seemed best when the time came.

When Lincoln's Cabinet was announced, the *Herald* made it known that the "Seward-Weed" slate had been smashed and that Lincoln had followed the fatal error of "poor Pierce" by trying to conciliate all elements, predicting that Cabinet clashes would wreck his administration. The predicted clashes occurred, but did not do the wrecking. Lincoln was too good a politician to permit that.

On April 8, 1861, Bennett saw that the crisis was reaching the acute state that could end only in war. He outlined three courses that lay before the administration, only one of which meant peace. That was: "First to yield to the Confederates and to all the slave-holding communities their just rights as co-equal partners in the Union." This he advocated as the best course and would have been "that of a statesman," and, he believed, would have had the effect of "healing the breach." On the ninth, not losing sight of its own success, the *Herald* pronounced itself "the most largely circulated journal in the world," with a daily print of eighty-four thousand copies. It had gone up twenty thousand copies in a month under the excitement—printing, as it did, the most complete chronicle of events.

April tenth, on the eve of Sumter, the *Herald* said: "Indeed our only hope now against civil war of indefinite duration seems to lie in the overthrow of the demoralizing, disorganizing, and destructive [Republican] sectional party, of which 'Honest Abe Lincoln' is the pliant instrument." It urged "all conservative citizens of all parties to exert themselves to this end. Naturally this sentiment did not go well in the strained situation, and the *Herald's* loyalty was at once under suspicion. Yet a further statement was but the truth. It read:

Anticipating, then, the speedy inauguration of civil war at Charleston, at Pensacola, or in Texas, or perhaps, at all these places, the inquiry is forced upon us, what will be the probable consequences? We apprehend that they will be; first, the secession of Virginia and the other border slave states, and their union with the Confederate States; secondly, the organization of an army for the removal of the United States ensign and authorities from every fortress or public building within the limits of the Confederate States, including the White House, the Capitol and other public buildings of Washington. After the secession of Virginia from the United States, it is not likely that Maryland can be restrained from the same decisive act. She will follow the fortunes of Virginia, and will undoubtedly claim that, in withdrawing from the United States, the District of Columbia reverts into her possession under the supreme right of revolution. Here we have verge and scope enough for a civil war of five, ten or twenty years' duration.

What for? To "show that we have a Government"—to show that the seceded states are still in our Union, and are still subject to its laws and authorities. This is the fatal mistake of Mr. Lincoln, and his Cabinet, and his party. The simple truth—patent to all the world—is, that the seceded states are out of the Union, and are organized under an independent government of their own. The authority of the United States, within the borders of this independent Confederacy, has been completely superseded, except in a detached fort here and there. We desire to restore this displaced authority in its full integrity. How is this to be done? By entering into a war with the seceded states for the continued occupation of those detached forts? No. A war will only widen the breach, and enlarge and consolidate this Southern Confederacy, on the one hand; while, on the other hand, it will bring ruin upon the commerce, the manufactures, the financial and industrial interests of our northern cities and states, and may end in an oppressive military despotism.

How then are we to restore these seceded states to

the Union? We can do it only by conciliation and compromise.

Still hoping, the *Herald* urged Virginia and the Border States to hold to the line, believing, truly enough, that this would limit the uprising to controllable proportions. By April twenty-second the Mother of Presidents had followed her sisters. Then the *Herald* took a stand. The Southern States, it declared, had "wantonly and wickedly inaugurated hostilities," and Lincoln's program "was founded upon this imperishable, inextinguishable love of country which will not permit the relinquishment of any of its parts."

As has been said, previous to hostilities the *Herald* was under suspicion. Its large circulation in Europe, as Thurlow Weed recites in his memoirs, was creating a dangerous public sentiment abroad. Our representatives in England, France, Belgium, etc., regarded the influence of the *Herald* upon Europe with apprehension. A reversal of its policy was imperative. Of Lincoln's approach to Bennett, Weed wrote.*

That circumstance, added to our disasters during the early months of the war, induced President Lincoln to bring the subject before his Cabinet. It was deemed important, if possible, to change the course of the *Herald* upon the question of secession and rebellion; but how this was to be accomplished was a question of much difficulty. It was agreed that an earnest appeal must be made to Mr. Bennett. Several gentlemen were named (myself among the number) for this delicate mission. The Secretary of State [Mr. Weed's old political partner, William H. Seward] re-

*From *The Life of Thurlow Weed.* Courtesy of Houghton-Mifflin Company.

marked that my relations with Mr. Bennett were such as to insure the failure of the object contemplated, but it was finally determined that I should be summoned to Washington by telegraph. On my arrival, while at breakfast with Secretary Seward I was informed of the business in hand. Calling after breakfast upon President Lincoln, he remarked, in his peculiar way, that he understood I had had "considerable experiences in belling cats," and with this introduction proceeded to say that, in view especially of the influence the *Herald* was exerting in Europe, he deemed it of the greatest importance that Mr. Bennett should be satisfied that the course of the *Herald* was endangering the government and Union, adding his belief that if Mr. Bennett could be brought to see things in that light he would change his course. While appreciating the importance of the mission, I assured Mr. Lincoln I was the last person in the country to be selected for such a duty, but he insisted that I should make the trial, and I departed on the first train for New York.

My acquaintance with Mr. Bennett commenced in 1827, when he was the Washington reporter of the New York *Enquirer*, then conducted by the late M. M. Noah. I was in Washington several weeks during the session of Congress for the purpose of adjusting then existing political complications which, as I hoped, might result in the election of Mr. Henry Clay for president. Mr. Bennett, in his letters to the *Enquirer* attributed acts to Mr. Clay which, in the excited state of the public mind, defeated the hopes and efforts of his friends. . . . Out of those charges grew a conflict between Mr. Bennett and myself which entirely separated us politically, personally, and socially, for more than thirty years, during which time, although living much together at the Astor House, we had not spoken. Notwithstanding this embarrassment, remembering that General Miller, when asked if he would take a British battery at Lundy's Lane, replied he would "try," I determined to face my enemy. Upon my arrival in New York I called upon my friend Richard Schell, between whom and Mr. Bennett I knew intimate relations existed. Mr. Schell readily undertook to arrange an interview, and in a couple of hours afterward called at the Astor House with a message from Mr. Bennett, inviting me to dinner that afternoon. In stepping out of the cars at the Washington Heights Station I met Mr. Bennett, who had gone out in the same train. After a cordial greeting we were driven in his carriage to his mansion on the Heights. We then walked for half an hour about the grounds, when a servant came and announced dinner. The dinner was a quiet one, during which, until the fruit was served, we held a general conversation. I then frankly informed him of the object of my visit, closing with the remark that Mr. Lincoln deemed it more important to secure the *Herald's* support than to obtain a victory in the field. Mr. Bennett replied that the abolitionists, aided by the Whig members of Congress, had provoked a war, of the danger of which he had been warning the country for years, and that now, when they were reaping what they had sown, they had no right to call upon him to help them out of a difficulty they had deliberately brought upon themselves. I listened without interruption for ten minutes to a bitter denunciation of Greeley, Garrison, Seward, Sumner, Giddings, Phillips, and myself, as having, by irritating and exasperating the South, brought the war upon the country. I then, in reply, without denying or attempting to explain any of his positions, stated the whole question from our standpoint. I informed him of facts and circumstances within my knowledge, showing conclusively the deliberate design of severing the Union to prevent California from coming into it as a free State. I gave him the then unknown particulars of an interview of Messrs. Toombs, Stephens, and Clingman, members of Congress from Georgia and North Carolina, with General Taylor. The object of that interview was to induce General Taylor, a Southern man and a slave-holder, to veto the bill permitting California to enter the Union as a free State. It was a stormy interview, with threats of disunion on one hand and of hanging on the other. The facts were communicated to Senator Hamlin of Maine, and myself, within ten minutes after the interview closed. Jefferson Davis, General Taylor's son-in-law, though not present was, as Taylor believed, the master spirit in the movement. General Taylor's death and the compromise measures under the auspices of his successor, Mr. Fillmore, bridged over rebellion for the time being. I then called Mr. Bennett's attention to the condition of things in 1860, when the results of the census disclosed the fact of an unmistable numerical and political ascendency of freedom over slavery. This ascendency crushed the Southern hope of extending slavery into free territory, that having been the object of the repeal of the Missouri Compromise and the only national issue then pending. I then reverted to the Democratic National Convention of 1860, startling Mr. Bennett with the assumption that that convention was deliberately demoralized by its leaders for the purpose of throwing the government into our hands, and thus furnishing the pretext desired for secession. I claimed that the harmonious nomination of an available candidate would have insured the success of the Democratic ticket, but that the convention was broken up by leading Southern men, into whose hands General Butler and Caleb Cushing played. Two Democratic candidates for president were placed in the field, with the knowledge and for the purpose of giving the election to Mr. Lincoln, and then before a word was spoken, or an act performed by the incoming Adminstration, a predetermined course of secession and rebellion was entered upon.

No one knew better than Mr. Bennett the truth, the force, and the effect of the facts I presented, but his mind had been so absorbed in his idea of the pernicious character of abolition that he had entirely lost sight of the real causes of the rebellion.

Mr. Weed observes further that Mr. Lincoln and his Cabinet were "greatly gratified" at the report he brought back to them. It is hard to perceive from his written account of the interview what he had to report that could be gratifying. Bennett knew him thoroughly as a professional "fixer" and lobbyist, and quite naturally evaded being delivered at his hands. Weed also overstates the strength of the *Herald's* "support." Aside from the New York *Times*, as Weed says, Lincoln had no thick and thin backers in the New York press, or anywhere else in the North for that matter. All the great editors tried to be great generals.

It is easy to assume that the wise and far-seeing President sensed perfectly the way Bennett had baffled Weed. There is plenty of evidence that thereafter he dealt with him directly.

When the news that Fort Sumter had been fired upon reached the North, the *Herald* made no editorial comment, contenting itself with a plain statement of the event, the first line of which was: "Civil war has begun."

The *Herald's* loyalty was so much doubted that a crowd marched to Fulton and Nassau Streets to demand that "old man Bennett" show his colors, which, to be satisfactory to the enthusiasts, had to be the Stars and Stripes. There was great excitement within as well as without the office. It was feared the building would be invaded and that vengeance might be wreaked on Bennett himself. One old printer who looked like him volunteered to appear at a window, but this he would not permit. He concluded, however, that it was time the colors went up. There was no flag in the place so Edward Townsend Flynn, then office boy, scurried out the rear entrance and, reaching a Broadway bunting store, hurried back with a banner in the nick of time. It was duly displayed and Bennett made his bows to the mob beneath its flaunting folds.

Fearing assaults by mobs, as a precaution he bought a liberal supply of the best rifles to be had and stored them away in the *Herald* office. They were transferred to the new building where they remained hidden long after the elder Bennett was dead and the dangers past. The library and council room on the second floor, where father and son also had their offices, was paneled to the ceiling with walnut, and behind this paneling was the arsenal. The rifles were always in order, being kept beautifully clean and polished, with an abundance of ammunition ready at hand. They were there up to the time the *Herald* abandoned the Broadway and Ann Street building to move up-town.

It chanced at the moment that Henry Villard, then an enterprising young reporter, who had become acquainted with American affairs under Oswald Ottendorfer, on the influential *New Yorker Staats-Zeitung*, had, after some experience as a traveling correspondent for Murat Halstead's Cincinnati *Commercial*, set himself up as the first "syndicate" writer in Washington. He offered copy to the *Commercial*, the Chicago *Tribune* and the New York *Herald*.

Both Bennett and Frederic Hudson, his managing

editor, accepted Villard's proffer, with the understanding that he "should be free to speak through the *Herald* as a sympathizer with the Republican party." They also contributed twenty-five dollars per week for their share. Villard had been in touch with Lincoln at Springfield, and was now proposing to cover events at the capital—from a Republican standpoint, as noted. He had got his work well under way when the storm broke. Following Lincoln's proclamation, on April 15, 1861, calling for seventy-five thousand men to put down the rebellion, Villard states in his autobiography:*

I received a despatch from James Gordon Bennett asking me to come at once to New York. I obeyed the summons by the night train. On reaching the *Herald* office, I found an invitation to accompany him in the afternoon to his residence at Washington Heights and to spend the night there. As was my host's regular custom, we drove from the office up Broadway and Fifth Avenue and through Central Park to the Heights. I had seen Bennett only twice before, and then but for a few minutes each time, and the opportunity to learn more of this notorious character was therefore not unwelcome to me. I must say that his shameful record as a journalist, and particularly the sneaking sympathy of his paper for the Rebellion, and its vile abuse of the Republicans for their anti-slavery sentiments, made me share the general prejudice against him to such an extent that I had been thinking for some time of severing my connection with the *Herald*, although the agreement that all I telegraphed should be printed without change or omission had been strictly kept. With his fine tall and slender figure, large intellectual head cov-

---

*From *The Memoirs of Henry Villard.* Courtesy of Mr. Oswald Garrison Villard and Houghton-Mifflin Company.

ered with an abundance of light curly hair, and strong regular features, his exterior would have been impressive but for his strabismus [Philip Hone's "squinting"], which gave him a sinister, forbidding look. Intercourse with him, indeed, quickly revealed his utterly hard, cold, utterly selfish nature and incapacity to appreciate high and noble aims.

His residence was a good-sized frame house in park-like grounds, with no great pretensions either outwardly or inwardly. On the drive and during the dinner, at which his one son—a fine-looking, intelligent youth of twenty—was the only other person present, he did nothing but ask questions bearing upon the characteristics and doings of President Lincoln and the circumstances of my acquaintance with him. After dinner he disclosed his true purpose in sending for me. First, he wanted me to carry a message from him to Mr. Lincoln that the *Herald* would hereafter be unconditionally for the radical suppression of the Rebellion by force of arms, and in the shortest possible time, and would advocate and support any "war measures" by the Government and Congress. I was, of course, very glad to hear this, and promised to repeat these assurances by word of mouth to the President. The truth was, that the *Herald* was obliged to make this complete change in its attitude, there having been ominous signs for some days in New York of danger of mob violence to the paper. Secondly, he wanted me to offer to Secretary Chase, his son's famous sailing yacht, the *Rebecca,* as a gift to the Government for the revenue service, and to secure in consideration thereof for its owner the appointment of lieutenant in the same service. This last wish I thought rather amusing, but I agreed to lay it before Secretary Chase, to whom I had ready access as the representative of the Cincinnati *Commercial,* his strongest supporter in Ohio. My host retired early, and was ready before me in the morning for the down drive, on which I accompanied him again. Mr. Hudson—the managing editor, a fine-looking man, and one of the most courteous and obliging I ever met, with extraordinary qualifications for newspaper management—told me in the course of the day that Mr. Bennett was very much pleased with me and had increased my weekly allowance to thirty-five dollars.

Villard does not give any account of the delivery of the several messages or further information about the episode. That he kept his promise, however, is evident from this letter now on file in the Treasury Department's historical collection:

Executive Department
May 6, 1861.

Hon. Sec. of Treasury
Dear Sir:
The Secretary of State this moment introduces to me Mr. James Gordon Bennett, Jr. who tenders to the U. S. the service, a fine Yacht of 160 tons burthen. If you allow him an interview, which I ask for him, he will talk with you about putting some other vessels of the same class into the service. We send this subject to you because we believe these vessels may be made most available in the Revenue service.

Yours truly,
A. LINCOLN.

It will be perceived that William H. Seward was given the duty of steering the young man to Salmon P. Chase. The Lincoln letter carries this indorsement:

President Lincoln in relation to the offer of James Gordon Bennett, Jr. to furnish his yacht for the Revenue Cutter Service.

May 6, 1861

Commission as Third Lieutenant in Revenue Cutter Service sent to Mr. Bennett May 15, 1861.

W. H.

The yacht in question was not *Rebecca* as Villard states, but *Henrietta,* named after the young man's mother. The Treasury Department records show that the vessel was equipped with two six-pound rifled bronze guns, cast at Chicopee, Massachusetts. Later a brass twelve-pounder was added to her equipment. Bennett's commission was dated May 14, 1861. The cutter cruised off the Long Island coast during the summer of 1861, and in February, 1862, was reported at Port Royal, South Carolina. April 29, 1862, she was withdrawn from the service, and on May 11, 1862, Lieutenant Bennett tendered his resignation, which was accepted. No glory appears to have been acquired, but he ever after loved to dwell upon the fact that he had served his country upon the sea.

The days of wabbling and wavering ended with Bull Run, on July 21, 1861. "Then," Walt Whitman wrote in his *Specimen Days,* "the great New York papers at once appear'd, (commencing that evening, and following it up the next morning, and incessantly through many days afterwards,) with leaders that rang out over the land with the loudest, most reverberating ring of clearest bugles, full of encouragement, hope, inspiration, unfaltering defiance. Those magnificent editorials! they never flagg'd for a fortnight. The *Herald* commenced them—I remember the articles well."

Sumter was not a test of strength. Bull Run was, and the South showed both generalship and power. It really looked as though one southerner could "lick" five Yankees. Yet until the last quarter of an hour of the conflict when panic seized the northern forces, it was anybody's fight. Indeed the first news of the battle was favorable to the army of the North. This alone got to the newspapers of the twenty-second. It was head-lined in the *Herald* as a "Brilliant Union Victory." The next day it became "Desperate Conflict and Repulse of Union Troops by an Overwhelming Force." In the instant consternation that followed, the *Herald* alone of the New York papers did not lose its head. It printed in the usual first column of the editorial page under the standing line "The Situation," a clear cold analysis of what happened. Its editorial was of the sanest sort. After reviewing the conditions accurately, the article concluded:

The war now ceases to be an uninterrupted onward march of our forces southward. The government in a single day and at the Capitol of the Nation, is thrown upon the defensive, and under circumstances demanding the most prompt and generous efforts to strengthen our forces at that point. Every other question, all other issues, and all other business, among all parties and all classes of our loyal people, should now be made subordinate to the paramount office of securing Washington. The loyal states within three days may dispatch twenty thousand men to that point; and if we succeed in holding the Capitol for twenty days we may have by that time two hundred thousand men intrenched around it.

Action, Action, Action! Let our Governor, and state and city authorities, and the state and city authorities of every loyal state come at once to the rescue and move forward their reinforcements without waiting for instructions from Washington.

Following Bull Run, the North found itself friendless in the world at large. In England, the *Times*, *Punch* and the *Spectator*, each potent in its field, were viciously pro-southern. They saw no purpose on the part of the North save to protect its tariff. The friends of anti-slavery in England could find no evidence of any intent to free the black bondmen. In short, there were no moral visualities.

The *Herald* met this storm with one of its own making. It arraigned a monarchy as against a republic, desirous that the only one of consequence in existence should be snuffed out. As the *Herald* was the journal best known in Europe, what it had to say carried far. It proudly proclaimed that it had "unmasked" and then "spiked" the batteries of the English aristocrats, aimed at the liberties of the remnant of the United States. This was demagogic, of course, for before the end came it was the aristocratic rather than the Liberal end of England that prevented recognition of the Confederacy with all the direful consequences that would have followed. The great Gladstone, for example, was strongly against us. So truculent was the *Herald* that John Bright wrote Charles Sumner: "It is unfortunate that nothing is done to change the reckless tone of your New York *Herald;* between it and the [London] *Times,* there is great mischief done in both countries."

James Ford Rhodes holds that friends of England in America underrated the power of the *Herald,* in deprecating the influence of its attacks. This was undoubtedly correct. As he says further:* "This journal

*From *History of the United States from the Compromise of 1850,* by James Ford Rhodes. Courtesy of The Macmillan Company.

spoke for a potent public sentiment outside of New England. By its large news-gathering agencies, and by its unvarying support of the administration, it had a large and increasing circulation. Men who were eager for the latest and fullest news from the field, and who wished to stand loyally by Lincoln against the fault-finding of peace Democrats on one side and of Frémont radicals on the other, read it gladly. It had a body of devoted readers whom it could influence, and in working up animosity towards England it played upon an oft-used string."

Yet, read to-day, the *Herald's* editorials on our foreign relations are fine examples of up-standing, self-respecting Americanism. One finds nothing in them that ought not to be cheerfully submitted to as the right sort of doctrine.

According to the Russian Minister, Count Gurowski, Lincoln read no paper except the *Herald.* John Hay is authority for the statement that he scarcely ever looked at one unless his attention was called to it. Just the same he knew what was going on and took great care to keep in touch with Bennett—probably because he realized his capacity for mischief. For one thing, Bennett did not try to force his hand as did Horace Greeley, Murat Halstead and Joseph Medill.

The Bennett collection before mentioned included a number of letters from Abraham Lincoln and his wife, indicating a cordiality hardly to be expected toward one who had so staunchly supported Buchanan and upheld the attitude of the South. Written in Lincoln's own hand and marked private, they renew one's respect for his skill as a politician and navigator of the ship of State. Toward his party papers he felt no concern apparently beyond, perhaps, annoyance at their efforts to "run" him. But Bennett's following was outside of party lines and in such, Lincoln saw, rested the balance of power. It is easy to understand therefore, how he could write the following:

Private and Confidential.

Washington, D. C.,
Sept. 22, 1861.

Mr. James Gordon Bennett.

My Dear Sir: Last evening Mr. Wikoff solicited me for a pass, or permission to a gentleman whose name I forget, to accompany one of our vessels down the Potomac to-day, as a reporter of the *Herald,* saying the Sec. of the Navy had refused, while he had given the privilege to reporters of other papers. It was too late at night for me to see the Secretary, and I had to decline giving the permission, because he, the Sec., might have a sufficient reason, unknown to me. I write this to assure you that the Administration will not discriminate against the *Herald,* especially while it sustains us so generously, and the cause of the country as ably as it has been doing.

Your Obt Servant,
ABRAHAM LINCOLN.

Could there have been devised a more clever step to head off attacks and implant the wisdom of support in the editor's mind? Lincoln knew his man and dealt with him accordingly. He had read the Sermon on the Mount and knew how to take an enemy with him. The shrieks of Greeley, the howls of Halstead and the meddlings of Joseph Medill passed unnoticed as a rule, but he would not permit the *Herald* to go unleashed.

This close touch continued. Note this of a few months later date, when Bennett had been pounding

Edwin M. Stanton over the shoulders of General Hunter for his proclamation uttered at Harper's Ferry, freeing slaves:

Private. Executive Mansion,
May 21, 1862.

James Gordon Bennett, Esq.

Dear Sir: Thanking you again for the able support given by you through the *Herald* to what I think the true course of the country, and also for your kind expressions toward me personally. I wish to correct an erroneous impression of yours in regard to the Secretary of War. He mixes no politics whatever with his duties; knew nothing of Gen. Hunter's proclamation; and he and I alone got up the counter proclamation. I wish this to go no further than to you, while I wish to assure you it is true.

Yours truly,
ABRAHAM LINCOLN.

The Emancipation Proclamation was but four months off, but was yet an unrevealed and, perhaps, an unthought purpose. It was more important to keep the *Herald* and the northern Democrats in line than to appease the abolitionists. These could be relied upon to do nothing for the South. Not so Bennett and the others.

Henry Wikoff, the singular Chevalier, who flitted mysteriously in and out of the chancellories of Europe and about our White House, gets into the picture first in making peace with Buchanan. He was a squire of dames as well as of diplomats and wrote a book to justify the vain pursuit of an heiress that had a rather humiliating outcome, when the rich maiden got away. That he was a go-between is certain. Lincoln knew how to use men, and Wikoff was the sort of tame knave Bennett could utilize with his inside contacts on many things, social, political and international.

Indeed, Bennett was something of a godfather to Wikoff, having pinned "Chevalier" to the amiable adventurer for the rest of his life. He was a passenger with Bennett on the return trip of the *Sirius* to Europe in 1838, when that vessel, together with the *Great Western* had just pioneered the ocean. The two got on well together and formed an acquaintance that remained close. The Chevalier has left this account of their meeting:

I was startled to hear that Bennett was on board; for at that time, May, 1838, he gave free scope to his slashing powers and satirical vein, and everybody trembled lest it might be his turn next. I looked anxiously round on the upper deck where I was standing, as we steamed down the bay, and sidling up to a quiet and inoffensive looking man near me, said—

"Do you know the editor of the *Herald* is on board?"

"I believe he is," he answered.

"I only wish I knew him by sight."

"What for?" queried the gentlemanly sort of person I was talking to.

"Why, that I might keep out of his way. He will be sure to stick me in that confounded *Herald* of his."

"He doesn't confer that honor on everybody," said my facetious friend, laughing.

"Egad, I would not trust him. . . . Have you ever seen him?" I asked.

"Very frequently," was the reply.

"That's lucky. Do point the ogre out to me if you see him near us."

"I don't see him, but you may if you look at me; I am the Editor of the *Herald*."

VOL 6. VANITY FAIR NO. 138.

Saturday, AUGUST 16, 1862.

PUBLISHED EVERY SATURDAY, AT 116 NASSAU STREET, N. Y.

PRICE TWO DOLLARS PER ANNUM—SINGLE COPIES SIX CENTS.

The Chevalier Henry Wikoff,

As the Political Paul Pry.

Published for the Proprietors, by Louis H. Stephens, at 116 Nassau Street N. Y.

Cartoon of the Chevalier Wikoff in *Vanity Fair,* August 16, 1862

The blithesome Wikoff lived until May 3, 1884, when he died of paralysis at Brighton, England.

Wikoff dabbled in many things besides amours and amateur diplomacy. Among other items he brought Fanny Elssler, the celebrated dancer, to America and managed a successful tour. He tried to keep Jenny Lind from signing up with P. T. Barnum, representing that Barnum was a mere showman and would not scruple at exhibiting her in a cage at twenty-five cents a head!

When the crisis developed in December, 1862, Secretary of State William H. Seward and Secretary of the Treasury Salmon P. Chase, resigning after a Senate caucus had decreed Mr. Lincoln's Cabinet a failure, the *Herald* was the first paper to have the news, by chance this time, not by enterprise. George E. Baker, disbursing agent of the Department of State, was a fellow-townsman of Seward, from Auburn, New York. So was J. C. Derby, the New York publisher who was then government dispatch agent in New York. To him Baker sent the news while it was still secret. He took the tidings to Frederic Hudson, managing editor of the *Herald,* who, in turn, conducted him to Mr. Bennett. The astute editor could not believe it. "Scanning me closely with those penetrating eyes of his," wrote Derby, in his recollections, "that could see in two directions, he finally said: 'I guess it's true; we'll print it.' "

So the *Herald* scored a great "beat." Lincoln refused to accept the resignations, and legislative power continued to grow less in Washington.

It has been seen in Mr. Villard's recollections how Bennett sought contact with Lincoln. The activities of Wikoff have also been noted. Lincoln's cognizance of the Bennett desire to be "close up"—to use a modern phrase—is made clear in the following extract from a letter written by Leonard Swett, an intimate associate, to William H. Herndon, dated at Chicago on January 17, 1866, concerning Lincoln's political course in securing his renomination to the presidency:*

His rivals were using money profusely; journals and influences were being subsidized against him. I accidentally learned that a Washington newspaper, through a purchase of the establishment, was to be turned against him, and consulted him about taking steps to prevent it. The only thing I could get him to say was that he would regret to see the paper turned against him. Whatever was done had to be done without his knowledge. Mr. Bennett of the *Herald,* with his paper, you know, is a power. The old gentleman wanted to be noticed by Lincoln, and he wanted to support him. A friend of his who was certainly in his secrets, came to Washington and intimated if Lincoln would invite Bennett to come over and chat with him, his paper would be all right. Mr. Bennett wanted nothing, he simply wanted to be noticed. Lincoln in talking about it said, "I understand it; Bennett has made a great deal of money, some say not very properly, now he wants me to make him respectable. I have never invited Mr. Bryant or Mr. Greeley here; I shall not, therefore, especially invite Mr. Bennett." All Lincoln would say was, that he was receiving everybody, and he should receive Mr. Bennett if he came.

This attitude, while well enough as viewed from the Swett view-point, does not remain adamant in view of

*From *Abraham Lincoln: The True Story of A Great Life,* by William H. Herndon and Jesse W. Weik. Copyright 1892. Courtesy of D. Appleton and Company.

the offer to make Bennett minister to France, which certainly followed the support the latter gave Lincoln in 1864. The President could be, and often was, disingenuous.

Therefore, there remains something untold and unascertainable in the relations between the editor and the President, that brought the *Herald* to Lincoln's support in the election of 1864. Colonel Alexander K. McClure, celebrated later as the able editor of the Philadelphia *Times,* was much about the White House at the period, and performed many confidential errands for Lincoln. Of the incident in question he writes in his *Lincoln and Men of War Times*:

One of the shrewdest of Lincoln's great political schemes was the tender, by autograph letter, of the French mission to the elder James Gordon Bennett. No one who can form any intelligent judgment of the political exigencies of that time can fail to understand why the venerable independent journalist received this mark of favor from the President. Lincoln had but one of the leading journals of New York on which he could rely for positive support. That was Mr. Raymond's New York *Times*. Mr. Greeley's *Tribune* was the most widely read Republican journal of the country, and it was unquestionably the most potent in moulding Republican sentiment. Its immense weekly edition, for that day, reached the more intelligent masses of the people in every State of the Union, and Greeley was not in accord with Lincoln. Lincoln knew how important it was to have the support of the *Herald,* and he carefully studied how to bring its editor into close touch with himself. The outlook for Lincoln's re-election was not promising. Bennett had strongly advocated the nomination of General McClellan by the Democrats, and that was ominous of hostility to Lincoln; and when McClellan was nominated he was accepted on all sides as a most formidable candidate. It was in this emergency that Lincoln's political sagacity served him sufficiently to win the *Herald* to his cause, and it was done by the confidential tender of the French mission. Bennett did not break over to Lincoln at once, but he went by gradual approaches. His first step was to declare in favor of an entirely new candidate, which was an utter impossibility. He opened a leader on the subject thus: "Lincoln has proved a failure; McClellan has proved a failure; Fremont has proved a failure; let us have a new candidate." Lincoln, McClellan, and Fremont were then all in the field as nominated candidates; and the Fremont defection was a serious threat to Lincoln. Of course, neither Lincoln nor McClellan declined, and the *Herald,* failing to get the new man it knew to be an impossibility, squarely advocated Lincoln's re-election.

Now up to December 1, 1864, William L. Dayton of New Jersey was minister to France. He had been candidate for vice-president with John C. Frémont, in 1856, and was far too eminent to have been removed to make way for the editor of the *Herald.* He died suddenly on the evening of the above date in the apartment of a Mrs. Eckels, at the Hotel du Louvre, Paris. He had eaten a very hearty dinner before making his call, including a super-portion of pumpkin pie. John Bigelow then Consul General, made a confidential report of the circumstances to Secretary Seward, with the request that it be burned after its contents had been communciated to the President. This was done. Bigelow, in his *Retrospections of An Active Life,* cites the fact that nine months before he had given a dinner in Mr. Dayton's honor, at which by evil inadvertence, thirteen were seated at the table, and wonders whether the superstition that one would die within the year had operated. Mr. Lincoln could hardly have been forewarned of the combination of pie, lady, and Number 13, in furnishing a vacancy which could be used to soothe the editor of the *Herald*. Moreover, the "confindential tender of the French Mission" was not made until February 20, 1865, a fortnight before the second inauguration. It read:

Executive Mansion,
February 20, 1865.

Dear Sir: I propose, at some convenient and not distant day, to nominate you to the United States Senate as Minister to France.

Your obedient servant,
A. LINCOLN.

The President kept this offer secret from his Cabinet. There is nothing in Seward's memoirs that sheds any light on the subject. That it was officially in the dark is shown by the entry in the diary of Gideon Welles, Secretary of the Navy, written on March 15, 1865, nearly a month after the date of the offer:* "A rumor is prevalent and very generally believed that the French mission has been offered Bennett of the *New York Herald*. I discredit it. On one or two occasions this mission has been alluded to in Cabinet, but the name of B. was never mentioned or alluded to."

The next day Welles continues: "Blair believes the

*From *The Diary of Gideon Welles*. Copyright, 1909. Courtesy of Houghton-Mifflin Company.

President has offered the French mission to Bennett. Says it is the President and not Seward, and gives the reasons which lead him to that conclusion. He says he met Bartlett the (runner) of Bennett here last August or September; that Bartlett sought him, said they had abused him, B., in the *Herald* but thought much of him, considered him the man of most power in the Cabinet but were dissatisfied because he had not controlled the Navy Department early in the Administration and brought it into their (the *Herald's*) interest."

The first Lincoln letter throws light on this. Bartlett, says Welles, went on to tell Blair that he was in Washington watching movements and that "they did not mean this time to be cheated," whatever that may have meant. Bartlett was charged by Welles with vindictiveness against the Navy Department, because he would not purchase vessels through Bartlett's agency. He gives Bartlett credit for controlling the New York press, even the "pliant" Raymond of the *Times*. He excepts the *World* from this mysterious mastery. Welles "was sorry to hear Blair speak approvingly of the appointment of Bennett,— . . . an editor without character for such an appointment, whose whims are often wickedly and atrociously leveled against the best man and the best causes, regardless of honor or right."

"I dare not tell all about the Bennett matter on paper," wrote Thurlow Weed to John Bigelow, April 26, 1865. "It was a curious complication for which two well-meaning friends were responsible. Seward knew nothing about it until the Election was over, when he sent for me. I was amazed at what had transpired."

This was eleven days after Lincoln's death. The

surmise left open is that "the two well-meaning friends" may have conveyed some word of the President's intention to honor the editor during the campaign and so brought about the switch in the *Herald's* attitude; that certainly occurred as McClure recites. It is known that Lincoln angled for Horace Greeley and caught him with an offer to make him postmaster-general when he reorganized his Cabinet, if reelected. The promise had not been kept up to his death. It does not follow that it would not have been, though Greeley characterized the promise as a "lie." Therefore, it is not at all impossible that an intimation of coming honors flattered Bennett into outright support, and that the death of Dayton gave the President a chance to make good, which he did after a decent interval. This is pure surmise. The known facts are that the offer was made and declined.

According to Frederic Hudson:

> When Abraham Lincoln was elected President for the second term, what did he do: What was his opinion of a leading journalist? He unreservedly offered this great prize—the French mission—to Mr. Bennett and with what result? It was respectfully and positively declined. In his letter to the President the editor said his editorial mission was high enough and honorable enough for him; that he could do more good in the *Herald* than in France, and did not want office. Thus ended all the talk and gossip of the French mission.

Lincoln was not alone in keeping *en rapport*. Even the iron-minded Edwin M. Stanton, Secretary of War, bent to approach the editor of the *Herald*. He wrote Bennett, May 2, 1862, in these terms:

Dear Sir:—I take the liberty to inclose to you some observations respecting the present state of things as they appear to me. The great question involved in the rebellion has always seemed to me in a great measure a commercial question, and the history of the Federal Union shows that the commercial interest was one of the strongest inducements to the formation of the government. We have experienced the misfortune of the dissolution of the Union in our Commercial interests most sensibly (using that word in its most general sense), and have proved the wisdom of the framers of the Constitution by our loss in the destruction of their work—a wise and liberal system of domestic and foreign commerce. To the re-establishment of commercial relations I look, under Providence, for the restoration of the government, and that work, I regard, in a great measure, accomplished by the opening of the ports occupied by our forces. Of course, I consider the destruction of the enemy at Yorktown and Corinth as necessary conditions.

Holding these views, I think the public mind should be directed to this state of the question, and therefore venture to submit it to you.

Yours truly,
EDWIN M. STANTON.

Yet Anthony Trollope, the English novelist, writing in 1862 of a visit to America, made this off-the-track observation: "No newspaper in America is really powerful or popular; and yet they are tyrannical and overbearing. The New York *Herald* has, I believe, the largest sale of any daily newspaper; but it is absolutely without political power, and in these times of war has truckled to the Government more basely than any other paper. It has an enormous sale, but so far is it from having achieved popularity, that no man on any side ever speaks a good word for it."

When Lee surrendered, the *Herald* indorsed Grant's terms, observing further: "We apprehend no danger from a pardon to the Confederate leaders, political or military. They have played their game of rule or ruin and have lost it. Refuse them the honors of martyrdom. They may be left to the judgment of the people they have so cruelly and selfishly betrayed. With the violent death they have brought upon their institution of slavery, the cause, the argument and the party of a Southern Confederacy cease to exist. If four years of this terrible war have done the work of a century of peace, we must advance a century now that the work is done."

In this Bennett was in strict accord with Lincoln. Unfortunately for his country, the assassination of the President by John Wilkes Booth and the resulting political conspiracy spoiled the temperate procedure that would have followed had Lincoln lived. The *Herald* editorial on Lincoln's death was a fine tribute; no hysteria, but a just estimate. It said in summing up: "He may not have been, perhaps was not, our most perfect product in any one branch of mental or moral education; but, taking him for all in all, the very noblest impulses, peculiarities and aspirations of our whole people—what may be called our continental idiosyncrasies—were more collectively and vividly reproduced in his genial and yet unswerving nature than in that of any other public man of whom our chronicles bear record."

The assassin's bullet made Andrew Johnson, a southern Democrat, president, April 15, 1865, and the *Herald* came at once to his support. The man needed it. Elected on a Republican ticket, the radical leaders of the party, Thaddeus Stevens, Benjamin F. Wade, Zach Chandler and their like were bitterly opposed to him from the start. Here again we find the Chevalier Wikoff in evidence. This letter written by President Johnson was found among the papers of the Bennett estate:

Executive Mansion,
Washington, D. C.
October 6, 1865.

(Private)
James G. Bennett, Esq.
Dear Sir:

Your note of recent date by the politeness of Mr. Wikoff was received and read and the suggestions made in reference to our foreign policy considered.

This is a subject I would be pleased to confer with you upon freely and fully. This letter, however, is not written for that purpose but simply to tender you my thanks for the able and disinterested manner in which you have defended the policy of the Administration since its accession to power. It is the more highly appreciated because it has not been solicited.

I feel grateful for your timely help and confidence and hope to prove in the end that they have not been misplaced. The *People Proper* who need friends—who need honest and able advocates to defend their rights and interests in all government affairs—will in due time appreciate those who firmly and faithfully stand by them while passing through this dreadful ordeal.

If the patriotic impulse of the national heart is consulted and obeyed and carried out in good faith, regulated by law and the Constitution which should be held sacred and dear by all the friends of free government, all the former relations of the States in the Union will be restored, with all the associates of peace and sincere devotion to a Union that will be as enduring as time. This will be so if we perform our parts as patriots.

I entered upon this presidential term with a fixed and unalterable determination to administer the government upon the principles which will bring the people as near as may be in close proximity with all the acts and doings of their public servants thereby enabling them to determine understandingly all questions of public policy. So far in public life the people have sustained me. I have never deserted them and if I know my own heart I will stand by them now. Hence in the peoples' cause I need and ask your aid. You can now indelibly fix upon the hearts of this people who will be grateful that you are their friend and benefactor.

Now is the time for the principles upon which the government is founded to be developed, discussed and understood. There is no man in America who can exercise more power in fixing the government upon a firm and enduring foundation than you can. With such aid the task will be made easy in the performance of this work. I do not intend to be drawn from my purpose by taunts and jeers, coming whence they may, nor do I intend to be overawed by pretended or real friends, or bullied by swaggering or pursuing enemies. If truth is made our guide, the public Good our aim the Union will be restored, attended with all the blessings of a prosperous peace.

Accept assurance of my sincere esteem,

ANDREW JOHNSON.

N. B.

By the meeting of Congress the work of restoration will, I think, be nearly complete. Post Offices, Federal control, navy, etc., will be established.

"He begins well," had been the *Herald's* comment on the manner in which Johnson took over the presidency. It even sided, for the moment with his fierce announcement of his purpose to avenge the murdered Lincoln. When, however, his vagaries threatened the country by reason of party opposition and undue oppression in the South, the *Herald* turned against him and took the side of sanity, something that was very much lacking in the period of Reconstruction.

CHAPTER IX

WAR-TIME AND AFTER

So CLEARLY had Bennett envisaged the coming of the conflict between the states that he was much better prepared than any of his contemporaries to meet the news emergencies created by war. He gathered together a force of forty men and sent them to the various "fronts." All were splendidly equipped with horses and camp equipage. Many made remarkable records. Doctor George W. Hosmer, for example, reported the Battle of Gettysburg and discovered the Confederates moving through the darkness on Cemetery Ridge in time to warn its defenders against Longstreet's fierce assault. This act on his part saved the line and had much to do with Union success on the field. Charles H. Hart and a companion were captured by Mosby. The Guerrilla kept their horses but sent the pair safely to Richmond.

After the close of the Rebellion Frederic Hudson, managing editor of the *Herald,* figured out that the paper had spent five hundred and twenty-five thousand dollars in covering the four years' conflict. The staff in the field grew to sixty men and special dispatches were liberally paid for, a few exclusive lines that were worth one dollar and fifty cents at space rates often bringing twenty-five dollars as a reward for the sender's enterprise. Thus it was that the *Herald* always was the first choice among men on the spot as a market for their news.

One exploit that astonished the War Departments both at Richmond and Washington was the publishing of an almost correct roster of the Confederate Army. Richmond thought it had been done by some traitor to the cause and Washington suspected the *Herald* of improper intimacy with the South. In fact, the achievement was the result of close calculation in the compiling of carefully gathered facts. The results were astonishingly accurate.

When the wicked and needless war, which he had so deplored and had so sturdily tried to prevent, ended in 1865, Bennett was threescore and ten. For fifty years he had toiled as few men do, and was old. Accordingly he determined to put his son into harness. With the incoming of 1866 the young man began to take his turn. He was kept closely under the paternal eye, continuing to live with his father in the Washington Heights and Fifth Avenue mansions. The mother and daughter remained abroad. The elder Bennett advised and counseled but was no more in the limelight. The *Herald* had become an institution, solid and substantial, earning a new fortune for the owner each year.

The junior was twenty-five and had already sowed a liberal crop of wild oats to which his father seemingly took no exception. Indeed the canny old man had every confidence in the capacity of his son both to get and keep money. His extravagance was safely within the income of the *Herald*, and it may be that the father, knowing the son regarded the paper only as an agency for the making of money, relied upon this trait to keep up the *Herald's* steam. When the second Atlantic cable proved successful he began the costly habit of using it liberally. On its opening, the *Herald* and *Tribune* each endeavored to be first with a message under the sea on July 28, 1866. Both claimed the distinction. The *Herald* seems to have earned it.

The young man began his career with a coup. He caused the speech of King William of Prussia, after the battle of Sadowa, upon the making of peace with Austria, to be cabled in full to the *Herald*. The tolls totaled seven thousand dollars in gold. He bought smart steam craft to waylay vessels at quarantine, or farther out, as, for example, when the Grand Duke Alexis arrived on his celebrated visit to America, a steam scout intercepted the frigate *Sveltland*, on which his Highness traveled, at midnight, well off Sandy Hook, and the *Herald* thus "scooped" its contemporaries. He considered the use of balloons to carry messages, but found them too uncertain for the purpose.

July 1, 1867, the son started the *Evening Telegram* as an expensive independent effort. He maltreated the bantling from the start; never gave it a chance either with men or money and kept it in evidence mainly by printing it on pink paper.

The elder Bennett often changed his place of residence during the 'thirties. After his marriage the New York directory locates him at 114 Chambers Street. Upon Mrs. Bennett's departure for Europe with the children he gave up his home and resided at the Irving House until 1858 when he purchased a handsome country seat with large grounds at Fort Washington, near the present One Hundred and Eighty-first Street. In

1864 his town residence was at 379 Fifth Avenue. This was shifted the next year to 425 Fifth Avenue which remained his city domicile until his death.

In 1868 the Washington Heights mansion caught fire. The New York department rallied bravely to the rescue and succeeded in stopping the flames with but twenty thousand dollars damage. Bennett was very grateful and gave the men fifteen hundred dollars in rewards. He also established a fund at the expense of which a medal is given each year to the most heroic fireman. The bestowal of this award has become an annual ceremony of great moment to the fire-fighters of the city. It was first made through his son.

People thought the younger Bennett would not care to take on the *Herald* after his father's hands dropped from the rudder. They were mistaken. Several attempts were made to buy the paper—one of them by a syndicate in 1869, which made an offer of two million, two hundred thousand dollars for the property. It was promptly declined. Mr. Bennett met proffers with the remark that, "There is not money enough in the world to buy the *Herald,*" but it "could be had for 3 cents a copy any time."

Even in his quasi-retirement the old gentleman preserved his appearance of energy, bodily and mentally. Edward Townsend Flynn once recalled his coming to the *Herald* office one morning soon after the war ended, full of vim and carrying an old silk umbrella, time worn and faded. To this he was much attached. He busied himself issuing instructions and asking questions, one of which, addressed to Frederic Hudson, the managing editor, was as to how much he had paid E. A. Pollard, the former editor of the Richmond *Enquirer* and author of *The Lost Cause,* for an article that had just been published under the caption, "The Evacuation of the Confederate Forces from Richmond." Hudson replied, "One hundred twenty-five dollars." This was at the rate of fifty dollars per column, the space occupied being two and one-half of these units. "You must give him one hundred dollars more a column," commanded Mr. Bennett. He knew Pollard was desperately poor and took this way of aiding him, supervising the drawing of the check. Then he decided to go home. Looking about, he failed to find his ancient umbrella and made a prodigious row. It could not be found. He went off full of wrath over its disappearance. He could pay Pollard splendidly, but to lose the old friend of silk and whalebone upset him.

He was inclined to be kind to all of his old southern acquaintances, sunk as they were in misfortune and defeat. Despite the view of Jefferson Davis expressed in the *Herald* when the war broke, Mr. Bennett was not personally estranged from that personage. Mrs. Harriet Stanton Blatch, who as a little girl lived near the Bennett mansion on Washington Heights, recalls that after Jefferson Davis was liberated on the bail bond signed by Horace Greeley among others, he came north and there was considerable mystery as to his whereabouts. One day, with her elder sister, she ran across to a neighbor's and on the piazza were two distinguished-looking men. One she knew as James Gordon Bennett. The neighbor, Mr. Lane, introduced the stranger to the little ladies as Mr. Jefferson Davis. The sister stepped forward and shook hands. She, abashed, put her hands behind her back. Mr. Davis laughed and remarked, "Aha! a little Yankee!" So it was that while the reporters were seeking Davis he was lodging quietly with James Gordon Bennett.

John Russell Young has left a good picture of the elder Bennett in his declining years:*

My earliest impression of Bennett was that of a vast, sinister shape which had come out of the infinite, like some genii of the Arabian Nights, to overspread and darken the heavens. There was an aspect of terror in what young eyes saw of this, a lawless, eccentric influence sweeping a wayward orbit, and above human conditions and limitations, breathing wrath upon those who would not bow down and worship. I first saw the elder Bennett one bleak snowy night toward the close of Lincoln's presidency. A guest with my ever hospitable and gentle friend, Mr. [J. B.] Haskin, at his Fordham residence, nothing remained after dinner but that we should speed over the snow with tingling sleigh-bells to the Bennett home on the Hudson. If my imagination had gone into darkened fancies over the ideal Bennett, the man as I saw him drove them away. Hair white and clustering, a smooth face soon to have the comfort of a beard, prominent aquiline nose, a long, narrow head with abundant development in perceptive faculties, a keen boring eye which threw arrowy glances, bantering rather than hearty laughter, a firm masterful jaw, talk in a broad Scottish accent, which he seemed to nurse with a relish. His speech had the piquant, saucy colloquialisms which stamped his individuality on the *Herald*. His manner stately, courteous, that of a strenuous gentleman of unique intelligence giving opinions as though they were aphorisms, like one accustomed to his own way. Whatever he may have seemed in the columns of his journal, the man as he welcomed us was wreathed in courtesy and good will.

---

*From *Men and Memories,* by John Russell Young. Copyright, 1901. Courtesy of Major Gordon Russell Young.

I was to see Bennett on many occasions between this winter's night encounter, in 1864, until our last meeting in May, 1872, one month before he died. You felt in his company, the impression of a man of genius; humor, apt to run into mockery,—until it seemed almost as if it were the spirit of Voltaire breathing through him.

His mind teemed with ideas, which streamed into his talk,—saucy phrases, invectives, nick-names, keen bits of narrative surcharged with cynical pessimism, which remained, one might fancy, as a legacy of early days of disappointment and trial. For this man had fought the world—had fought it down! The world would not come to his need, and now he reigned apart, looking down upon it with scorn.

Bennett admired Andrew Jackson, and next to Jackson his admiration was Grant. He was the first of the great editors to recognize Grant. There was the affinity of the Scottish blood, and the attraction of Grant's Scottish tenacity of character.

The editor had an eye for results, and the campaigns of Grant were ripe in results. Bennett did not have a cheerful view of war; he could see no outlook but irretrievable bankruptcy, against which, as he said with a smile, he had provided by keeping a special deposit of gold in the Chemical bank. When the bottom fell out he would have swimming-gear of his own, and substance likewise, and not go down in a sea of paper currency and inflation.

There were no reasons in those days why even a more cheerful man than Bennett should be deep in gloom. The concern of Lincoln was lest the Union would be destroyed in a self-imposed bankruptcy before the army overcame secession. The military problem was solved when I saw Bennett in later days, and no one could have a more cheerful view of the national future. I remember some *Herald* articles published in the weeks succeeding the surrender of Lee, which I used to dig out of the files and read for the splendor and breadth of their foresight. And, in many conversations in his closing years, I recall the enthusiasm with which the venerable man would dwell upon the assured glory of the Republic. This was shown especially on one of my last visits. He had surrendered to his son the practical control of the *Herald*, and received his friends in a small richly-garnished corner-room of his New York house, in the second story, looking out upon Thirty-eighth street and Fifth Avenue. He was very old and feeble,—old in everything but genius. The face was scantily bearded, and, as he sat folded in the ample chair, with quilted gown, his head bent with years, his keen eyes gleaming through heavily rimmed spectacles, and heaped about him a pile of newspapers, there was a sense of majesty, even as that of the king on his throne. On this occasion I found him reading a report, several columns long, from a military officer, detailing a reconnaissance in the Yellowstone Park. And had I read it? I presume not. Some immediate story of the foolish fleeting hour had intervened, and military reports were not exhilarating. But I must read it! What a marvel that Yellowstone, and what a land, and what a country, with those awakening wonders day by day!—geysers spouting at times, and ceasing to spout, radiant clays with their pinks and blues, their crimson and saffron and pearl, and the rainbow phenomena; the hot steaming springs with healing in their waters. Such fertility, such beauty! and not the half was known. What this wise man saw in the officer's story was an object lesson. Living in his serene atmosphere of hope and contemplation, there was no romance like a fact. The things we called men, and the grasshopper brawls we called events, how small and mean to one who revelled in this revelation of Nature in sumptuous, gaudy mood! Bennett, as I used to read him, was the intellectual child of Walpole and Cobbett. He was an accomplished man. Although, for the first generation of its existence he made the New York *Herald* a journal which the humblest could comprehend,—although he understood the value of the journalistic axiom never to shoot above the heads of the people,—I question if any of his peers were better educated. He had lectured on political economy, had taught the languages and the higher mathematics, had written Byronian verses, and stories of the Maria Edgeworth school. He had studied the world from the moors of Scotland, the wharves of Boston, the academies of Charleston, the composing rooms of Philadelphia, the lecturer's pulpit in New York, and the Congress galleries of Washington. The lesson he had learned,—the stern lesson, that the world was a masked battery which must be carried at the point of a bayonet,—the fierce lesson that his one appointed duty in this existence was in the fortunes of James Gordon Bennett,—this he preached in the *Herald*. He preached amid derision and contempt, amid misrepresentation and personal violence; he preached and won.

The world knelt to his sceptre, and when I saw him he reigned as no man has reigned since, or, to my fancy, ever will, in the kingdom of journalism. A pupil of Walpole and Cobbett in literature, the political ideas of Bennett were influenced by the tremendous upheaval of Napoleonism. He was a contemporary of Napoleon, and his plastic mind had taken from, and hardened under, the bewildering influence of the French Emperor. Napoleon,—what he did or would be apt to do,—was among Bennett's familiar forms of illustration. He told me that one of the first articles he had ever written was an editorial upon the battle of Waterloo and the fall of Bonaparte, for a newspaper in Aberdeen.

After Napoleon, Bennett, like most students who had studied under the super-classical traditions of the earlier century, was immersed in Roman history. His parallels and illustrations, his moral and historical reflections were apt to come from Plutarch and the classic fathers. He would cite them in defence of a paradox, for his genius was quite capable of believing one thing in June and the contrary in July. "I print my paper every day," he was wont to say, when charged with inconsistency. And when some strange unexpected sensation in the *Herald* would burst upon the town to its wonderment, Bennett would tell the story of the dog of Alcibiades whose tail was docked to the end that Athens might talk about its master.

Bennett senior died at his Washington Heights residence at twenty-five minutes past five on Saturday, June 1, 1872. He had not been ill, though for five years inactive. The cause of his death was a stroke of apoplexy, which first befell a week previously. In its editorial mention of his death the *Herald* said:

The *Herald* was his creation; the embodiment of his long cherished idea of justice, owing allegiance to no party and laboring singly for the advancement and happiness of the people. The power he thus called into being and established as a wonderful success has exercised for more than thirty-five years a healthful influence over the politics and public men of the country, and has been instrumental in hastening the development and securing the triumph of many of those great undertakings that have added so much to the progress and prosperity of the American nation. In the advocacy of novel and comprehensive projects Mr. Bennett's broad views took no heed of obstacles that to ordinary minds seemed insurmountable; and his strong will manifested through the columns of the *Herald* infused into many a wavering enterprise a spirit that carried it successfully through all difficulties.

Oddly enough the *Herald* carried no biographical account of its founder in the issue of June second, which printed the news of his decease. On Monday it republished several biographies printed by other papers. None of them gave the date of his birth correctly. "About 1800," was the closest most of them came to it; the *Sun* gave the year—1795—accurately, but not the day. Mr. Bennett's New York contemporaries bade him good-by with the utmost respect.

"In the chief function of modern journalism," said the *World*, "that of promptly supplying the public with important news, Mr. Bennett stood not only in the first rank but at the head of that rank."

"As a successful journalist and man of business," said the *Times*, "James Gordon Bennett will be remembered among the representative men of the city of New York."

The *Sunday News* called him "the greatest journalist the world ever produced."

The *Sun* credited Mr. Bennett with the "invaluable service" of emancipating the press from "the domination of sects, parties, cliques and what is called society."

"He had no aim other than to make a great and lucrative newspaper," was the *Tribune's* comment.

It will be seen that the animosities engendered on his way up to the top of his profession had disappeared. Indeed, the directors of the New York Associated Press united in this tribute to his memory:

Resolved: That his long and eventful connection with the newspaper press of the country in a career of unexampled success and prosperity was the result of his great foresight, energy, and industry; that in all these qualities the example of Mr. Bennett inspired the greatest enterprise in journalism in the United

States and throughout the world, and must, therefore, for all time, leave their impression for good in the diffusion of knowledge and the advancement of the press.

It had been planned to hold the funeral in St. Patrick's Cathedral with Archbishop McCloskey officiating. Perhaps this was thought too great an honor for one who had so frequently flouted the hierarchy. So the services were held instead at the Fifth Avenue house, Vicar-General, the Reverend Doctor Starrs, conducting them. Horace Greeley, of the *Tribune,* George W. Childs, of the Philadelphia *Ledger,* Erastus Brooks, of the *Express,* George Jones, of the *Times,* Charles A. Dana, of the *Sun,* Hugh J. Hastings, of the *Commercial Advertiser,* David M. Stone, of the *Journal of Commerce,* Major J. M. Bundy, of the *Mail* and Frederic Hudson, managing editor of the *Herald* acted as pall-bearers, escorting the body to Greenwood Cemetery in Brooklyn—not Catholic ground. The *Herald* carried no account of the obsequies.

Mrs. Bennett did not long survive her husband. She died at Sachsen, Germany, March 28, 1873. John Bigelow, writing to W. H. Huntington, the New York *Tribune's* Paris correspondent, from Sachsen, April 18, 1873, remarks: "Mrs. J. G. Bennett died here about three weeks ago, the whole middle part, or axis of her body consumed by a confluent cancer. Like her husband, she died in the arms of mercenaries; she would not allow her son to be sent for while she was conscious; and she had long been unconscious of anything when he did arrive about two hours before she expired. She would not allow the doctor to speak of her danger, seemed unwilling to contemplate death, even when he was standing in her presence. The daughter, who is at school at Versailles arrived the day after her mother's death."

Frederic Hudson in his *History of American Journalism* sums up the *Herald* platform as developed under the elder Bennett in these terms:

First. The Constitution and prosperity of the United States under all circumstances.

Second. The growth and prosperity of the City of New York.

Third. To give all the news, freshly, fully, and faithfully, from all parts of the world.

Fourth. To comment clearly, freely and independently on the events of the world as they daily developed themselves.

Fifth. To sustain every enterprise that would elevate the human race, and unite all the nations in commerce and civilization.

Sixth. To make the *Herald* a cosmopolitan journal *par excellence.*

Bennett's will gave James Gordon Bennett, Jr., full and complete ownership of the *Herald* properties. He was enjoined, however, to pay for his sister Jeanette's education and maintenance.

CHAPTER X

BENNETT THE YOUNGER

JAMES GORDON BENNETT, the younger, was born May 10, 1841, with a silver spoon in his mouth—a spoon which he lived to turn into gold. Belying the tradition that second-growth timber is inferior, he did things which dwarfed the accomplishments of his parent. His arrival was made much of by his father, who inducted him into "the business" at an early age. Both the *Herald* and the *Sun* carried on sidelines in the way of special publications and each conducted a book store. There was much rivalry between these shops. In advertising his own, Mr. Bennett made mocking use of his first-born, then nineteen months old, by announcing him as proprietor of a better book stall than that maintained by his rival, Moses Y. Beach.

Three more children were born to the Bennett family, one charming boy named Cosmo Gordon Bennett, after the elder Bennett's much-loved brother. This child died when five years and three months old. The others were a daughter who died at eight months, and Jeanette, who became Mrs. Isaac Bell, Jr.

It has been shown that the savage attacks on Mr. Bennett were showered upon his wife as well. She stood the social storm until the two surviving children were eligible for school and then departed to live much of the remainder of her life in Europe. This move arose from her determination to educate her children "out of the sphere of misrepresentation, calumny and reckless wit, to whose insulting frequency her own name has been subjected for no other cause than to gratify the spleen of assailants, alike destitute of magnanimity of disposition and good taste in literature, when they despaired of wounding Mr. Bennett in any other way," as it was written by Isaac C. Pray, in 1855.

All this was true. It is a poor tribute to a day in which "chivalry" and "gallantry" were overworked words that in the slurs on her husband Mrs. Bennett was constantly linked with the lowest and meanest forms of innuendo or downright insult. That all were infamous calumnies is beyond question. The seasoned soldier who was her mate knew that to give meant to take, and never shrank from blows. But she, a high-minded, intelligent woman, was literally driven from the country.

So it befell that "young Jim," as he was then known, had a queer sort of bringing up. There was probably wisdom in thus exiling the youth, even if the after-effects on his character were bad. Because of the intense feeling against his father in the upper circles, he would hardly have been welcomed at any institution of learning in America where boys of the wealthy class were harbored.

Private tutors provided him with as much learning as he cared to accept. He acquired French, but his education was not elaborate, nor did he inherit his father's facile skill as a writer. He wrote in labored fashion quite lacking in sparkle or wit, and often groped for the point he wanted.

At times Mrs. Bennett returned for short residences,

bringing the children with her. New Yorkers of the 'fifties, who were sometimes bidden within the doors, found "young Jim" a strange and ill-mannered youth. One of these, the late Frank Squier, Park Commissioner of Brooklyn, and brother of Ephriam George Squier, the explorer and archeologist, once told the writer of attending a party for the young folks at which James Gordon, Junior, aged sixteen, gave an exhibition of himself such as his father, even in the unregenerate days of the penny *Herald,* would hardly have cared to publish. Isolation abroad, combined with plenty of money, made him dissolute when very young.

But as he had given his son the book store when an infant, the father made the growing wilful boy the center of his thoughts. In the *Herald* office he had a room fitted with a desk, on either side of which he installed two lesser ones. Here during his son's stay in New York he would place the lad and Edward Townsend Flynn, another youngster of the neighborhood whom he favored as a playmate, with the purpose of bringing up the pair to "run" the *Herald,* as indeed they were destined to do. Flynn was a bright boy with brilliant red hair and a resourceful mind. He was a born New Yorker, the family having come from Schenectady in the troubled days of revolutionary border warfare to locate on Manhattan Island, where his grandfather "farmed" in the vicinity of the present Thirtieth Street.

Inheriting from his father decision, boldness and enterprise, the younger Bennett multiplied all three. Doctor George W. Hosmer, who served under both father and son, and who detested the latter, used to

The Three Bedlams

Showing Horace Greeley, of the *Tribune,* Henry J. Raymond, of the *Times,* and James Gordon Bennett. Cartoon in *Vanity Fair,* October 5, 1861

declare that the boy, half Irish and half Scotch, embodied the worst qualities of both races. He could be as generous as an Irishman and as close as a Scot, with upsetting suddenness. No one ever knew what he would do next—least of all himself.

As he grew up the youth speedily became a member of the New York fast set—and it *was* pretty fast. It centered at Delmonico's for luncheon and gathered at the Union Club in leisure hours. For boon companions young Bennett found here the Heckshers, the Howlands, the Osgoods, Lloyd Phœnix, Frank Work, Gunning S. Bedford, whom he made a judge; Herman Oelrichs, Pierre Lorillard, Jr., Arthur Leary, William P. Douglas, William R. Travers, the stammering wit of Wall Street; Lawrence R. Jerome and Leonard Jerome—and other blue-blooded New Yorkers of their type. Most of the gentlemen named were his elders, but they saw in him one of their kind.

New York then supported a Jockey Club, the present home of the Manhattan Club, at Madison Avenue and Twenty-sixth Street, which contained a theater and many adjuncts of good living. Here Leonard Jerome was supreme. Jenny Jerome was his daughter. She captured the brother of the Duke of Marlborough with her wit and beauty, and became the mother of the brilliant Winston Churchill of our day.

Ladies of the stage interested young Bennett, and when Lydia Thompson brought her bevy of British blondes to America, he impartially annexed them, notably Pauline Markham, she of the "voice of velvet and the lost arms of the Venus of Milo," as Richard Grant White described her. Poor damsel! When she went into a decline after her dazzling days, people soon forgot that James Gordon Bennett had drunk champagne from her slipper! Having disappeared completely, she turned up in New York in the late 'nineties, wife of a printer, and soon thereafter died. I have in my autograph collection a letter from her denying some statement affecting her personally. It was the last note heard.

Aristocracy in New York made its last stand in the Union Club. It still exists on memories. But in Bennett's day the club house at Fifth Avenue and Twentieth Street was the citadel of the *jeunesse dorée* and, open all night, it afforded a refuge for the gilt-edged, who did not care to go home. That the son of the person most detested by the preceding generation of New York's social set could pass into its exclusive precincts illustrated the gilding power of money. He kept up his membership all his life, and members of the club were sacrosanct in the *Herald* office. They were accursed of copy readers, who were pretty sure to be wigged if the mention of one under unfavorable circumstances got by. I recall the late William C. Reick, so long the head of the *Herald*, asking me mournfully if we had in the *World* office any list of "sacred cows" who had to be treated with discretion. I said no. He said he had a full stable, and remarked: "How in hell can I be expected to carry the names of all the members of the Union Club in my mind?"

Next to Commodore Vanderbilt and William B. Astor, the younger Bennett, after his father's death, probably possessed for the period the largest assured income in America. The certainty of resource made him a good spender. He had no taste for piling up millions and never tried to.

While the elder Bennett had been in the background

for five years, and the son was more or less in the harness, the public did not hold him in full responsibility until the death of the father, when the thought that so powerful an engine as the *Herald* was to fall into reckless hands brought on a sense of dismay, enhanced by the fact that a sort of twilight of the gods had fallen upon New York journalism. Henry J. Raymond had died and left the *Times* to his commercial associates, who had put an astute Englishman, Louis J. Jennings, in his place. Horace Greeley and the elder Bennett died within a few months of each other. Manton Marble navigated an able, but not widely circulated, *World.* Charles A. Dana was putting life and intellect into the *Sun,* but always as a devil's advocate. Frederic Hudson, the *Herald's* competent managing editor, went into retirement and the young man picked Thomas B. Connery to take his place, a mild and gentle individual, entirely at his master's service. People expected the *Herald* to do strange things—and it did.

The young man was difficult to approach and hard to deal with. John Bigelow, in his diary, under date of September 4, 1874, records going with Samuel J. Tilden to call on the distinguished Charles O'Conor, at Fort Washington, for the purpose of getting him to "see Bennett and straighten out the *Herald* on the Governorship"—Tilden being the Democratic candidate for that office. "O'Conor," says Bigelow, "worried a good deal over the difficulties of manipulating a man wholly given up to pleasure, but he showed by the faces he made over it that he should not fail for want of trying."*

*From *Retrospections of an Active Life,* by John Bigelow. Copyright, 1913. Courtesy of Doubleday, Doran and Company.

Bennett had that curious contempt for men which seems inherent in those who have inherited wealth. Captain A. J. Keanealy, once yachting reporter, son of the celebrated Queen's Counselor, who wrecked his fortunes on behalf of the Tichborne claimant, made an appeal for better financial recognition. It was denied with the blunt remark that "all the brains I want can be picked up any day at twenty-five dollars per week." The captain left to adorn the newly established New York *Recorder,* and ended his days prosperously on the *World.* Oddly enough, this indifference of Bennett did not extend to the mechanical departments. John Henderson, Mannis J. Geary, foreman of the *Herald* composing-room, and John Hays, who bossed the presses, were well paid and were treated as persons of distinction. Their several domains of authority were never invaded. They were given the best of tools to work with, and rigid rules as to closing forms were enforced upon the editors to serve their convenience. Each page had its fixed minute for departing from the composing-room floor, and woe betide the make-up man who was guilty of delay. In all other offices going to press was a scramble; in the *Herald* it was governed with military precision, under carefully drawn and printed schedules.

Beside the scorn of the proprietor, the *Herald* men had to endure a system of espionage. The suspicious satrap had a system of spying that brought constant trouble to the staff. He insisted on elaborate reports, which he rarely read, but he was keen on gossip and matters at which he chose to take offense. "White mice," the reporters called the spies.

As the result of this espionage Bennett received

many unsigned letters. On one occasion he cabled Edward D. DeWitt, his very capable advertising manager, to come to Paris by the next French steamer. Mr. DeWitt sailed and in due season presented himself before his employer at his apartment in the Avenue d' Iena.

"DeWitt," was the greeting, "I have been receiving some anonymous letters about you. They say you are getting fat and lazy. Napoleon and his marshals won their victories when they were lean. If you have become fat you are of no use to me."

Now it happened that Mr. DeWitt was a Princeton athlete not long enough out of college to have lost his taste for exercise. He had played "squash" all the way across and was agile as an antelope. Bennett scrutinized him closely for some time and dismissed him without further ceremony to make his way back to America. Nothing more was heard on the subject of avoirdupois. DeWitt had passed the inspection. Later he was considered sufficiently slender to be made general manager.

The results of the spying were not always adverse to the intended victim. In 1917 when the Wilson administration issued its order curbing the use of coal in the interest of war industries, there was alarm among the newspaper publishers lest paper mill fuel should be cut off. I wrote a protest, after an informal conference of New York publishers had authorized such a step. When it came to signing the document Oswald Garrison Villard of the *Evening Post,* H. F. Gunnison of the Brooklyn *Eagle,* Frank B. Flaherty of the *Herald* and myself were the only ones to put down our names. Flaherty had just been appointed general manager of the *Herald* and had some doubts as to his status. He thought this would be a good way to find out where he stood, so he affixed "General Manager" after his signature. In due season Mr. Bennett was apprised of his act in the usual fashion. Instead of the expected explosion he remarked mildly, "Well, Flaherty *is* general manager."

It may be remarked that the remonstrance was effective, despite the timidity of those who failed to join in it after urging such a step.

So far as Bennett could make it, the *Herald* was a one-man shop. In the Paris office this was especially the case. "I want you fellows to remember," he once said to the executive staff, "that I am the only reader of this paper. I am the only one to be pleased. If I want it to be turned upside down, it must be turned upside down. I want one feature article a day. If I say the feature is to be Black Beetles, Black Beetles it's going to be."

Once the Paris edition published a letter that came in by mail, signed "Old Philadelphia Lady," asking some way of transmuting the movements of a Centigrade thermometer into Fahrenheit. By a composing-room blunder this was repeated a second day. The oddity of the inquiry and the repetition made talk. Bennett ordered the letter reprinted continuously. So it ran on and on, but sometimes he used her signature himself to propound puzzling inquiries. People would answer the Old Lady's plaintive inquiry from all parts of the world.

Two men who detested each other were linked together, to their mutual distaste, in the London office. One had a penchant for periodical sprees. The other was aware of this tendency, and, hoping through it to rid himself of an objectionable associate, hired at his own expense a private detective to trail the frail gentleman. The sleuth followed his subject for some time without result, but was at last able to report him delinquent from drink. His employer at once telegraphed the fact to Bennett in Paris, to the tune of being crippled for lack of reliable help. Bennett replied: "You are not even a good reporter. I knew three days ago that B——— was drunk."

It seems that the thirsty one, aware of the net spread for him, had prudently advised headquarters that he was about to have a "periodical" and had been forgiven in advance!

Colloquially Bennett was the "Commodore" to *Herald* men, on account of his three terms in command of the New York Yacht Club squadron. The title lent itself better to their relationship and his own view of them than the implied servility of "Chief."

Men were often cruelly demoted. For example, George J. Taylor, whose name stood long with others at the head of the editorial page as News Editor, was suddenly shifted from that high estate to Brooklyn, supervising the few small-pay reporters who covered that bedroom. Taylor, father of Bert Leston Taylor, the "Line O' Type" man of the Chicago *Tribune*, was a valuable aid, devoted to the *Herald*. He never knew the reason for the change. Besides humiliation, the evil of the system was that salaries were lowered as well as rank. Pay went with the place, not with the man. This was quite different from Joseph Pulitzer's custom; however he might shift men he did not alter their rewards.

According to Thomas G. Alvord, who was much in Bennett's confidence:

> The seemingly erratic, unjust, contemptible conduct now and then shown the most deserving members of the staff was designed to put to the severest test the loyalty of the individual whose seeming fealty, expecting a reward, had been proven a dozen times. Came he through demotion, reduction of pay, undeserved suspension, designed humiliation, and still remained, steadfast in his devotion to the *Herald* and its master, taking his dose without complaint or the seeking of a place on some other paper, then Mr. Bennett believed he might be trusted in great temptation and relied on in all emergencies. In no other way, in his opinion, could a thoroughly reliable corps of newspaper employees be built up and maintained.

So it was that despite ill-usage men stood a service as desperate in ways as that in the French Foreign Legion. Indeed, some who were discharged or demoted were never themselves again. They missed their shirts of hair and the excitement of accomplishment which was always plentiful in the *Herald* office.

Thus for all of their contemptuous ill-treatment, men were attracted to the *Herald*. There was something compelling about the tigerish proprietor with his fickleness and brutality. Women are said to be fascinated by such characters. Certainly, newspaper men were. Besides, the *Herald* was a conquering force and they liked to be associated with victory and achievement. Of course, no one with real sense or any hope of the hereafter, would work for a metropolitan daily, even of the best sort. Journalists are, however, seldom sensible persons. They prefer irregularity to routine, and excitement to ease. Money is secondary in their eyes, else they would never yoke themselves as slaves of the lamp. This trait kept the *Herald* staff full of capable men. The candle flame never lacked its attendant array of admiring moths. One who came under the spell was Mark Twain, who, when he returned to New York on November 17, 1867, after the novel voyage on the *Quaker City*, which produced *The Innocents Abroad*, and so laid the foundation of a fame that was preeminent, made for the *Herald* office and deposited there the last of many letters describing the trip. The others had been written to the *Alta California*, which paid for the excursion, and the New York *Tribune*, then in its great Horace Greeley days. Mark Twain was out for business, as he wrote home from Washington a week later: "Am pretty well known now—intend to be better known." He knew the *Herald* was the best publicity medium in America. Indeed, the same letter chronicles one result of his forethought: "Belong on the *Tribune* staff, and shall write occasionally. Am offered the same berth to-day on the *Herald* by letter. Shall write to Mr. Bennett, and accept as soon as I hear from the *Tribune* that it will not interfere." Evidently the *Tribune* did not object for Clemens records under date of January 24, 1868:*

This is a good week for me. I stopped in the *Herald* office as I came through New York to see the boys on the staff and young James Gordon Bennett asked me to write twice a week, impersonally, for the

*From *Mark Twain's Autobiography.* Copyright, 1924. Courtesy of Harper and Brothers.

Herald, and said if I would I might have full swing, and about anybody and everything I wanted to. I said I must have the very fullest possible swing, and he said "All right." I said, "It's a contract—" and that settled that matter.

He noted a purpose to "write *one* letter a week anyhow." Thus began a connection that endured as long as Mr. Clemens lived. The *Herald* was always his friend, and he the *Herald's*. I possess a list of nearly two hundred articles, letters, interviews and references dating from this beginning that appeared in its columns.

Naturally, men studied Bennett's humors and turned their discoveries often to advantage. He was very fond of small dogs and kept a troop of the little animals about him. One of his fancies was that animals were good judges of human character, and he was given to guessing the qualities of callers by the manner in which they were received by his favorites. It chanced that a shrewd Irish attaché of the London office fell into disfavor. He judged by the tone of notes from his employer that a crisis was near in their relations, and receiving a summons to Paris, which indicated a nearness to the end, he bethought himself of the dogs and took measures to win their esteem. Wearing the customary garb of Fleet Street—a tall hat and long frock coat, the "Prince Albert" of those days,—he pinned a slice of raw liver in the topper and scented a handkerchief with anise, tucking the same in a coat-tail pocket. Thus armed, he went into the haughty presence of the boss, who received him coldly. Not so the pups. Scenting the delicacies, they swarmed upon the visitor, fawning and frolicking about him, to the deep delight of the Commodore, who, whatever he had in mind, laid it aside, treated his visitor cordially and sent him away warmed with every evidence of esteem. The dogs parted from him with lavish regret. It might be said that he held his hat firmly against his chest during the stay.

This love of canines—Pomeranians, Pekinese and Cocker spaniels were his favorites—made Bennett a fervid foe of vivisection. He steadily fought the practise in the *Herald* and never lost an opportunity to utter a protest. Once he presented an Egyptian princess with a prize pup. For days after its arrival the Paris *Herald* carried bulletins concerning the state of its health.

John Habberton, author of *Helen's Babies,* spent many years on the *Telegram's* editorial page, and for a while before his death Walt Whitman's name had a place on the *Herald's* pay-roll.

It would require a long list to cover the talented men who saw service on the *Herald* in Bennett's younger days. One name stands out with Henry M. Stanley's—that of Januarias A. Mac Gahan, who rode to Khiva with the Russians in their advance on the Oases of Turkestan in 1873. Mac Gahan reported the Carlist contest in Spain in 1874 and the Turco-Russian War of 1877. Among the men who counted through the years were Ivory Chamberlain, Joseph I. C. Clarke, Julius Chambers, Ballard Smith, William J. C. Meighan, Charles H. Hart, Robert Hunt Lyman, Charles Nordhoff, Thomas Gold Alvord, Thomas J. Cummins, James Creelman, Samuel S. Chamberlain, Robert E. Livingston, S. J. E. Rawling, Doctor E. P. Cohen, Nicholas Biddle, DeFrancias Folsom, L. A.

Hendrick—who covered the Beecher-Tilton trial with Albert Pulitzer, then fresh from Budapest, as an assistant; A. O. Plunkett—a veteran in the Brooklyn field; E. A. Rockwell, William O. Inglis, Frank H. Pierson, Robert S. Yard, H. L. Marshall, William M. Fuller, J. C. Klein, Edward M. Brant—expert yachting reporter; James F. Gill, John Grant Dater, Nelson Hersh, James Clancy—whose specialty was inside Irish news; George R. Miner, Kate Masterson, Max F. Ihmsen, Harry S. Brown, J. W. Slaght, Frank Leslie Baker, Hamilton Peltz, John T. Burke, Paul Krotel, John R. Caldwell, William B. Bininger—the most accomplished society reporter New York ever knew; and H. L. Mayhew, an authority on dogs, as good as was the Commodore himself; George B. McClellan, afterward mayor of New York; Ashley W. Cole, Maurice M. Minton, James Luby, Samuel Walter Taylor, Arthur Bartlett Maurice, James L. Ford, H. W. B. Howard, Byron P. Stephenson, A. S. Crockett, Leo L. Redding, James Fisher and John H. Tennant, later managing editor of the *Evening World.*

The artists included H. C. Coultaus, W. Goater, J. W. Trowbridge, Ripley Osgood Anthony, C. H. Wright, Louis Biederman and Harry Grant Dart.

The cartoonists numbered such notables as Baron C. de Grimm, Charles G. Bush and W. A. Rogers.

On the editorial side, George H. Hepworth and E. S. Drone, were in turn chief leader-writers; Charles Nordhoff, Thomas W. White, Charles Edward Russell, Charles M. Lincoln and William C. Reick figured largely, especially Mr. Reick who earned the distinction of becoming closer to his employer than any other man who ever served him, and who was a potent factor in the paper's history for nearly two decades. For years he wielded powers not before given another, though his title never got beyond city editor. Bennett once explained to Joseph Pulitzer that he had found titles swelled the heads of executives and he thought this would keep down the size of this particular gentleman's occiput. Reick began his career by sending in items from his native place, Burlington, New Jersey. Soon he did so well that he became state reporter, winning Bennett's attention during a mad-dog scare in Newark in 1889, with a suggestion that five children who had been bitten be sent to Paris by the *Herald* to undergo the new serum treatment discovered by Pasteur. This was done. Thereafter his progress was rapid and he took on the city desk. In reality he was Bennett's main connecting link with the office. He stood to a degree between master and men, taking many blows that should have reached others. Bennett was more than liberal with him and gave him the foundation of a considerable fortune. A block of uptown lots had been eating themselves up with taxes. He presented them to Mr. Reick. The building of the first New York subway expanded their value to a top notch. He acquired affluence in other ways and got into society, losing caste with the Commodore by moving too much in what reporters call "financial and social circles." His powers were restricted and his activities curbed. Bennett would also prescribe hours for him and have some one else report whether or not they were kept. These hours were sometimes arranged most uncomfortably, as, for example, from noon to midnight. In Mr. Reick's last years on the paper he was sentenced to keep this schedule without having anything to do. Ennui drove him forth to success as a stockholder and associate editor of the *Times* and to failure as owner of the *Sun.* He was a very able man who could transform the owner's orders into action without demoralizing the staff—something Bennett himself could not always do.

Next to Mr. Reick, Charles M. Lincoln stood a lengthy test, until an offer from the *Times* relieved him from a relationship that had become irksome. The last man to serve Bennett as an editorial executive was Joseph K. Ohl, who had much experience in the Far East and was a capable, amiable man.

Sometimes when the Commodore was unduly exhilarated he would write strange things into articles on the proof sheets. These were usually caught up-stairs, until he learned the trick and got into the habit of standing over the forms to see that what he wanted was in place. J. I. C. Clarke, then night editor, relates that he appeared one night in a merry mood and drifted up to his desk to say:* "I want this correction made in old Mr. Thingimbob's editorial. I want this inserted; give it point." Clarke read a scrawl on the proof: "This is the last dying kick of the Tammany anaconda!"

"What do you think?" queried the young man. "M' friends uptown say anaconda can't kick; got no legs. That's the fun of it. I want it in, and I'll have it in."

"Suppose," suggested Clarke, "you say squirm?"

"H'm. Squirm, squirm. Yes, squirm is disagreeable, but I want to give Tammany a kick; so I'll stick to kick." To make sure, he followed the proof to the composing-room and saw it "in."

*From *My Life and Memories*, by Joseph Ignatius Constantine Clarke. Copyright, 1925. Courtesy of Dodd, Mead and Company.

When Bennett wrote an editorial it was his custom to have it printed in double-leads, so that it stood out on the page. He liked double leading as a form of emphasis, which it is. He would also sprinkle his copy liberally with capitals, which had to be sifted out in the composing-room, and delighted in writing letters to the editor, calling attention to poor service in popular restaurants like Sherry's or Delmonico's when a meal did not happen to suit him, just as his father before him puffed those he patronized.

The effect of his potations was usually to evolve some out of the ordinary physical action, but sometimes it confused his head work. On one of his spells of exhilaration his father's anti-Catholicism gave through him an atavistic performance. Summoning Samuel S. Chamberlain, then his secretary, he remarked:

"Sam, I am tired of all this talk of the *Herald* being controlled by the Roman Catholic Church and of the number of Trinity College men on its staff. Now, I want you to write an editorial that will put us right before the public and show that we have no affiliations with Rome. Attack the Catholic Church, its monasteries, nunneries and schools and make it as strong as you can: Write the editorial and bring it to me this evening."

Mr. Chamberlain labored dutifully, turning up at eventide with a blistering "leader." It was headed "To Hell with the Pope," and contained such burning phrases as, "Tear down the Monasteries," "Drive out the Monks," "Let us have no politics from Rome" and much more of the like. Bennett was delighted.

"Now, Sam," he observed, "you've fooled me many

times before but you're not going to do it this time. We'll cable this to-night."

Together they drove to the Paris *Herald* office and duly delivered the editorial for transmission to New York, Bennett personally handing in the copy. His faithful secretary had used forethought, however, and passed the word that it was to be held for him. This was duly done. Bennett went home highly pleased with himself and proceeded to extend his period of inebriety. Some ten days later he came to himself and dimly recalled the indiscretion. He summoned Sam to his bedside and nervously asked if something had not been sent to the *Herald* abusing the Catholic Church. The dutiful secretary replied that it had not seemed strong enough and he had recalled the article for further revision. Bennett blessed him for his action, took him to ride and during the course of it stopped at a jeweler's shop to buy a cat's-eye ring which he placed on the secretary's finger as a reward for his judgment!

"Sam" was the son of Ivory Chamberlain, one of the ablest of *Herald* men, and was an ideal secretary for such an employer. He knew all the ropes of newspaperdom, but even he could not stand everything. The end of their relations came in the harbor at Nice where Bennett, commanding his yacht, persisted in a course that would have rammed a United States man-of-war, insisting that the latter was in the wrong place. He was dissuaded with difficulty from having a collision. Mr. Chamberlain joined the remonstrants and lost so much favor that he left the entourage, to found *Le Matin,* since become one of the most successful Parisian papers under the ownership of Maurice Bunau-Varilla and his brother Philippe, of Panama Canal fame. Chamberlain did some great work for William R. Hearst in San Francisco and New York, also aiding Thomas B. Wanamaker in building up the Philadelphia *North American.* He learned to imitate his first employer in various ways and ended his stay in Philadelphia with an expression of opinion about shop-keepers that was hardly warranted in Mr. Wanamaker's case. Then he returned to Mr. Hearst and died in his employ.

Bennett's vagaries brought him into frequent contact with the New York police. They usually treated him with consideration, but one wild ride in a fore-in-hand led to his being clubbed a bit by Police Captain Alexander S. Williams, who was given to that form of discipline in dealing with the unruly. Bennett pounded him for years in the *Herald,* but at last they made up. Williams became in time an inspector, and was hailed up on charges before the Police Board, of which Major-General Fitz John Porter was a Democratic member. Williams was a Republican with a pull. Porter felt that Williams was guilty and said so in an interview given Thomas Gold Alvord, of the *Herald's* staff, covering police headquarters. It was printed. Ballard Smith, then in charge of city news on the paper, knowing that Williams had been placed on the immune list, suspended the reporter, while the two Republicans on the Police Board insisted that Porter should not sit in the trial. As a result Williams was acquitted. Meeting Alvord he told him that he had saved him and expressed deep gratitude. Alvord replied that he had lost out himself. At that Williams boarded the Police Boat *patrol,* and, knowing that Bennett was nearing land on a home trip, met the yacht at Fire Island, whence there came at once a telegram reinstating the innocent offender. Alvord rose high in Bennett's favor, being paid twelve thousand dollars a year, a mighty price for the day, as head of the Washington Bureau.

It would take an Arabian Night's volume to chronicle all the mad doings of the young man and his "set" in the early 'seventies. They tell a tale of his dining one night at the up-town Delmonico's with Colonel James Fisk, Jr., Edward Townsend Flynn and Edwin Booth, when an alarm of fire sounded. Though he was full clad in evening clothes some erratic impulse led him to go out and assume direction of the firemen. He was soon in the way and so much of a nuisance that one company turned the hose on him. The jet of water struck him in the chest and flattened him into a sitting posture on the pavement, from which situation he was rescued by his companions and taken home, very damp, inside and out.

The next day, on reaching the *Herald* office, he sent for Flynn. "What did I do last night?" he queried.

"Made a big fool of yourself," was the frank response. "You interfered with the firemen by trying to tell them how to do their work, about which they know a good deal more than you do."

"Order a rubber overcoat for every man in the department," said Bennett. "Send the bill to me. I was never so wet in my life."

Once at Delmonico's, the young man, in company with Mr. Flynn, annoyed at the delay in bringing on a bottle of champagne, shouldered his way through a double line of men fronting the bar and called out:

"I ordered a bottle of champagne fifteen minutes ago! Where is it?"

"You would have thought he'd ordered a case," observed a small man in the cluster. Bennett aimed a resentful blow at the commentator. It was gracefully warded off, and then a return clip under the jaw landed him insensible on the floor.

Flynn fled the scene discreetly and left his companion to the well-ordered waiters of Delmonico's. The next day he was summoned to the Bennett presence, and asked if he had not been with him at Delmonico's. Flynn said he had, but left when the other started for the bar.

"Who hit me?" was the next question. "It was a knockout."

Flynn promised to find out, and did. It was "Billy" Edwards, a light-weight boxer of the day, later, and for a long time, the "bouncer" at Edward S. Stokes' Hoffman House bar. When his indentity was known, Bennett invited him to call, highly delighted to know that the "knockout" was professional. They became quite friendly.

Another tale of interest in pugilism avers that he once set up a "ring" on *Lysistrata* and personally illustrated the merit of the newly discovered "solar plexus" blow, using the yacht's butler as an example. By good luck he was able to flatten out that rather beefy personage to his own great satisfaction. The butler, as a measure of safety, chose to remain unconscious for half an hour.

Sometimes an employee took liberties successfully. George Cooper, a rough and ready Paris *Herald* man, coming in one day found Bennett poking around the office looking sour. He slapped him on the back cordially and shouted: "Come along, Bennett, I'm going to show you Paris." To the amazement of beholders the Commodore assented. The pair went off gaily together on a tour of the town. Cooper had his salary doubled as the reward for his sociability.

It is related that some time after Charles Henry Meltzer, the musical critic, joined the New York *Herald* staff a curt cable came, reading:

"Tell Meltzer to cut his hair."

Meltzer was duly advised. He declined to submit to the shears. Soon there came the query:

"Has Meltzer cut his hair?"

"No," was the reply.

"Send him to St. Petersburg," was the reaction.

Meltzer, it should be explained, had a shoe-brush hirsute adornment, cut schoolboy fashion, just above his coat collar. He went to St. Petersburg. The correspondent at that capital received the same order with the same result and inquiry. The obdurate critic was next forwarded to Berlin, and possibly other continental capitals. In the end he reached New York unshorn—and without a job. He sued, and received damages.

If the elder Bennett admired Grant, the son did not. It was he who, during the President's second term, warned the country against Cæsarism, for which he was roundly cartooned by Thomas Nast.

An abrasion on the bridge of his nose caused by a polo accident forced Bennett to wear a patch for some time on that rather prominent organ. Nast seized upon it and added it to the caricatures of the "young man" in *Harper's Weekly*. He also contrived

Courtesy of James Melvin Lee, Department of Journalism, New York University

James Gordon Bennett, the Younger, in his prime

to make him look a sap-head, which in no way was part of his character.

Men of consequence from abroad sought out the young *Herald* proprietor when they came over to see America. A notable who visited New York in the early 'seventies was A. P. Primrose, to be better known as Lord Rosebery. The two made New York glow together. Bennett and his English guest, both scintillating with champagne, saw the *Herald* to press one night with a degree of éclat that quite upset the usually well-ordered establishment. The rosy-cheeked, fair-haired Primrose was at the time of this American visit accounted the most brilliant young man in England, quite capable of accomplishing anything he might set his mind upon. He was credited with three high purposes—to marry a great heiress, win the Derby and became prime minister of England. He did all three, the heiress being Rothschild's daughter. Bennett always had a warm corner for him in the *Herald*.

The *Herald* office teemed with tales about the Commodore. He required that all things should be made known to him before they were attempted, and the office council, playing safety as much as possible, laid everything in his lap. Most of it stayed there, but now and then some odd responses came to the waiting wise men. On one occasion a matter of importance had waited for a week. The cables were watched with expectancy, but remained dumb. At last a message came. The watchers opened it eagerly, hoping to have their desires endorsed. Instead, came this cryptic mandate:

"Send two mocking-birds by special messenger."

The Dog and Bird columns of the *Herald* produced a dealer who sold mocking-birds. Two splendid specimens were secured and sent by a faithful hand to Paris. This spoiled another fortnight. Still no response came to the council's communication. Silence continued for a few days more. Then the cable spoke:

"Send mocking-bird food."

Again a messenger was dispatched with a supply of bird fodder. When he came back he shed light on the mystery. The Commodore had been expatiating at a dinner on the melodious merits of the American mocking-bird. A lady guest was skeptical. To prove that he was right the Commodore at once called for the birds. When they arrived it was found that they required a special diet, such as was not to be found in France. Hence the second cable. No reply ever came to the council's propositions.

Daniel McCarthy had been a locomotive engineer on the Auburn branch of the New York Central Railroad. He developed a talent for drawing and making cartoons that secured him a place on the *Herald* staff. After a while, he was sent to France to liven up the Paris *Herald,* then newly established. One day an order came assigning him to Trouville. He went, expecting instructions to follow. None came. So he drew some local washerwomen and sent them on. A sharp rebuke was all he got in reply. Having nothing else to do thereafter, he took to brandy and became comfortably drunk. One day a coach and four, driven by the Commodore, rolled up to the inn, well laden with fast specimens of European nobility, male and female. They were gorgeously arrayed and looked right royal to the ex-engineer's eyes. It was this arrival he had been sent to depict. Sour with drink, McCarthy ambled up to the proprietor of the equipage and queried.

"Say, Bennett! How much do you pay those kings for riding around with you?"

In reply he was told to return to Paris. Reaching Paris, the journey was continued to New York. In New York he was given the key to the street. His talents shone variously long afterward in the *Recorder* and the *World,* but never again graced the columns of the *Herald.*

One of the satrap's amusements in Paris when inspired by wine was to walk the length of a narrow restaurant, pulling the table-cloths off the tables on both sides of the aisle as he passed, crunching the crockery under his feet. The proprietor would send in a handsome bill to his patron. It was always paid. Wall mirrors in public places also often came in for a smashing at his hands.

His movements were highly uncertain. Every morning his room in the *Herald* building was dusted and put in order against the chances that he might walk in. Woe betide the luckless janitor were he caught in arrears with dust or litter.

Bennett's generosities to the staff were fitful and tantalizing, and were usually followed by some vexatious offset in the way of criticism or humiliation. He tossed away huge sums in his way of living. When his nephew, Isaac Bell, Jr., was born he called to see the infant in its cradle and laid a check for one hundred thousand dollars at the youngster's feet. As he grew up the nephew found the uncle very difficult.

Plovers' eggs were a dainty that much pleased Bennett's palate. It was a *Herald* tradition that James Creelman, the paper's star reporter, was invited to remain at luncheon where the delicate ovules were served. They had been brought at great expense from far up on the Orinoco, and represented about four dollars each. Mr. Creelman was invited to try one. It made an instant appeal. He took another, and another, until he was credited with consuming about fifty dollars worth of the rarities. Bennett grinned grimly, and restrained both his temper and his appetite. In a way he was pleased at Creelman's endorsement of his taste in eggs.

There are weird tales a-plenty—of wild night rides in Newport and Paris, and startling adventures that do not seem quite sane when narrated in cold blood. Indeed, he was not in his right mind when wine had had its way. Sober, the coldest and most calculating of men; drunk, he was a madman. Once, it may be noted, he undertook to drive a coach and four through a low and narrow archway in Paris, in which venture he was scraped off the box and nearly killed, lying for weeks under surgical treatment. At other times he sat on the box stark naked and dashed along the darkened highways. In his younger days in New York, in company with Gunning S. Bedford he would hire a carriage and pair from some livery stable and dash off on reckless rides that would sometimes last for a week. He liked scenes along country roads and took this way of gratifying his taste.

Bennett's charities were large. He once contributed one hundred thousand dollars to relieve distress in Ireland. The *Herald's* free ice fund brought much hot weather relief in New York's crowded tenements. Further he built the memorial that marks the site of Fort Washington on upper Manhattan Island.

The Commodore was a man of moods, and seldom made any effort to restrain them. Men were sent scampering about the earth only to find themselves on fools' errands. This was often the case with members of the staff incontinently summoned to Paris, there to be kept dancing attendance for many weary days, and then ordered home summarily without even seeing Bennett. On one occasion two important men were called oversea by cable. They departed hurriedly, and on reaching Paris, polished up to meet the Boss. He was found seated at a desk in the office of the Paris *Herald,* busily writing. The pair draped themselves in the doorway and respectfully awaited attention. It soon came.

"What in hell are you doing here?" Bennett queried, as he raised his eyes from his work.

"You sent for us," one stammered.

"Go back to New York," was the curt command.

They went!

The chief editorial writers of the *Herald* in the palmy days of its junior proprietor were the Reverend Doctor George H. Hepworth, an independent parson who had failed to hold a large congregation in a corrugated iron church near the Grand Central depot, in what is now New York's highest priced area, and Charles Nordhoff. Hepworth was a handsome man, with flowing side whiskers and some considerable attainments, who abased himself at the feet of his proprietor and tried to meet every whim of his swift-changing mind. Not so Nordhoff. He was a sturdy and much beloved character in American literary life.

As an editorial writer on the *Herald,* he stood up stoutly for the things he believed to be right. He would come to work with a large supply of pencil stubs with which he always wrote his copy.

Robert Hunt Lyman, then new on the night desk, whither he had advanced from Yale and the Springfield *Republican,* recalls a council called by the Commodore to determine the *Herald's* course a few days before the national election of 1888. Bennett was inclined to come out for Benjamin Harrison as against Grover Cleveland, who was running for reelection—because of the Sackville West incident and partly because he thought the former would win. Lyman and S. J. E. Rawling, a talented young Englishman, were added to the conference, largely because Bennett wanted to test their judgment. Doctor Hepworth, Charles Nordhoff, Doctor George W. Hosmer and John Russell Young were the elders. Bennett stated his views and called on Lyman and Rawling first for opinions. Both were adverse. Hepworth and Young were acquiescent—eager to bend to the imperial will. Bennett accordingly ordered Nordhoff to write a leader coming out for Harrison. He quietly declined, remarking that the agreement under which he came to the *Herald* prescribed that he should never be asked to write in support of things to which he was opposed. To this Bennett gave cheerful assent and instructed Young, a Republican, to produce the editorial. This he did. It was put into type, but never printed.

Once when Bennett summoned a member of the staff to Paris the editor in charge demurred, cabling that the man was "indispensable." Bennett sent for a list of men who were presumed to be in this class. A dozen names were forwarded to him. He discharged them all, with this grim comment: "I will have no indispensable men in my employ."

Some of the night editors on the Paris *Herald* were fond of beer. They stacked the empty bottles on a shelf above the desk of a teetotaler. One evening Bennett came in and observed to the startled writer that he seemed fond of refreshment. Having no explanation the man admitted the fact. Remarking that he could hardly afford so much beer on his salary, the proprietor amiably raised it one hundred francs per month on the spot.

By some wise provision of nature it took but little liquor to upset the younger Bennett. Two glasses of champagne would completely destroy his equilibrium, so it followed that his potations did little interior damage though they often imperiled his person.

"In 1900," related William Dinwiddie, an active *Herald* man of that day, "when I came out of South Africa, via Paris, after the Boer War, I followed the usual policy demanded by Mr. Bennett of obsequiously calling his private secretary, Mitchell's, attention to the fact that I was in Paris, and that I would esteem it an honor if I might, at Mr. Bennett's convenience, see him personally. Mr. Bennett was a great stickler as to the form of approach made by men who were on his pay-roll.

"Within an hour I had received word that I was to dine with the Commodore at his Louis XIV estate in Versailles, and that Mitchell was to take me down that evening, by motor. I still rather vividly remember the horrors of that first early motor experience. The Commodore owned a French make of car said to be the most powerful of its kind, at that time. It had four cylinders, was chain-driven, had a rubber-bulbed horn and was cranked by hand. The roaring engine was so badly balanced that when it was not moving forward it actually quivered and shimmied over the pavement. I think we touched the unheard speed, at times, of forty miles an hour, and I have a dazed recollection of women and children and pigs and chickens fleeing out of our path, in the narrow twisting streets of some of the little French villages, as we went roaring by with a spasmodically sounding horn.

"Two years of war and being shot at occasionally had not had half the terrors of that trip.

"When the lodge gates had been thrown open and we had passed inside the huge grey and moss-grown walls which surrounded the Commodore's estate, a dialogue took place between Mitchell and one of the Commodore's men servants, in exclamatory French which I did not understand. Mitchell laughingly interpreted that the servants were all worried because Mr. Bennett had climbed on top of the wall, at a broken-down place, and that they could not get him to come down. Following the man, under the shade of the huge trees of the park, we reached the spot on the wall where the Commodore was precariously teetering along the narrow top, some twelve feet off the ground. An old gardener, carrying a light ladder which barely reached the top of the wall, was begging the Commodore to descend by its aid. Mr. Bennett was protesting that he never would come down until he found the place where he went up. I personally never did see the breach in the wall where he had ascended. As he caught sight of me, he exclaimed 'Hello, Dinwiddie, I am glad to see you.' Then the excited, trembling old gardener placed the ladder, and the Commodore, nimbly if a little uncertainly, climbed down, to shake hands with me.

"The dinner that night under an immense tree, lit with electric bulbs, was another and interesting story."

When the new *Herald* building was completed at Broadway and Thirty-fifth Street no feature of its choice design attracted more attention than the owls that blinked at nightfall over its portals. There was much puzzlement as to why the owner of the *Herald* had chosen Minerva's bird for a totem. Certainly the paper did not typify any high-brow grade of wisdom. No explanation was forthcoming, but a good reason lay behind the unique decoration. When Bennett was a young officer on the *Henrietta,* cruising to Port Royal, he fell asleep on watch. The hooting of an owl awoke him just in time to save the yacht from running ashore on a sandy reef, where, if she had not been lost, *he* would have been. In grateful memory he adopted the solemn bird as an omen of luck.

As Bennett insisted on having all things about the *Herald* personal unto himself, all messages were sent and received in his name. Orders to correspondents were signed "Bennett." The *Herald* never appeared as such in this phase of its administration. Men who wrote letters in the course of *Herald* business signed them "J. G. Bennett." He never used the full cognomen, as did his father. Mastery was, of course, behind all this. There could be but one known man in the shop—Bennett. If others bobbed up their heads they were speedily knocked back into proper obscurity or lopped off. This desire to dominate extended to his possessions generally. He was captain of his yacht, the professional seamen being subordinates, whom he frequently startled with his vagaries.

He persisted in preserving his imperiousness at any cost. Once in his apartment at Paris he was annoyed by a roll of bank-notes that interfered with the use of his pocket, and, in a fit tossed the bundle into the fireplace. A guest rescued the bundle and when the fit wore off returned it with a remark that he had saved it from the flames.

"Perhaps that is where I wanted the roll," said Bennett. With that he threw the bothersome bills into the fire. This time they were consumed.

Bennett could be gracious, and sometimes was—when he had a motive. Emma Eames, the American prima donna, in her *Some Memories and Reflections* recites a case in point.* Returning to Paris in 1901 after a year and a half among the leaves of Vallombrosa she "was amazed" one afternoon to have Mr. Bennett's card brought up to her. "I read his name unbelievingly," she narrates, "as it was a matter of common talk that he did not like me—although no one knew why, least of all myself—and had given the New York Herald emphatic instructions to dismiss any operatic success of mine with a bare mention, and not to print my name if it could be helped."

Curious to know the object of the call she caused the visitor to be shown into her presence. "I have come," he remarked, "to make you my deepest apology." He then went on to explain that a rival singer had, seven years before, cabled him from New York

*Copyright, 1927. Courtesy of D. Appleton and Company.

to Paris that her reception in America had been spoiled by intriguing on the part of Miss Eames. He had regarded this as "contemptible" and had cabled the boycotting order to the *Herald.* Having just learned by merest chance that "this singer had deliberately lied" he had come that afternoon "to place the *Herald* at my feet."

The lady describes her visitor's appearance as "hard, austere," and remarks that a *Herald* reporter told her that the facts of the bogus cable were known in the office, but no one dared tell the truth to the proprietor. Despite his austerity, Miss Eames testifies: "Nevertheless, he possessed a keen sense of justice, as the foregoing proves, and a very tender heart. He adored animals, and perpetuated his affection for them in a motley array of china and painted iron figures of every size which took up a large part of his lawn at Beaulieu. Every time he went to Nice he added to his collection by purchasing a new specimen from a poor old woman who sold such wares."

To add to the amende, Bennett commissioned Julian Story, who was then the singer's husband, to paint his portrait. The sittings were given at Beaulieu, where the prima donna was regaled with further gossip concerning her rival, who, Bennett said, was disposed to accumulate obligations when she visited his villa by giving impromptu song recitals, accompanying herself at the piano. Then she would collect by making requests which he found hard to honor and impossible to refuse. As a last resort he found protection by sending the piano into storage.

Two years later—in 1903—Bennett called again to tell Miss Eames that her rival had circulated a rumor that she (Eames) could sing no more because of an attack of paralysis, and to suggest that she do something to bring herself prominently before the public.

"What can I do?" she asked. "I am far from well, though I am equally far from being paralyzed."

"You can give some parties," he replied. So the parties were given in the shape of four musicales which were copiously reported in the Paris and New York *Heralds,* so much so that a flattering friend described the latter sheet as "Your New York *Herald.*"

Madame Nordica, another Maine nightingale, enjoyed substantial favors. On one of her visits to New York she found a house awaiting her on Murray Hill, and Nicholas Biddle, the *Herald's* society expert, was commissioned to provide her with horses and a barouche. Bennett paid the bill.

Bennett disliked tenants. He sold the Bennett Building in Nassau Street, but did tolerate Hudnut's drug-store in the Herald Building at Broadway and Ann Street, mainly because the lease had been made by his father. Robert E. Livingston, of the *Herald* staff, suggested that a branch Federal post-office would be a good thing for the new home in Herald Square. The New York Postmaster E. M. Morgan made the necessary arrangements. Then came the rub. Bennett would accept no rental and the government would not move in without paying it. A compromise was finally affected at the nominal rate of fifty dollars per month. The station speedily became one of the most useful in New York.

In 1894 Ralph D. Blumenfeld tried to manage the uneasy *Herald.* The new building was being furnished, and Stanford White, the architect, suggested buying a silver desk set he had seen at Tiffany's, somewhat shop-worn, for which they asked two thousand five hundred dollars, to adorn the Bennett room. He thought Blumenfeld could beat them down to one thousand dollars. Ralph called at the store, offered five hundred dollars and came away with the goods for seven hundred and fifty dollars. His weekly report to Bennett showed the item among others. A fierce cable came telling him to pay for the silver out of his own salary. It had been delivered and duly placed on the autocrat's desk. The bill had also been paid by the *Herald.* There Blumenfeld let it rest. He soon left the paper, but later met Bennett in Paris, and was asked if it was true he was running a cigar store in London, as his former employer had heard. He replied that he wished he was. Bennett offered to be of any service he could to him outside of the *Herald.* When Blumenfeld rose to power in London journalism, he was able to do the *Herald* several good turns, for which he refused to accept pay. So they were friendly, but not sociable. After Bennett's death Mrs. Bennett wrote Blumenfeld to say that her husband had had the desk set on his conscience and wished it sent him. In due time it arrived from New York. Incidentally, the price had never been taken out of Blumenfeld's salary.

Personally, I never met the Commodore. After the reorganization of the Associated Press in 1900, when I insisted that the *Herald* and all other New York papers should enjoy equal rights with the *World,* for several years he sent me the *Herald's* proxy to represent in the annual meeting of the organization. His attorney, Colonel William Jay, would bring me the precious paper in person and deliver it with the air of one bestowing a great confidence. It was the Commodore's grand way of saying thanks.

"Mr. Bennett," wrote John Russell Young of the *Herald* proprietor, "is a man of strong character. He has courage, clearness, a quick mind, a thorough knowledge of his profession, generous and resolute qualities, and great independence." Young was "astonished" when he came on the *Herald* staff "at his princely way of exceeding my own expectations."

CHAPTER XI

SPORTSMAN AND DUELIST

No MAN did more to stimulate interest in the costly sports of America's gentlemen than James Gordon Bennett, the younger. He took part in or backed yachting, polo, coaching and aviation all his life. There are a legion of "Bennett Cups" to be competed for each season here and abroad. He encouraged aviation with the Coupe Internationale des Aeronauts for balloonists and the Coupe Internationale d'Aviation for the aviators. Polo, horse-racing and field sports in general received rewards at his hands. He also bestowed a *Lysistrata* cup for the stimulation of steam-yachting.

Bennett began his sporting career very early. His father was extravagantly liberal in allowing him pocket money enough to meet every desire. In 1857 he built the seventy-seven-ton sloop *Rebecca* and soon made himself known in yachting circles. The youthful skipper was elected a member of the New York Yacht Club, a little irregularly it may be observed, at a council of captains held August 12, 1857, at New Bedford, where the fleet had parked on its annual cruise. He was probably the youngest skipper ever accorded this fellowship, being but sixteen years and three months old. From that date till the end of his life he was an active factor in the affairs of the organization. The boy was a fearless navigator. On June 24, 1858, in a race around Long Island, he led all the entries at Montauk Point, only to be ruled out for taking a short-cut through Plum Gut instead of the Race as provided in the articles of agreement. The other yachts engaged were the schooners *Haze, Silvie, Favorite,* and *Widgeon;* the sloops *Madgie, Una* and *Minnie. Silvie* and *Minnie* were awarded the prizes. His performance was not due to sharp practise but to bold seamanship. Plum Gut had been cut out of the course because of the risk involved.

The next year he challenged the schooner *Restless,* five hundred dollars a side, to race from Brenton's Reef off Newport, to Thogg's Neck in Long Island Sound, a distance of one hundred and fifty-four miles. *Restless* was eighteen tons heavier than *Rebecca* and won by twelve minutes. Besides much racing with other yachts he sailed the little *Rebecca* across the Atlantic to the Isle of Wight and back again—no small feat at that or any other time.

Extending his ambitions he put *Rebecca* aside and built the one hundred and seventy-ton *Henrietta.* An earlier chapter details his service during the war in this trim schooner. The conflict over, he renewed his career as a yachtsman. He literally sailed into the upper circles of New York clubdom from which his father would have been ignominiously excluded had he so much as tried to enter. No doubt the old gentleman chuckled to himself when he saw his headstrong offspring go over the top so easily into the New York Yacht Club, the Union Club and the Jockey Club, domains then limited to the elect.

The Yacht Club elected him vice-commodore in 1867.

He was then twenty-six, and served from 1867 to 1870 inclusive. In 1871 he was elected commodore, serving through to 1874 inclusive. In 1884-1885 he was again commodore.

The most notable cross-Atlantic race ever contested was that between *Henrietta, Vesta* and *Fleetwing,* owned respectively by Bennett, Pierre Lorillard, Jr. and George Frank Osgood. The three sailed from Sandy Hook on December 11, 1866, in the face of wintry weather. *Henrietta* arrived at Cowes on Christmas Day, having made the trip in the amazingly short time of thirteen days, twenty-one hours and fifty-five minutes. *Fleetwing* and *Vesta* showed up on December twenty-sixth, Boxing Day, close together. The time of the former was fourteen days, six hours and ten minutes; of the latter, fourteen days, six hours, fifty minutes.

Each of the young gentlemen owners put up thirty thousand dollars to back the speed of his craft. Mr. Bennett took along for company Charles Longfellow, Lawrence Jerome and Stephen Fiske, the dramatic writer. So notable was the voyage of *Henrietta* and her competitors that I deem it worth while to reproduce the Logs, kindly furnished me by Secretary George A. Cormack of the New York Yacht Club, in whose custody the record remains. They follow:

OCEAN RACE
(Sandy Hook to the Needles)
Start December 11, 1866.

Daily log of:	*Henrietta*	*Fleetwing*	*Vesta*
Date	Miles	Miles	Miles
December 12	237	239	240
13	232	249	205

Daily log of: Date		*Henrietta* Miles	*Fleetwing* Miles	*Vesta* Miles
December	14	203	220	205
	15	——	186	227
	16	246	218	234
	17	280	240	236
	18	250	160	207
	19	——	188	222
	20	260	260	277
	21	157	136	165
	22	252	232	253
	23	——	215	201
	24	172	194	165
	25	——	270	209

Henrietta anchored Dec. 25 at 5.32 p. m. in Cowes Roads. Distance 3,106 miles. Time, 13 days; 21 hours; 55 minutes.

Fleetwing anchored Dec. 26 at 1.30 a. m. in Cowes Roads. Distance, 3,135 miles. Time, 14 days; 6 hours; 10 minutes.

Vesta anchored Dec. 26 at 2.10 a. m. in Cowes Roads. Distance, 3,144 miles. Time, 14 days; 6 hours; 50 minutes.

This contest between the three vessels has never been equaled. High westerly winds prevailed all the way across. There was no beating to windward, and the race was an unremitting drive. It remains one of the most difficult ever sailed by pleasure craft. Moreover it was marked by a dreadful tragedy. On December nineteenth, *Fleetwing* was swept by a heavy sea which picked six seamen out of the cockpit and carried them to a watery grave.

The daring of the bold young gentlemen roused tremendous interest both here and abroad. Bennett, finding *Henrietta* too small for his growing ambitions, bought the schooner *Hirondelle* from Dexter Bradford, Jr. of Newport, Rhode Island. She was lengthened some fifteen feet and renamed *Dauntless.* Coming down from Nyack on the Hudson on board the river steamer *Chrystenah,* on which I was the newsboy for two seasons, I used to see the *Dauntless* lying off Fort Washington, a thing of beauty aglow with brass, the deck polished until it shone and every strand of cordage as taut as the strings of a fiddle.

There had been no International contest since August 22, 1851, when *America* won the cup which has since borne her name, but, following the sensational race between Bennett and his rivals, the splendid schooner *Sappho,* built in Brooklyn at the yard of C. and R. Poillon, for William P. Douglas, ventured across the sea in 1868, only to be beaten by four other schooners in a run around the Isle of Wight. She sailed in cruising rig and with sea-ballast aboard. Encouraged by her poor showing, James Ashbury, owner of *Cambria,* one of the victors, on behalf of the Royal Yacht Squadron and the Royal Victoria Yacht Club, invited the New York Yacht Club to participate in the races held by the two bodies in August, 1869, around the Isle of Wight. He coupled this with an offer to contest for the *America's* cup on his own behalf, or to race across the Atlantic for a cup or silver service valued at two hundred and fifty sovereigns. The New York Yacht Club declined the trans-ocean challenge but expressed a willingness to defend the *America's* cup. Ashbury responded that he would sail under the flag of the Royal Thames Yacht Club but sought modifications in the deed of gift, which were rejected by the New York Yacht Club. Bennett meanwhile became interested in pitting *Dauntless* against *Cambria,* and an ocean race was arranged to be sailed in September, 1869. Bennett was unable to get *Dauntless* into shape. Ashbury and the New York Yacht Club came to terms as to the *America's* cup and he agreed to bring the *Cambria* over in the season of 1869 for a try at that elusive trophy. Bennett now added to the interest by arranging to carry out his cross-Atlantic challenge, sailing to the other side to meet his antagonist. *Dauntless* was a keel schooner one hundred and twenty-three feet ten inches over all, twenty-six feet seven inches beam and twelve feet six inches in draught. *Cambria* was of two hundred and forty-eight tons displacement, built by Michael Ratsey at Cowes. She was one hundred and eight feet in length, over all, twenty-one feet beam and drew twelve feet of water.

Bennett took every precaution that could attend assurance of victory. The crew was a picked one. Richard Brown, a Sandy Hook pilot who had been sailing master of *America* nearly two decades before, and Samuel Samuels, who had driven the clipper ship *Dreadnaught* from New York to Liverpool in thirteen days, without ever shortening sail, went along as advisers. Martin J. Lyons, a Sandy Hook pilot, with a reputation as a smart seaman, was sailing master.

The trip across was pleasant and *Dauntless* reached Cook Harbor, Ireland, in good order, from which point the start was to be made. The course was laid from Daunt's Rock to Sandy Hook. On July 4, 1870, the two yachts were towed to Daunt's Rock where the race started at two thirty-five P. M. The signal to get under way was given by H. B. M. S. *Mayflower* hoisting the Blue Peter. A steady west wind blew and the sea was hazy. The race was a tame affair, won by *Cambria* in twenty-three days, five hours, seventeen minutes and fifteen seconds. *Dauntless* made port off Sandy Hook in twenty-three days, seven hours. As a matter of fact she should have won but some error of seamanship sent her over a longer course. Their respective logs follow:

OCEAN MATCH RACE
CAMBRIA vs DAUNTLESS
Start July 4, 1870, 2.38 p. m.

Cambria—Commo. James Ashbury.

Dauntless—Vice Commo. James Gordon Bennett, Jr.

Start from Daunt's Rock, Cook Harbor, Ireland, to Sandy Hook Lightship

LOG

	Cambria miles	*Dauntless* miles
July 5	56	103
6	179	90
7	142	140
8	77	210
9	220	120
10	97	122
11	133	155
12	140	91
13	141	130
14	174	155
15	214	148
16	92	150
17	61	70
18	180	68
19	104	145
20	144	225
21	169	110
22	158	191
23	75	52
24	158	120
25	85	93

	Cambria	*Dauntless*
	miles	miles
July 26	82	95
27	36	180

Cambria sailed 2917 miles in 23 days, 5 hours, 17 min., 15 sec.

Dauntless sailed 2963 miles in 23 days, 7 hours.

The three captains and the owner did not get on well. Captain Samuels once threatened to put his employer in irons and was quite capable of having done so. Lyons in after years observed that "there were too many amateurs on board," referring to Bennett and his friends.

Mr. Ashbury had waived his point which was for a race of vessel against vessel and agreed to sail against a fleet for the *America's* cup. The event came off on August 8, 1870, and *Dauntless* was one of the defenders. The old *America* was also among the eighteen starters. *Magic* came in first, *Dauntless* fifth, just behind *America*. *Cambria* finished eighth.

The undiscouraged Englishman sought for another trial but with a new schooner, *Livonia,* as the contestant. Bennett was now commodore of the club and the correspondence was between the two, Ashbury being commodore of the Royal Harwich Yacht Club. After much bickering, the New York Yacht Club committee reserved the schooners *Columbia, Dauntless, Palmer* and *Sappho* as possible defenders in a series of races that seem now to have made Ashbury's task unduly hard. *Columbia* won two and *Sappho* two out of the four races sailed. *Dauntless* was out of it by reason of a rent in her mainsail. The committee accordingly had planned to have her sail the decisive race, and waited for repairs. When being towed to position the fouling of a hawser with one of her stays broke it, and she was compelled to drop out in favor of *Columbia.* Commodore Ashbury had asked for a twelve-contest race. The Yacht Club insisted on seven. When *Livonia* had been defeated four times out of seven,—her one victory being due to an accident to *Columbia,*—the Yacht Club declared the affair ended. This was in October, 1871. Ashbury informed the club that he would be at the line on October twenty-third. No one met him. The next day, October twenty-fourth, Bennett accommodated him with a run of twenty miles to sea and back, starting from Sandy Hook Lightship. *Dauntless* came in first, beating *Livonia* by ten minutes, thirty-one seconds. The rivals agreed to try it over the next day, but bad weather prevented sailing. Ashbury claimed to have won four out of seven races on technical points—no contestant showing up part of the time. Returning to England he accused the New York Yacht Club of "unfair and unsportsmanlike proceedings." Before the races he had presented Commodore Bennett with three cups to be contested for by New York Yacht Club members. These were now rejected, the club resolving: "That they cannot with any respect compete for the cups deposited with Commodore Bennett by Commodore Ashbury, to be sailed for by the yachts of the New York Yacht Club, and that the secretary be instructed to return the cups to Commodore Ashbury." This was done.

In 1885, while Bennett was serving his second term as commodore of the New York Yacht Club, Sir Richard Sutton, owner of the fast British cutter *Genesta,* challenged for the *America's* famous cup. Yachting circles in America were vastly stirred and steps were taken to provide defenders. Bennett and William P. Douglas furnished the money to construct *Priscilla.* Opposing her in the tryout was *Puritan,* built by a Boston group headed by General C. J. Paine and Malcolm Forbes. *Puritan* proved to be the better boat and successfully defended the trophy. Following the defeat of *Genesta* by *Puritan,* Bennett and Douglas offered a consolation cup to be sailed for on September 23, 1885. Sir Richard Sutton, owner of *Genesta,* had proved himself a true sportsman, and there was much rejoicing when she won. Incidentally, *Genesta* beat the old *Dauntless* for the Brenton's Reef and Cape May cups, both Bennett trophies. He gave the first to the New York Yacht Club on March 23, 1871, and the latter (gold) in 1872. The first named required sailing: "From the Lightship off Newport to and around the Lightship off Sandy Hook and outside of Long Island and return." The second: "From an imaginary line between the Judges' Steamer and Buoy 5 off Sandy Hook to and around the First Fathom light-vessel off Cape May, leaving it on the Port or Starboard hand at will, and back to Sandy Hook light-vessel, passing the same to the Southward and Eastward within one hundred yards distance."

Bennett had sold *Dauntless* in 1879 to Commodore John Waller of the New York Yacht Club, who in turn disposed of her to Caldwell H. Colt, of Hartford, a member of the famous arms family, under whose ownership she was often heard from. He then gave up sails for steam, and in 1882 built at the Newburg, New York, yard of Ward, Stanton and Company a swift screw-propeller named *Namouna.* After two years he tired of her and she was disposed of through Charles R. Flint to become a South American gunboat. Bennett also built a small steamer, *Polynia,* which he did not use much. She became the property of his friend William P. Douglas.

For some years he experimented with light craft—speed-boats on the Thames and Seine. Finally in 1900 G. L. Watson designed a splendid steamer named *Lysistrata,* after a Greek lady reputed to be very beautiful and very fast. She was built by Denny and Brothers, at Dunbarton, at a cost of six hundred and twenty-five thousand dollars. "Palatial" was the proper word to use in describing the vessel. No royal yacht was so splendidly equipped. The owner had a suite of rooms on each of her three decks, to use as best suited his fancy, besides ample quarters for guests. There was also a complete Turkish bath outfit. She carried a crew of a hundred men and an Alderney cow comfortably quartered in a padded stall, whence she supplied the cabin table with milk and cream. Bossy and her predecessor on *Namouna* were probably the only cows to enjoy such an experience. An electric milker extracted the lacteal fluid from the cow's udder. An electric fan over her stall, kept the Alderney cool in warm weather.

Like the lamb in the circus "Happy Family," the cow had to be renewed now and then. On one of these occasions Mr. Bennett made an inland tour by auto from his yacht, taking along one of his Paris *Herald* editors. After a considerable search among the peasant farms, the right sort of animal was found and bought. Then Bennett handed the tow-rope to the editor, remarking: "Here, ——, you'll have to lead the cow back to the yacht." The employee dutifully took the tether and after a wearisome walk brought the heifer safely to the landing. To have balked would have cost him his job.

Lysistrata was in active use until shortly before the World War broke out. Then Mr. Bennett's physician advised him that his health was harmed by cruising, and he gave up what had been his chief delight. The yacht was finally sold to the Russian Government.

One of the laws on shipboard was that there should be no gambling. The Commodore saw to it that the baggage of guests and crew was regularly searched for cards. He would have the packs brought to him and personally tear up the four aces, thus rendering the rest of the pasteboards useless for playing purposes.

Guests on the yacht could never be certain what the next freak of their host would be. On one occasion, while in port at Amsterdam, he engaged a theatrical company to give a special performance on board. Liking their talent, he put to sea, to the great dismay of the actors. They were kept performing to his delight, bountifully paid for their inconvenience and safely returned to shore. The episode broke up the program of the Amsterdam manager who, however, managed to turn it to account in advertising.

Once James Creelman, who held a roving commission for many years, was called from Paris to join his employer on *Lysistrata,* at Leghorn. He put out in a wherry and soon reached the companionway over the side. As he was about to come on board he was stopped by a quartermaster.

"You can't come on board," said the man, who knew him well.

"Why not?" asked Creelman. "I have been ordered here."

He wore a fine brown beard.

"You see," replied the quartermaster, "you will have to take off that beard. The Commodore will permit no one on the ship who isn't shaved clean."

Creelman refused to be shorn. He went ashore and there learned that all hands had been scraped clean of hirsute adornments, from the captain down. He got hold of the yacht's itinerary and followed her to every port as far as Fiume. At every one of these he was refused permission to board, and returned to Paris unshorn without ever laying eyes on his employer. Bennett never mentioned the episode and their relations continued until Creelman left the *Herald* at his own volition to join the *World.*

Bennett once explained this freak to George A. Cormack, Secretary of the New York Yacht Club, as due to his admiration for the clean-shaved, square-jawed officers and men of the British Navy. He therefore determined to have the crew of *Lysistrata* smooth-faced, consoling the sailors for their shearing by allowing extra pay in atonement for their sacrifice.

It will be seen that to be his guest was not always an unalloyed pleasure in his more active days. But in his last years he mellowed and became a delightful host; also more moderate in his handling of men.

In the course of his yachting experience he attended a German regatta at Kiel and encountered what he considered a severe snub from the then Emperor William II. To this was credited some of the animosity he showed toward that unlucky potentate when the World War began.

Bennett's devotion to the sea took the further form of minute supervision of nautical items printed in the *Herald.* Each day a copy of the paper was sent him with the name of the writer of each article written on it in red pencil and that of its editor in blue. Woe betide the wight who perpetrated lubberly errors in technique. The instant one caught the Commodore's eye there would come a blast by cable: "Why was that damned fool Blank allowed to write that shipwreck story? Doesn't he know the wind and tide in that neighborhood never perform as he states it? Never let him touch a sea story again."

Mistakes in terms were equally sinful. To erect a crow's nest on ships that do not carry that form of convenience for look-outs was to be for ever excommunicated from anything pertaining to navigation.

He always had some naval officer on the pay-roll. One of these, Lieutenant J. L. Stickney, stood by Admiral George Dewey on the bridge of the *Olympia* the day of the battle of Manila Bay. His cable dispatch to the *Herald* describing the event cost eight thousand dollars in tolls.

Commander J. D. Jerrold Kelly was another Navy man greatly esteemed by the Commodore.

Bennett's passion for the sea was always manifest. He carried a master's license, charted his own courses, and had a tell-tale in his stateroom that gave the alarm when the helm shifted unduly. He would soon be on the bridge laying down the law to the official skipper.

When Lord Dunraven withdrew *Valkeyrie III,* from the International Yacht Race for the *America's* cup in 1895, he charged that he had been the victim of false measurements. The New York Yacht Club investigated. Robert E. Livingston, one of the *Herald's* best reporters, got hold of the testimony. It filled four or five pages of the paper and made a prodigious row inside the club, of which Bennett had twice been commodore, and to which he had always been more than kind. A flood of cables went to Paris and an effort was made to expel him. This was headed off by Herman Oelrichs and some of the older set. William C. Reick, the city editor, was summoned to the awful presence oversea and kept waiting a month before Bennett would see him. By that time the excitement had died down and the subject was dropped.

Bennett's voyagings carried him far across the Atlantic and back, many times to Bermuda and New York. The Mediterranean was his favorite cruising ground, but the yacht now and then found her way into the Indian Ocean, going at least once to Ceylon.

Wherever the yacht went it was followed by news summaries sent from the *Herald* office in New York, so that the proprietor and his guests always knew what was going on in the world. The cablegrams even pursued the yacht up the Nile where frequent telegraph stations permitted constant contact with events.

Bennett took deep interest in the development of American shipping, and the *Herald* was foremost in favoring measures to keep the flag upon the sea. Thus it was that its ship news occupied a space not given the same intelligence by any other newspaper anywhere.

Bennett's playfulness could find outlet in less heroic games than yachting. E. P. Mitchell, long of the *Sun*, in his *Memoirs of an Editor,** recalls him as "a tall

*Copyright, 1924. Courtesy of Charles Scribner's Sons.

youth of nineteen or twenty" whom he "saw often and admired reverently as the beau ideal of the man of the world and all around dare-devil. In the neighborhood [of Thirty-eighth Street and Fifth Avenue] he was generally credited with the invention of the new form of sport then popular thereabouts; for instance, such as the game of breaking up the long processions of boarding-school young ladies promenading the avenue two by two, at about four o'clock on sunny afternoons. The demoralization and stampede were effected with *schrecklichkeit* by plunging between the foremost couple, enfilading the entire line and throwing it into confusion, and then dodging to escape the duenna at the rear."

This amusing exercise came to be called "Bennetting" and was much practised by emulative youths.

Together with William P. Douglas, Bennett brought polo to America and when young was an enthusiastic player of the kingly game. Coaching became his fad when years took him away from the polo field.

Riding once in Bar Harbor with the late Joseph Pulitzer, we stopped before the post-office. During the pause, a tall striking chap in his mid fifties came up and began gaily chaffing the owner of the *World*. Mr. Pulitzer was nervous under the encounter and made haste to end the interview. As we drove off he said: "That handsome scamp was Fred May, who fought a duel with Bennett. He is trying to sell me some real estate, and I am afraid he will if I am not careful."

Mr. Pulitzer's usual precaution preserved him from the purchase, but the figure of the "handsome scamp" remains in memory. So does the duel. It came about in this fashion: Doctor William May, of a distinguished Baltimore family, was a physician in New York, residing at 44 West Nineteenth Street, then in the fashionable belt and not far from the Union Club. Besides the son Frederick, aged twenty-six in 1876, several daughters of unusual beauty graced the household. One of these, Caroline, was noted for charm and daring. The Mays were persons of spirit. Doctor May's brother, Charles, had been a very gallant Colonel of Dragoons at Buena Vista and had married a daughter of George Law, the New York street-car and shipping magnate, who gave him the prosaic job of superintendent of the Eighth Avenue horse car line, a profitable parental possession. Charles May, when a dashing dragoon, had once startled Baltimore by riding his horse up three flights of stairs in Barnum's hotel, then the palatial hostelry of the town. One of the privileges of belonging to the Union Club was that of being wild and respectable at the same time. Hence it was that Bennett, junior, could pass doors where his father, who lived cleanly, could not so much as touch the knob. One of these doors was that of Doctor William May. Indeed, it was thought that Caroline had captured the younger Bennett—though he was not so young, having passed thirty-five. The habit of calling on New Year's Day had not ceased when the New Year of 1877 came into being. It was the excuse for much drunkenness. Hostesses kept open house and flowing punch bowls. Bennett had already acquired his limit when he called on Miss Caroline, on the afternoon of January 1, 1877.

What happened can not be told politely. Suffice

it to say, Bennett forgot where he was, under circumstances such as had convinced Alexander the Great that he was not the god his courtiers conceived him to be, and became guilty of conduct unbecoming a gentleman—or any one else.

As a result, Frederick May waylaid Bennett on January 3, 1877, right before the sacred edifice of the Union Club, as he was about to step into his sleigh after luncheon, and proceeded to beat him with a cowhide, to the horror of some, and possibly to the delight of other gentlemen who looked out of the windows upon the spirited spectacle.

Bennett was heard to ask: "Why don't you kill me while you are about it?" but made no attempt to ward off the blows. They clinched, however, and rolled together in the snow. At this point William P. Douglas and John G. Hecksher rushed from the club and pulled the combatants apart. Bennett drove away to seclusion and May went about his business. The morning papers of January fourth printed the story decorously, though the *Herald* for once left out a piece of news. Its owner kept out of sight and sent for his friends. One of these was Charles Longfellow, son of the gentle bard of Cambridge. The outcome was a challenge. May accepted, chose pistols at twelve paces, and named his cousin, Doctor Frederick May of Baltimore, as his second. Bennett chose S. Howland Robbins of New York. The place selected for the meeting was Slaughter's Gap, in Delaware, where passes the Maryland line, across which the duel was fought. The customary retinue of surgeons attended. Politeness and the utmost ceremony prevailed, and the "affair" came off on the afternoon of January 7, 1877. Mr. May fired with the intent to miss, and Bennett, whatever his purpose, was too nervous to aim accurately and his shot went wild. Both parties expressed themselves satisfied. Bennett and his second came back to New York, where he remained unseen and away from the sound of the laughter, the scorn and the scandal. The episode ended his life in America save for what were usually brief and infrequent visits.

Even though Fred May had fired in the air at Slaughter's Gap his antagonist held him in fear. A woman who chose to call herself "Camille Clermont," and with whom Bennett was once intimate in Paris, wrote *The Confessions of Gentle Rebecca,* which was published in London not long after his decease. In this book she thinly disguises him as "J. G. Burnett," and tells this tale:*

Burnett [Bennett] was nearly undressed and appeared resplendent in a coat of mail which for the last few weeks he had worn underneath his clothes. The reason for wearing the coat of mail was that he had been told that one of his compatriots, Mr. May, had arrived recently in Paris with the determination to avenge his sister, to whom B. had behaved in a particularly disgraceful way. He feared Mr. May would probably shoot him "on sight" according to the American fashion of settling differences. J. G. B. valued his life far too highly to be thus lightly disposed of, so he ordered a magnificent coat of mail to wear under his clothing, and with his long, lanky figure he looked supremely ridiculous. He wore the coat of mail for a month or so, until he grew tired of carrying the abnormal weight, so sent two of his friends to Mr. May to ask what his intentions were, preferring the risk of

*Copyright, 1922. Courtesy of Drane's "Danegeld House."

a duel to the constant fatigue imposed by the medieval armour. Mr. May declared that he had no homicidal intentions, so, to his great relief, J. G. B. discarded the cuirass.

While chagrin had much to do with his determination to reside abroad, there was a further reason, as he once explained—a desire to escape process servers and annoyance in connection with petty libel suits that tipped the scales in which he weighed the pleasure to be got out of life, with the greater certainty of increasing prominence in the world's eye. He could also do things in Paris that would not have been tolerated in New York, where moral standards do prevail in the open—in evidence whereof the lady continues:

Beneath his thin veneer of civilisation J. G. B. was in reality a Barbarian, and education had done little to modify his nature. He had not been tenderly reared, and had never known the gentle culture imparted to most children by their mother. Delicacy and sensitiveness were alike strangers to him, and he had never learnt the precious maxim: "Never hurt those who love us."

CHAPTER XII

GO AND FIND LIVINGSTONE

Beyond reporting events the art of creating them is the greatest of journalistic attainments. By this is meant the ability to seize upon dormant situations and bring them to life. Bennett possessed this quality to an exceptional degree.

In 1869 David Livingstone, the Scotch-Presbyterian missionary, who for thirty years had kept Europe informed and interested with the results of his travels, dropped out of sight in darkest Africa. No word of any sort came from him and the belief spread that he was dead or so situated as to be helpless. Though he was acting for the Royal Geographical Society that rather lame body did nothing toward finding out the facts. As the sequel showed, Livingstone was all the while striving to follow out the instructions of its head, Sir Roderick Murchison, in tracing the route the wide and strong Lualaba River took to reach the sea. Public interest in Livingstone's fate grew, but no effort was made to ascertain whether he was dead, or his whereabouts if living, until the proprietor of the *Herald* found a human instrument fit for the task and sent him to its fulfillment.

There had come into the world at a lying-in hospital, in London in 1841, one John Rowlands, whose father died before he saw the light and whose mother had gone to the metropolis from Denbigh, Wales, for her accouchement. She took the baby back and left him with his grandfather, then vanished from his history. The grandfather was very old and his death, when the boy reached four, caused the little lad's transfer to the workhouse where two uncles paid his slender sustenance. In this demoralizing charitable establishment he grew into a sturdy, square-shouldered boy, with a singular conscience and virtue of body. Becoming stout enough to beat a tyrannical teacher he fled from the charity school and, after some small experimenting, reached Liverpool and took to the sea as cabin boy of the bark *Windermere.* He did not fit the place and was soon kicked forward into the forecastle, where he abided until the ship reached her destination at New Orleans. Then he deserted and tramped the streets, penniless and starving. Forlornly looking about for work he caught the eye of a middle-aged merchant, Henry Morton Stanley, who secured him employment with a shipping firm, and saw that he was comfortably lodged and fairly paid. The grateful boy worked hard in New Orleans until yellow fever broke up the firm and cost his benefactor his admirable wife. The protegé was then sent to manage a store in a plantation section of Arkansas, where he was doing well when Mr. Stanley died and the Confederacy took him from counter-jumping and made him a soldier.

The waif had not been at all interested in becoming a warrior, but his hesitancy came to an end on the receipt of a woman's skirt in a sealed package. The hint was obvious, and he enlisted for the hard campaign ending at Shiloh.

Here he was taken prisoner and sent to the wretched pen at Camp Douglas, near Chicago. Much has been written of the horrors of life in southern war prisons. The sufferings of the Confederate captives were just as great in the North, where climate, ennui and discomfort took the place of starvation and fever in the South. Plagues of smallpox and typhoid raged, and pneumonia sent scores to their graves. Neither side can look back upon this phase of the great conflict with any other sense than that of shame.

After enduring his share of misery for a few months, he who had been John Rowlands escaped from Camp Douglas by the process of enlisting in the Federal artillery. Here he never served. Illness followed him from Camp Douglas, and, reaching Harper's Ferry, he was discharged as unfit for service. He had taken the name of his benefactor and from the day of his dismissal began one of the most extraordinary careers in the history of men of action, that of Henry Morton Stanley.

His discharge was dated the twenty-second of June, 1863. He describes himself as a physical wreck, who somehow tramped his way to Hagerstown, Maryland. Here a kindly farmer took him in. He was able to do a little work in return for the care given him. The farmer paid his fare to Baltimore when he was fit to travel in mid-August. From Baltimore the ship *E. Sherman* bore him to Liverpool, thence he made his way to Denbigh expecting the sort of welcome a mother should give a long-absent son who had become a real man. Instead, he was turned away from her door, with the word that he "was a disgrace to them in the eyes of the neighbors," and bidden to leave "as speedily as possible," according to his own report.

Thus rebuffed, the adventurer, with a sore heart, turned again to the sea, enduring shipwreck and the usual hardships. In August, 1864, he joined the Union Navy as a ship's writer on a tub called the *Moses H. Stuyvesant,* where he viewed the futile attack on Fort Fisher, made under the plans of Major-General Benjamin F. Butler. He sent letters to various newspapers, which found a ready market, and so took his first step in journalism.

Leaving the navy at the close of the conflict, he made his way west, as far as Denver, and came back via a skiff on the Platte River, so reaching Omaha, with W. H. Cook as companion. The pair took it into their heads to explore Asia Minor. With very little money they sailed from Boston in July, 1866. The expedition came to grief at the hands of Turkoman robbers, who relieved them of their funds and turned them back. Somehow they got to Constantinople and thence to America.

Heading out from St. Louis in 1867, he "wrote up" northwestern Missouri, Kansas and Nebraska for the St. Louis *Democrat* and was assigned to follow General Winfield Scott Hancock's campaign against the Sioux and Cheyennes. This lasted until the beginning of 1868.

The *Democrat* paid him fifteen dollars per week and expenses. He was at liberty to write for other journals and did so, sending letters to Chicago and New York papers, sometimes collecting eighty dollars per week. In this fashion of working hard and living frugally, he had accumulated three thousand dollars when he came to New York after the Indian campaign in January, 1868, looking for a chance to join the pending British expedition under Lord Napier against King Theodore of Abyssinia. He sought an assignment from the *Tribune,* but in vain.

John Russell Young, then its managing editor, paid him well for his letters from the plains, but did not think *Tribune* readers would be interested in Abyssinia. Accordingly, as recorded by Stanley in his journal:*

Bowing my thanks, I left the *Tribune* and proceeded to the *Herald* office; by a spasm of courage, I asked for Mr. Bennett. By good luck, my card attracted his attention, and I was invited to his presence. I found myself before a tall, fierce-eyed, imperious looking young man, who said, 'Oh, you are the correspondent who has been following Hancock and Sherman lately. Well, I must say your letters and telegrams have kept us very well informed. I wish I could offer you something permanent, for we want active men like you."

"You are very kind to say so, and I am emboldened to ask you if I could not offer myself to you for the Abyssinian expedition."

"I do not think this Abyssinnian expedition is of sufficient interest to Americans, but on what terms would you go?"

"Either as a special at a moderate salary, or by letter. Of course, if you pay me by the letter, I should reserve the liberty to write occasional letters to other papers."

"We do not like to share our news that way, but we would be willing to pay well for exclusive intelligence. Have you ever been abroad before?"

"Oh, yes. I have travelled in the East, and been to Europe several times."

*From *Autobiography of Sir Henry Morton Stanley.* Courtesy of Houghton-Mifflin Company.

"Well, how would you like to do this on trial? Pay your own expenses to Abyssinia, and if your letters are up to the standard, and your intelligence is early and exclusive, you shall be well paid by the letter, or at the rate by which we engage our European specials, and you will be placed on the permanent list."

"Very well, Sir. I am at your service, any way you like."

"When do you intend to start?"

"On the 22nd, by the steamer *Hecla.*"

"That is the day after to-morrow. Well, consider it arranged. Just wait a moment while I write to our agent in London."

In a few minutes he had placed in my hands a letter to "Colonel Finlay Anderson, Agent of the New York *Herald,* the Queen's Hotel, St. Martin's Le Grand, London," and thus I became what had been an object of my ambition, a regular, I hope, correspondent of the New York *Herald.*

One line sticks out strongly in Stanley's journal concerning relations with the *Herald* from that time on, even if his pay was small: "I have *carte blanche* at the bankers." While on assignment he could direct his own movements, do what he thought best, hire men if needed; in short, be free in his own judgment. "This," he adds, "I have done in the short space of eighteen months, when others have languished on at their business for fifteen years and got no higher than the step where they entered upon duty." That is, he had "arrived" on the *Herald* and was justly proud of his prowess.

Thanks to his thrift, Stanley was able to finance himself to Abyssinia, as Bennett had stipulated. He took with him letters from Generals Grant and Sherman that made him welcome at Lord Napier's headquarters, and though at first the English war correspondents were frosty with the American, as he had become, he soon thawed them out and easily outranked them in energy and achievement. Indeed, so well were his plans laid that he was first to get the fall of Magdala and its consequences on the wire at Suez. It had been no more than sent before the line was interrupted for two days, so it befell that the *Herald* dispatches were the earliest to tell the tale, not only to America, but to England.

He was now put on the *Herald* pay-roll at two thousand per year and kept wandering like Ulysses. He toured the isles of Greece, whence he bubbled sentiment in the *Herald*. He confesses in his journal that "the charm of Hellas fell upon me," and he even thought of marrying a Greek girl, but concluded it could not be done on his salary, though he appears to have had a narrow escape. He reported a royal baptism in Athens, glimpsed Smyrna, Rhodes, Beirut and Alexandria, to be suddenly shifted to Spain, where the Carlist war flamed up critically. He had no more than interviewed General Prim, who had placed Queen Isabella on a back seat, than he was recalled.

Stanley's own account of his sudden departure from Spain and his subsequent, epoch-making interview with Bennett is vivid. The summons came on October 16, 1869, at Madrid, in the form of a telegram reading: "Come to Paris on important business, J. G. Bennett." To read was to obey. He notes further:

Down come my pictures from the walls of my apartments on the second floor; into my trunks go my books and souvenirs, my clothes are hastily collected, some half-washed, some from the clothes-line half-dry, and after a couple of hours of hasty hard work my portmanteaus are strapped up, and labelled for "Paris."

The express-train leaves Madrid for Hendage at 3 P. M. I have yet time to say farewell to my friends. I have one at No. 6 Calle Goya, fourth floor, who happens to be a contributor to several London dailies. He has several children, in whom I have taken a warm interest. Little Charlie and Willie are fast friends of mine; they love to hear of my adventures, and it has been a pleasure to me to talk to them. But now I must say farewell.

Then I have friends at the American Legation whose conversation I admire—there has come a sudden ending of it all. "I hope you will write to us, we shall always be glad to hear of your welfare." How often have I not during my feverish life as a flying journalist heard the very same words, and how often have I not suffered the same pang at parting from friends just as warm as these?

But a journalist in my position must needs suffer. Like a gladiator in the arena, he must be prepared for the combat. Any flinching, any cowardice, and he is lost. The gladiator meets the sword that is sharpened for his bosom—the flying journalist or roving correspondent meets the command that may send him to his doom. To the battle or the banquet it must be all the same—'Get ready and go.'

At 3 P. M. I was on my way, and being obliged to stop at Bayonne a few hours, did not arrive at Paris until the following night. I went straight to the Grand Hotel, and knocked at the door of Mr. Bennett's room.

"Come in," I heard a voice say.

Entering, I found Mr. Bennett in bed.

"Who are you?" he asked.

"My name is Stanley," I answered.

"Ah, yes; sit down. I have important business on hand for you."

After throwing over him his robe-de-chambre, Mr.

Bennett asked me, "Where do you think Livingstone is?"

"I really do not know, sir."

"Do you think he is alive?"

"He may be, and he may not be!" I answered.

"Well, I think he is alive, and that he can be found, and I am going to send you to find him."

"What!" said I. "Do you really think I can find Dr. Livingstone? Do you mean me to go to Central Africa?"

"Yes; I mean that you shall go and find him wherever you may hear that he is, and to get what news you can of him, and perhaps"—delivering himself thoughtfully and deliberately—"the old man may be in want: take enough with you to help him should he require it. Of course you will act according to your own plans, and do what you think best—BUT FIND LIVINGSTONE!"

Said I, wondering at the cool order of sending one to Central Africa to search for a man whom I, in common with almost all other men, believed to be dead, "Have you considered seriously the great expense you are likely to incur on account of this little journey?"

"What will it cost?" he asked, abruptly.

"Burton and Speke's journey to Central Africa cost between £3,000 and £5,000, and I fear it cannot be done under £2,500."

"Well, I will tell you what you will do. Draw a thousand pounds now, and when you have gone through that, draw another thousand, and when that in spent, draw another thousand, and when you have finished that, draw another thousand, and so on; but FIND LIVINGSTONE."

The reporter was a bit dazed at the size of the assignment and a little uncertain as to his authority to invade a continent. "I have heard," he said, "that should your father die you would sell the *Herald* and retire from business ''

''Whoever told you that was wrong,'' came the quick rejoinder, ''for there is not money enough in New York city to buy the New York *Herald*. My father has made it a great paper but I mean to make it greater. I mean that it shall be a newspaper in the true sense of the word. I mean that it shall publish whatever news will be interesting to the world at no matter what cost.''

This declaration swept away Stanley's misgivings. ''After that,'' he remarked, ''I have nothing more to say. Do you mean me to go straight on to Africa to search for Dr. Livingstone?''

Mr. Bennett proceeded to outline a rather leisurely approach to the Dark Continent, ending:

> Bagdad will be close on your way to India; suppose you go there, and write up something about the Euphrates Valley Railroad. Then, when you have come to India, you can go after Livingstone. Probably you will hear by that time that Livingstone is on his way to Zanzibar; but if not, go into the interior and find him, if alive. Get what news of his discoveries you can; and, if you find he is dead, bring all possible proof of his being dead. That is all. ''Good night, and God be with you.''

As a first step the reporter went to Egypt and covered the opening of the Suez Canal on November 17, 1869. Then he enjoyed a twenty-three-day trip as the Khedive's guest to upper Egypt. Jumping from Cairo to Constantinople he visited Odessa, took in the Caucasus and went on to Persia, whence he crossed to Bom-

Courtesy Houghton Mifflin Company

Henry M. Stanley in 1872
From the *Autogiography of Sir Henry Morton Stanley*

bay, from which point he had determined to plan his search into the heart of Africa. During all this time—some fifteen months—since he had received his orders, no word had come from the missing missionary.

Stanley set out from Bombay on the bark *Polly,* for Mauritius, on a zigzag voyage to Zanzibar, sailing October 12, 1870. The stay on the *Polly* lasted six weeks. From Mauritius the brigantine *Romp* carried him to the Seychelles in seventeen days. The third lap was taken in the whaler *Falcon*—nineteen days more. Thus, at last, he reached Zanzibar!

The date of his arrival after this dispiriting voyage was December 31, 1870. He seems to have expected to find funds and further instructions awaiting him and wavered a bit when neither were on hand. With but a small handful of cash—eighty dollars—he found himself faced with both the organizing and financing of his expedition. Smaller men would have abandoned the task. The very neglect of his employer he interpreted into an attitude of confidence, which, indeed, it was. An appeal would probably have resulted in his recall and dismissal. Accordingly, he set valorously at work to overcome the obstacles in his path.

His first step was to sift all rumors extant about Livingstone. He learned nothing tangible. Not a word had been heard from him since he vanished into Equatoria years before. There was gossip, of course, most of it unfavorable to his project. The general belief was that the explorer was dead, or if living not worth finding; he was cross, old and hard to get along with; narrow-minded and unfit for the work he was engaged in; ought to give way to a younger man; took no notes, kept a faulty journal, and, moreover, did not want to be rescued; if he heard any one was coming for that purpose would probably run away from him. This, with the lack of funds and, apparently, of interest on the part of Bennett, was sufficiently discouraging. Stanley knew the law of the newspaper, however, that one stays on a story until he gets it, or the assignment has been replaced by another. In no office was this rule more mandatory than in that of the *Herald.* He had not a scrap of paper to verify his mission or backing, and eighty dollars was hardly convincing capital. Being the sort of man who inspires faith, he soon enlisted the support of Captain Francis R. Webb, the American Consul, who made the strength of the *Herald's* credit known to Zanzibar bankers. Drafts were cashed, which provided funds. By the twenty-first of March, 1871, he records, the expedition was ready—"a compact little force of three whites, thirty-one armed freemen of Zanzibar as escort, one hundred and fifty-three porters and twenty-seven pack animals for a transport corps, beside two riding horses," all assembled on the east coast of the continent at Bagamoyo.

"There was nothing aggressive" in the outfit Stanley records: "Its many bales of cloth, and loads of beads and wire, with assorted packages of provisions and medicine, indicated a peaceful caravan about to penetrate among African tribes accustomed to barter and chaffer; while its few guns showed a sufficient defensive power against bands of native banditti."

It was no holiday march, however, as the event proved. "I passed my apprenticeship in African travel," Stanley's journal continues, "while traversing the maritime region—a bitter school—amid rank jungles, fetid swamps and fly-infested grass-lands, during which I encountered nothing that appeared to favor my journey. My pack and riding animals died, my porters deserted, sickness of a very grievous nature thinned my numbers; but, despite the severe loss I sustained, I struggled through my troubles."

For solace in his manifold miseries the explorer had a Bible, which he read and pondered deeply, and a large number of New York *Heralds,* that the kindly consul had given him in which to wrap packages. "Strange connection," he exclaims. "But yet strangest of all was the change wrought in me by the reading of the Bible and these newspapers in melancholy Africa."

The fever took hard hold of him. For days he endured a temperature of one hundred and five, yet "when not light-headed" he read the good Book and the papers. He grew more resolute than ever, as he became more and more alone in thought and action. There "rose the ghosts of bygone yearnings, haunting every cranny of the brain with numbers of baffled hopes and unfilled aspirations," but there followed no echo of despair. Even though he was "only a poor journalist, with no friends," he had become "possessed by a feeling of power to achieve" which he never lost. This trial of fever and fatalities had upon him the effect of making a remolded man. Bonaparte once said that before crossing the bridge at Arcola in the face of the Austrian fire, it had never occurred to him that he could do anything; afterward it never occurred to him that there was anything he could not do. So it was with Stanley after his ordeal.

He became indifferent to all things but his purpose,

grew competent, decisive, masterful—like the man who sent him into the wilderness. Preconceived notions were cast out. He concluded that African fever was no worse than the ague of Arkansas; that his negroes were no more incompetent than could have been expected and were always amiable. "Troubles taught patience, and with the exercise of patience came greater self-control and experience."

By the eighth of May they were in a better country—the Usagara uplands—and advanced to Ugogo. Nine marches more took them to the land of the Moon, where they fell in with a colony of Arab traders, such as had befriended Burton and Speke. Although great travelers, they knew nothing of Livingstone. Stanley now made the mistake of joining forces with the Arabs in the hope of strengthening his own. Jointly, they engaged in a war with Mirambo, a native chief—queer business for a *Herald* reporter. It resulted in a demoralizing defeat. The combined forces were put to rout by Mirambo's warriors, and Stanley found his organization gone. In mid-Africa he had to pull another together—and did it. Where Burton had been forced to give up, he kept on. Three months were lost in putting things in shape, but on September 20, 1871, he was in motion again, and, avoiding Mirambo and his men, he crept cautiously to the south. At the best the situation was desperate enough: "One of my white companions was dead; the other had become a mere burden"—an all too frequent happening with "white companions" thereafter in his African adventures. Forty men had deserted; all but two of the pack-animals were dead, yet the expedition "numbered nearly sixty picked men, almost all of whom were well armed, and loaded with every necessary that was portable, bound to demonstrate if somewhere in the wild western lands the lost traveller lived, or was dead."

How fine his fixed purpose sounds! Yet behind it all, brave man that he was, is visible the fact that it would have taken more courage on his part to face James Gordon Bennett with a report of flight and failure. This was unthinkable in the mind of a man who thought much.

For twenty-six days the southwestern march went on, covering some two hundred forty miles. He early learned that twelve miles a day meant four thousand miles a year without exhaustion. They then went west thirty-five miles, to turn north for one hundred five miles more; thence northwesterly, heading for Lake Tanganyika, and the Arab colony at Ujiji. "With the exception of a mutiny among my own people, which was soon forcibly crushed," he notes, "and considerable suffering from famine," he met with no adventures on what was a rapid advance! The march was expedited by contact with an Arab caravan at the ferry over the Malagarazi River, from which he learned of "a white man having reached Ujiji from Manyuema, a country situated a few hundred miles west of the lake, which startled us all greatly," as indeed it might!

The stranger was reported to be elderly and gray-bearded, as well as white; he had been at Ujiji before, but had only recently arrived after years of absence. Stanley could think him none other than Livingstone. Sir Samuel Baker was somewhere in the country, but he was neither gray-bearded nor old. "Quickened," therefore, "by the hope that was inspired in my mind by this vague rumor," he speedily crossed the river and pushed on through warlike tribes, who demanded blackmail and endangered his progress. He bought his way on the best terms attainable and got on, burning with impatience at every blockade until he passed into the peaceful region of Ukaranga, six hours from Ujiji, where the gray-bearded white man was supposed to be. This was Friday, November 10, 1871. With a heart full of hope the expedition ate a good breakfast and set forth through an agreeable country, thickly wooded, with "towering trees nodding their heads far above, tall bush filling darkly the shade, the road winding like a serpent, narrow and sinuous, the hollows all musical with the murmur of living waters and their sibilant echoes, the air cool and fragrant with the smell of strange flowers and sweet gums." His mind, too, was "lightened with pleasant presentiment" and a "conscience complaisantly approving what I had done hitherto."

"About eight o'clock"—they had marched at dawn, he goes on—"we were climbing the side of a steep and wooded hill, and we presently stood on the very crest of it, and on the farthest edge looked out into a realm of light—wherein I saw, as in a painted picture, a vast lake in the distance below, with its face luminous as a mirror, set in a frame of dimly-blue mountains." They had come at last to Tanganyika, and to the borderland of their hopes.

Eagerly they pressed on, as did the Greek ten thousand and when the cries of the advance announced "Thalassa, thalassa—the sea, the sea!" Stanley looked "enraptured upon the magnificent expanse of fresh water, and the white tipped billows of the inland sea." Hard by he saw Ujiji sleeping amid palms in the noonday sun. A gentle slope led down to the town. At its crest the party halted to "re-unite and reform for an imposing entry." The men put on clean clothing, wrapped fresh snowy cloth around their heads and loaded their guns to awake Ujiji from its siesta with a thunderous salute that was to echo around the world. "It is," says Stanley, "an immemorial custom, for a caravan creeps not up into a friendly town like a thief. Our braves knew the custom well; they therefore volleyed and thundered their salutes as they went marching down the hill slowly, and with much self-contained dignity."

He himself, if less noisy, was equally decorous. The villagers poured out to meet the newcomers. They were scanned with eager eyes. He saw no gray-bearded white man, but "a tall black man, in a long white shirt, burst impulsively through the crowd" on Stanley's right and bowing low, said:

"Good morning, sir."

"Hello," replied Stanley, "who in the mischief are you?"

"I am Susi, sir, the servant of Dr. Livingstone."

"What! is Dr. Livingstone here in this town?"

"Yes, sir."

"But, are you sure; sure that it is Dr. Livingstone?"

"Why, I leave him just now, sir."

Just then another tall black man, clad in white, came up. "Good morning, sir."

"Are you also a servant of Dr. Livingstone?" Stanley asked.

"Yes, sir."

"And what is your name?"

"It is Chuma."

"Oh! the friend of Wekotani, from the Nassick School?"

"Yes, sir."

"Well, now we have met, one of you had better run ahead, and tell the Doctor of my coming."

Susi took to his heels. The crowd, quick to sense a great occasion, shouted, sang, tooted horns and beat upon drums. It was surely Ujiji's greatest day. The caravan passed on under this noisy escort into the town. Let Stanley tell the rest:

After a few minutes we came to a halt. The guides in the van had reached the market-place, which was the central point of interest. For there the great Arabs chiefs, and respectabilities of Ujiji, had gathered in a group to await events; thither also they had brought with them the venerable European traveler who was at that time resting among them. The caravan pressed up to them, divided itself into two lines on either side of the road, and, as it did so, disclosed to me the prominent figure of an elderly white man clad in a red flannel blouse, gray trousers, and a blue cloth, gold banded cap.

Had the quest ended in victory? Stanley was not sure. He had traveled the road of doubt so long that he failed now of conclusion. "It may not be Livingstone after all," he thought. "If this is he what shall I say to him?"

Stanley next says his imagination had not worked him up to the point of greeting, though "all around me was the immense crowd, hushed and expectant, and wondering how the scene would develop itself." What followed was so commonplace as to be memorable.

Under all these circumstances I could do no more

than exercise some restraint and reserve, so I walked up to him and, doffing my helmet, bowed and said in an inquiring tone,—

"Dr. Livingstone, I presume?"

Smiling cordially, he lifted his cap, and answered briefly, "Yes."

This ending all skepticism on my part, my face betrayed the earnestness of my satisfaction as I extended my hand and added,—

"I thank God, Doctor, that I have been permitted to see you."

"I feel most thankful that I am here to welcome you."

It was, indeed, only by rarest chance that they had met in this accidental, casual fashion. Had Stanley gone direct from Paris on receiving his command from Bennett, or had he not been delayed on his march, he would probably have missed his man. At any rate, he regarded the outcome of it all as providential.

They moved on to Livingstone's comfortable quarters, where Stanley was soon made at home. Here he delivered letters—the first that had reached Livingstone in years. Their contents did not appeal to their recipient. He wanted, instead, the news of the lost world. This Stanley gave him in quantities that filled the weary mind—all he could recall that had occurred since March, 1866, when Livingstone vanished in the wilds. This followed:

When I had ended the story of triumphs and reverses which had taken place between 1866 and 1871, my tent-boys advanced to spread a crimson table-cloth, and arrange the dishes and smoking platters heaped up profusely with hot dampers, white rice, maize porridge, kid kabobs, fricasseed chicken, and stewed goat-meat. There were also a number of things giving variety to the meal, such as honey from Ukawendi, forest plums, and wild-fruit jam, besides sweet milk and clabber, and then a silver tea-pot full of "best tea," and beautiful china cups and saucers to drink from. Before we could commence this already magnificent breakfast, the servants of Sayed bin Majid, Mohammed bin Sali, and Muini Kheri brought three great trays loaded with cakes, curries, hashes and stews, and three separate hillocks of white rice, and we looked at one another with a smile of wonder at this Ujiji banquet.

Truly Halima, the fat black cook of the household, had outdone herself. Such were the "hardships" Livingstone did not care to be rescued from!

Livingstone had reached Ujiji that November 1, 1871. He was fifty-nine, not old in any sense of years, but worn down by long life in the tropic lands and by much wandering. He could no more believe that he had been "found" when the servants came running with the news than could Stanley be certain that he had succeeded. The pair foregathered like a son and the father Stanley had never known, until March 14, 1872, when the latter again turned his steps to the coast. He reached Zanzibar in fifty-four days after leaving Ujiji, and sent back to Livingstone men and supplies for a two years' continuation of his explorations, at the *Herald's* charge. These reached him on August 11, 1872. Two weeks later Livingstone was again on the road. He was to live but eight months longer. But he had vastly impressed himself upon his young "rescuer," who was destined to take up and complete his labors.

The two men "took to each other," as the saying goes. Stanley had "expected and was prepared, to meet a crusty misanthrope" and was accordingly on guard, to be taken aback by finding instead "a sweet opposite," though confirmed in a certainty that he was individualistic and would be difficult to get along with—for a Stanley.

That Livingstone was not pining to be rescued is beyond doubt. But the world wanted news of him, and he was located. Stanley grew great in consequence. It is rather amusing to recall that he had similar, but more exasperating experiences when he was drafted in 1886 to "rescue" Emin Pasha, who was supposed to be suffering as the result of the Mahdist rising, and after enduring incredible hardships, found him more comfortable even than Livingstone had been.

But Livingstone was not ungrateful as this letter of acknowledgment to Mr. Bennett attests:

Ujiji, on Tanganyika,
East Africa, November, 1871

James Gordon Bennett, Esq., Jr.:—

My dear Sir—It is in general somewhat difficult to write to one we have never seen—it feels so much like addressing an abstract idea—but the presence of your representative, Mr. H. M. Stanley, in this distant region takes away the strangeness I should otherwise have felt, and in writing to thank you for the extreme kindness that prompted you to send him, I feel quite at home.

If I explain the forlorn condition in which he found me you will easily perceive that I have good reason to use very strong expressions of gratitude. I came to Ujiji off a tramp of between four hundred and five hundred miles, beneath a blazing vertical sun, having been baffled, worried, defeated and forced to return, when almost in sight of the end of the geographical part of my mission, by a number of half-caste Moslem slaves sent to me from Zanzibar, instead of men. The sore heart made still sorer by the woeful sights I had seen of man's inhumanity to man racked and told on the bodily frame and depressed it beyond measure. I thought that I was dying on my feet. It is not too much to say that almost every step of the weary sultry way was in pain, and I reached Ujiji a mere "ruckle" of bones.

There I found that some five hundred pounds sterling worth of goods which I had ordered from Zanzibar had unaccountably been entrusted to a drunken half-caste Moslem tailor, who, after squandering them for sixteen months on the way to Ujiji, finished up by selling off all that remained for slaves and ivory for himself. He had "divined" on the Koran and found that I was dead. He had also written to the Governor of Unyanyembe that he had sent slaves after me to Manyuema, who returned and reported my decease, and begged permission to sell off the few goods that his drunken appetite had spared.

He, however, knew perfectly well, from men who had seen me, that I was alive, and waiting for the goods and men; but as for morality, he is evidently an idiot, and there being no law here except that of the dagger or musket, I had to sit down in great weakness, destitute of everything save a few barter cloths and beads, which I had taken the precaution to leave here in case of extreme need.

The near prospect of beggary among Ujijians made me miserable. I could not despair, because I laughed so much at a friend who, on reaching the mouth of the Zambezi, said that he was tempted to despair on breaking the photograph of his wife. We could have no success after that. Afterward the idea of despair had to me such a strong smack of the ludicrous that it was out of the question.

Well, when I had got to about the lowest verge, vague rumors of an English visitor reached me. I thought of myself as the man who went down from Jerusalem to Jericho; but neither priest, Levite, nor Samaritan could possibly pass my way. Yet the good samaritan was at hand, and one of my people rushed up at the top of his speed, and, in great excitement, gasped out, "An Englishman coming! I see him!" and off he darted to meet him.

An American flag, the first ever seen in these parts, at the head of a caravan, told me the nationality of the stranger.

I am as cold and non-demonstrative as we islanders are usually reputed to be; but your kindness made my frame thrill. It was, indeed, overwhelming, and I said to my soul, "Let the richest blessings descend from the Highest on you and yours!"

The news Mr. Stanley had to tell was thrilling. The mighty political changes on the Continent; the success of the Atlantic cables; the election of General Grant, and many other topics rivetted my attention for days together, and had an immediate and beneficial effect on my health. I had been without news from home for years save what I could glean from a few *Saturday Reviews* and *Punch* of 1868. The appetite revived, and in a week I began to feel strong again.

Mr. Stanley brought a most kind and encouraging despatch from Lord Clarendon, whose loss I sincerely deplore, the first I have received from the Foreign Office since 1866, and information that the British government had kindly sent a thousand pounds sterling to my aid. Up to his arrival I was not aware of any pecuniary aid. I came unsalaried, but this want is now happily repaired, and I am anxious that you and all my friends should know that, though uncheered by letter, I have stuck to the task which my friend Sir Roderick Murchison set me, with "John Bullish" tenacity, believing that all would come right at last.

The watershed of South Central Africa is over

seven hundred miles in length. The fountains thereon are almost innumerable—that is, it would take a man's lifetime to count them. From the watershed they converge into four large rivers, and these again into two mighty streams in the great Nile valley, which begins in ten degrees to twelve degrees south latitude. It was long ere light dawned on the ancient problem and gave me a clear idea of the drainage. I had to feel my way and every step of the way, and was, generally, groping in the dark—for who cared where the waters ran? We drank our fill and let the rest run by.

The Portuguese who visited Cazembe asked for slaves and ivory, and heard of nothing else. I asked about the waters, questioned and cross-questioned, until I was almost afraid of being set down as afflicted with hydrocephalus.

My last work, in which I have been greatly hindered from want of suitable attendants, was following the central line of drainage down through the country of the cannibals, called Manyuema, or, shortly, Manyema. This line of drainage has four large lakes in it. The fourth I was near when obliged to turn. It is from one to three miles broad, and never can be reached at any point or at any time of the year. Two western drains, the Lufira, or Bartle Frere's River, flow into it at Lake Kamolondo. Then the great River Lomame flows through Lake Lincoln into it, too, and seems to form the western arm of the Nile, on which Petherick traded.

Now, I knew about six hundred miles of the watershed, and unfortunately the seventh hundred is the most interesting of the whole; for in it, if I am not mistaken, four fountains arise from an earthen mound, and the last of the four becomes, at no great distance off, a large river.

Two of these run north to Egypt, Lufira and Lomame, and two run south into inner Ethiopia, as the Leambaye, or upper Zambezi, and the Kaful. Are not these the sources of the Nile mentioned by the Secretary of Minerva, in the city of Sais, to Herodotus.

I have heard of them so often, and at great distances off, that I cannot doubt their existence, and in spite of the sore longing for home that seizes me every time I think of my family, I wish to finish up by their rediscovery.

Five hundred pounds sterling worth of goods have again unaccountably been entrusted to slaves, and have been over a year on the way, instead of four months. I must go where they lie at your expense, ere I can put the natural completion to my work.

And if my disclosures regarding the terrible Ujijian slavery should lead to the suppression of the East Coast slave trade, I shall regard that as a greater matter by far than the discovery of all the Nile sources together. Now that you have done with domestic slavery forever, lend us your powerful aid toward this great object. This fine country is blighted, as with a curse from above, in order that the slavery privileges of the petty Sultan of Zanzibar may not be infringed, and the rights of the Crown of Portugal, which are mythical, should be kept in abeyance till some future time when Africa will become another Indian to Portuguese slave traders.

I conclude by again thanking you most cordially for your great generosity, and am

Gratefully yours,
DAVID LIVINGSTONE.

This letter was printed by the *Herald* in facsimile and served to hush the usual doubters who were alert to discredit a great exploit; the chief of whom were in England, where there was much evidence of pique because the enterprise of an American had discovered the lost explorer, to whom of late his own countrymen had been so indifferent.

One of the disadvantages of unusual success is having to live up to it. There were no more Livingstones to find and so, after the semi-fiasco of Stanley's lecture tour in America, there was need of suitable occupation. British engaged in a witless war in West Africa, sending thither a force under Sir Garnet Wolseley. Stanley went with the army until Coomassie, the Ashantee capital, fell. He sent the *Herald* the best accounts extant, and put them together later in a book, which also contained his experience in Abyssinia, entitled *Coomassie and Magdala.*

Returning from Ashantee on the steamship *Dromedary,* he paused at the island of St. Vincent, on February 24, 1874, to be "shocked to hear on getting ashore of the death of Livingstone at Itala, near Lake Bangweolo, on May 4, 1873," and that his body was on the way to England via Aden on the steamship *Malwa.* "Dear Livingstone," he commented. "Another sacrifice to Africa! His mission, however, must not be allowed to cease; others must go forward to fill the gap. 'Close up, boys! close up! Death must find us everywhere!' "

He was marking out his own destiny, for continuing in the same strain he wrote further:

May I be selected to succeed him in opening up Africa to the shining light of Christianity! My methods, however, will not be Livingstone's. Each man has his own way. His, I think, had its defects, though the old man personally, has been almost Christ-like for goodness, patience and self-sacrifice. The selfish and wooden-headed world requires mastering, as well as loving charity; for man is a composite of the spiritual and earthly. May Livingstone's God be with me, as He was with Livingstone in all his loneliness. May

God direct me as He wills. I can only vow to be obedient, and not to slacken.

In this mood he reached London and logically became Livingstone's successor. He was "different," however, as he said he would be. An echo of him comes back to me from listening to his lecture on *Through the Dark Continent.* He had been describing the great equatorial forest: "And so we went on through the forest and ever and anon the dark people came out of its recesses and threw themselves across the path, barring our way. Then came the sound of an explosion and we went on, leaving them wondering and lamenting."

He attended Livingstone's funeral in Westminister Abbey and came from it full of Africa. The humor moved him to call at the office of the London Daily *Telegraph,* whose proprietor, Levy-Lawson, cooperated much with the *Herald,* and pointed out the vast uncharted spaces on the map of the Dark Continent, citing the things left in doubt by Livingstone, Burton, Speke, Grant and Baker.

"Do you think you can settle all these interesting geographical problems?" Levy-Lawson asked quizzically. That, Stanley answered, was not a fair question. He would, however, do his best. After some discussion the owner of the *Telegraph* said he would "cable over to Bennett of the New York *Herald,* and ask if he is willing to join in this expedition of yours."

The message was duly sent. "Deep under the Atlantic," records Stanley, "the question was flashed. Gordon Bennett tore open the telegram in New York City, and, after a moment's thought, snatched a blank form and wrote 'Yes! Bennett.' "

Thus it befell that Stanley became the successor of Livingstone, and succeeded where all others had failed.

In October, 1874, the *Herald* reporter began his work. His efforts continued until August, 1877, when he returned to civilization with a tale such as was never before given man to tell. He crossed the Continent from east to west, completely traced the Congo from source to mouth and made great geographical mysteries plain. It was the beginning of the opening of equatorial Africa. Soon the world rang with his praises. If Bennett did not share in the harvest of glory, the *Herald* did. It is proper that both should have their names written high in the records of human achievement, even though the lasting fame belongs to the bold and honest gentlemen who worked their will.

Three white men who went with Stanley into the wilds died there. He came out gray and old beyond his years, bent and blackened, but still indomitable. The King of the Belgians took up the opportunity which the English declined to grasp and made Stanley the creator of the Congo Free State. So, if there is any merit in civilizing Africa it dates from James Gordon Bennett's sententious command: "Go and find Livingstone!"

In the mighty acclaim that greeted Stanley on his several returns to civilization, Bennett learned that no proprietor, however despotic he might be, is greater than his newspaper. The *Herald* loomed large, with but a modicum of Bennett in the background, while Stanley stood in the center of the stage. England accorded him greetings such as it would hardly have given a conquering general, and the newspapers spread his fame around the world. Bennett became scarcely incidental. There sprang into his bosom a jealousy of Stanley that almost approached the dignity of hatred. That *his* hired man, whom *he* had sent on an errand, should, as a result, reach at one bound the summit of eminence was too much to be borne. That a *Herald* reporter should receive a jeweled snuff-box from the hands of Queen Victoria, be specially honored at great banquets, given the freedom of London and rewarded with other extravagant evidence of esteem, overwhelmed the owner of the *Herald.* The latter, of course, rarely escaped mention—its owner seldom received it.

Following his London triumph, Stanley came to New York to meet Bennett and enjoy further adulation. Here things were not so pleasant. The malicious *Sun,* rising fast under the spell of Charles A. Dana and Amos J. Cummings, scouted the merits of Stanley's exploit and tried to prove him a liar. Seeking the usual reward as a lecturer he failed; his untrained talk was a jumble, tainted with bitterness as he strove to refute the unfair and untruthful *Sun.* Bennett froze at his coming, and, while the first lecture was given praise when it deserved censure, the second was "roasted" in the *Herald* by one of the chief sycophants, George O. Seilhamer, who afterward confessed to Joseph I. C. Clarke, the night editor, that he "sensed" Bennett's displeasure, and wrote to gratify him. "I simply made the truth sound raw," he explained, "and when Bennett sent for me the next day to reproach me severely, as he did, I could see that he was really gratified."

Stanley's book, *How I Found Livingstone,* was well treated by the *Herald,* though, as Clarke relates, "Bennett let Stanley know he echoed the slighting attacks of some other papers on its want of literary style." This Stanley never acquired. Indeed, he was the sort of reporter who could be trusted to be on the spot, but was able to tell happenings only crudely, and wasted a good deal of space on the approach to his story.

The explorer does not seem to have been conscious of having offended Bennett by reaping the just reward of success. He could respect but never understand him. In his famous march through the Dark Continent, when under an escort of two thousand, three hundred men sent by Mtesa, King of Uganda, he "discovered the giant mountain Gordon Bennett, in the country of Gambaragara," and so immortalized his former employer, who seems to have little appreciated the eminence. The big peak should have been a volcano.

Men who were near Bennett have related how he would break out into fury at times when Stanley came into the news, reiterating what he thought was his unrequited share in the discovery of the discoverer. It was he who had given the distinction by making the opportunity. In this mood he would ask: "Who was Stanley before I found him? Who thought of hunting Livingstone? Who paid the bills?" The answer was Bennett, of course, but outside of himself and the sycophants few thought of that phase.

If Stanley ever suspected this jealousy he certainly gave it little heed. Indeed, he was too sincere a character to give a thought to such a thing and never posed in the background of his own story. He toiled too hard for all that, was deeply religious and loyal to all he undertook. Bennett was neither.

This smoldering animosity on Bennett's part lasted as long as the explorer lived. There once came to his ears after Stanley's late-in-life marriage to the lovely Dorothy Tennant, that he was treating her harshly. Aubrey Stanhope, who carried through some of Bennett's most offensive assignments, was at once sent to Stanley at a remote resort in the Tyrol, where he was vacationing with his wife, to ascertain by direct methods if Bula Matari, the Rock Breaker, had turned heart breaker. When he reached the resort Mrs. Stanley was ill and Stanley desperately lonesome. His heart warmed in welcome for some one to talk to and for two days he emptied his mind on the visitor.

On the third day he remarked contritely that he feared he had been very selfish in taking all the time, but he had been so bored that the company brought him a relief he could not resist. What, then, was Stanhope's errand? Did he want something about Africa?

"No," replied Stanhope. "It isn't Africa this time. It's something quite different," and then he gasped: "Do you beat your wife?"

"Now kill me," he said to himself. He saw Stanley's fingers tighten at the end of his long arms and nerved himself for the worst. There was a silence. Then Stanley said sadly:

"God! I used to do that myself."

"Mount Gordon Bennett" came up amusingly once in Stanley's career. He was invited to meet William E. Gladstone at a tea given at the home of Miss Tennant, to whom he was then betrothed, and loaded himself up with data to convince the statesman that some important things were yet to be done in Africa. Unrolling a map he narrates:

I landed him on the shores of the Nyanza and begged him to look at the spacious inland sea, surrounded by populous countries. When I came to Ruwenzori, his eye caught a glimpse of two isolated peaks.

"Excuse me one minute," said he, "what are those two mountains called."

"Those, sir," I answered, "are the Gordon Bennett and Mackinnon peaks."

"Who called them by those absurd names?" he asked with the corrugation of a frown on his brow.

"I called them, sir."

"By what right?" he asked.

"By the right of first discovery, and those two gentlemen were the patrons of the expedition."

"How can you say that when Herodotus spoke of them twenty-six hundred years ago, and called them Crophi and Mophi? It is intolerable that classic names like those should be displaced by modern names, and——"

"I humbly beg your pardon, Mr. Gladstone, but Crophi and Mophi, if they ever existed at all, were situated over a thousand miles to the northward. Herodotus simply wrote from hearsay, and——"

"Oh, I can't stand that."

"Well, Mr. Gladstone," said I, "will you assist me in this project of a railway to Uganda, for the suppression of the slave trade, if I can arrange that Crophi and Mophi shall be substituted in place of Gordon Bennett and Mackinnon?"

"Oh, that will not do; that is flat bribery and corruption," and smiling, he rose to his feet, buttoning his coat lest his virtue might yield to the temptation.

The road to Uganda was built as Stanley had planned and a considerable crimp put on the slave trade as a result.

Besides using his employer's name for adorning the admirable mountain, Stanley gave it to "a deep rapid stream of about forty yards in breadth at the ferry of Bwabwa Njali," which some "four miles lower down . . . descends a furious cataract by two mouths into the Congo about fifty yards below the first dangerous rapid" on the latter river. The "furious cataract" must have suggested the choice of its namesake.

Was the idea of sending Stanley to seek Livingstone original with Bennett? Possibly. My distinct impression is that the suggestion came from Colonel Finlay Anderson, the *Herald's* agent in London, where there was much public interest in Livingstone's fate, though it failed to rouse either the government or the Royal Geographical Society into action. Indeed, I recall his making some such statement to me shortly before his death. But Bennett seized the chance and backed his man unflinchingly. "What a romantic achievement, worthy to be sung in heroic verse, was the finding of Livingstone by Stanley," wrote Philip Gilbert Hamerton in *The Intellectual Life*. True enough, but there would have been no opportunity for an epic had not James Gordon Bennett made it possible.

CHAPTER XIII

THE WILD ANIMAL HOAX

New York, always most credulous of cities, awoke into wild alarm on the morning of November 9, 1874, when the *Herald* flung out a first page of solid nonpariel announcing that the "wild animals" in the Central Park Zoo had broken loose the night before with direful consequences. The city was thrown into a panic. A "proclamation" by the Mayor, warning people to remain in their homes until the "peril" was over, accompanied the tale and thousands kept within doors. The more valorous armed themselves to the teeth and sallied forth in search of big game. The city seethed with excitement, as well it might under the spell of such an announcement. That no other paper carried the tale was without effect—had not the *Herald* often beaten its slower contemporaries in big news? But few read the page through and so reached the anticlimax of what was the second most noteworthy "sell" on record—Richard Adams Locke's "Moon" Hoax, printed in the New York *Sun* on August 21, 1835, being the greatest. Well might panic follow a page headed with these lines:

AWFUL CALAMITY

The Wild Animals Broken Loose from Central Park.

Terrible Scenes of Mutilation.

A Shocking Sabbath Carnival of Death.

Savage Brutes at Large.

Awful Combats Between the Beasts and the Citizens.

The Killed and Wounded.

General Duryee's Magnificent Police Tactics.

Bravery and Panic.

How the Catastrophe was Brought About—
Affrighting Incidents.

Proclamation by the Mayor.

Governor Dix Shoots the Bengal Tiger in the Streets.

After the *Herald* custom, this was followed by a long and solemn introduction reading:

Another Sunday of horror has been added to those already memorable in our city annals. The sad and appalling catastrophe of yesterday is a further illustration of the unforeseen perils to which large communities are exposed. Writing even at a late hour, without full details of the terrors of the evening and night, and with a necessarily incomplete list of the killed and mutilated, we may pause for a moment in the widespread sorrow of the hours to cast a hasty glance over what will be felt to be a great calamity for many years. Few of the millions who have visited Central Park, and who, passing through the entrance at East Sixty-fourth Street, have stopped to examine the collection of birds and animals grouped around the old Arsenal building, could by any possibility have foreseen the source of such terrible danger to a whole city in the caged beasts around him as the trivial incidents of yesterday afternoon developed. The unfortunate man to whose fatal imprudence all accounts attribute the outbreak of the wild animals in the menagerie has answered with his life for his temerity, but we have a list of calamities traceable from his act which one life seems inadequate to expiate. We have a list of forty-nine killed, of which only twenty-seven bodies have been identified, and it is much to be feared that the large total of fatalities will be much increased with the return of daylight.

The list of mutilated, trampled and injured in various ways must reach nearly two hundred persons of all ages, of which, so far as known, about sixty are very serious, and of these latter, three can hardly outlast the night. Many of the slightly injured were taken to their homes, so that at least for another day the full extent of the calamity cannot be measured. We have only to hope that no further fatalities will occur. Twelve of the wild carnivorous beasts are still at large, their lurking places not being known for a certainty, but the citizens may rest assured that if they will only exercise ordinary prudence and leave the task of hunting down the animals to the authorities, who have somewhat tardily taken the matter in hand, there will be no further casualties to register as the outcome of the unauthorized act of a reckless keeper in Central Park.

It was an apparently small cause for a huge and horrible result, but the overturning of a kerosene lamp in a dingy cow shed in Chicago laid the Queen City of the West in ashes, and a spark from a hod-carrier's pipe was parent of the flames that consumed in a night the great granite buildings of Boston, as if the solid stones were fuel. It is not long since a herd of Texan cattle threw New York's million of human beings into consternation, defied the police force and injured so many. It was at least to be hoped that the somewhat similar, although more fearful, calamity of the breaking loose of the wild animals at Central Park would have found Superintendent Walling with some plan to meet the emergency. In all such cases, promptitude is invaluable, and although General Duryee deserves credit for his plan, formed, we are assured, on the instant and carried out so far with effect, we must regret that he was not earlier informed of the terrible event. A telegram from police headquarters to the general's residence did not reach him, and thus a valuable hour was lost, as he was first informed of the catastrophe by seeing the mutilated body of the unfortunate sewing girl, Annie Thomas, borne on an improvised stretcher to the Thirty-first Precinct station house, near West Eighty-sixth Street. He was visiting at the house of a friend, and the passing crowd with the mournful burden on the shoulders of the police attracted the attention of a young daughter of his friend's. Her screams brought the entire party to the windows. In an instant the General was in the street. Learning from a hundred tongues the horrible truth in the few words, "the wild animals at the park have broken loose," he ran like a deer to the station house, and seating himself by the telegraph instrument, directed from that point the operations which first resulted in staying the panic. Had he lost the time it would have taken to reach police headquarters, it is impossible to say where the panic and affright and their consequent fatalities would have ended.

Commissioners Matsell and Disbecker were heard from at various points throughout the evening, but their efforts were not of a nature to produce any good result. Orders and counterorders were issued by them in continuing succession. Happily, the steps taken by General Duryee made them practically subordinates and diminished their inefficiency—to give their stampeded zeal no harsher term. Commissioner Voorhis could not be found during the entire evening. To General Shaler, also, the thanks of the community are due. His promptitude in calling out the Seventh, Eighth, Ninth and Sixty-ninth regiments, a call manfully responded to, and placing them at the service of General Duryee deserves unqualified praise. It is to be hoped that the proclamation issued by Mayor Havemeyer after consultation with General Shaler and Commissioner Duryee, will meet with the obedience which its gravity merits. Discipline is the only means of meeting and conquering such an untoward chain of circumstances, and we here point out that the obedience which is given by the militia to General Shaler, by the police to General Duryee, the hero of the hour, should be cheerfully rendered by the citizens at large to the proclamation of his Honor the Mayor. The deaths and mutilations are already too numerous to risk their increase and the authorities will only serve the common cause by enforcing the law against those whose curiosity leads them to defy the mandates of the civil power.

The following is the Mayor's proclamation:

A PROCLAMATION

Mayor's Office, Sunday Night
Nov. 8, 1874

All citizens, except members of the National Guard, are enjoined to keep within their houses or residences until the wild animals now at large are captured or killed. Notice of the release from this order will be spread by the firing of cannon in City Hall Park, Tompkins Square, Madison Square, the Round and at Macomb's Dam Bridge. Obedience to this order will secure a speedy end to the state of siege occasioned by the calamity of this evening.

An account will be opened at the City Hall, of the City of New York, for contributions to the sufferers.

The "big story" then began under a single full face line:

THE CATASTROPHE

The location of the Zoological collection in the Park is well known to most New Yorkers; but it appears that changes were made recently in the disposition of the various animals, and to realize the exact nature of the catastrophe it becomes necessary to indicate where the various animals were situated yesterday when the frightful event occurred that spread such terror throughout the city. If you enter the menagerie from Fifth Avenue you will find on either hand, running parallel to the street, the houses where the herbivorous beasts were domiciled. In former times several bears from the northern regions occupied the right hand corner, where a few beautiful zebras lately gladdened the eye. To the extreme left were the cages of the several foreign birds, formerly devoted to a large collection of monkeys. To the extreme right were the vultures and eagles, and the visitor, by making a short circuit of the large building, known in times gone by as the Arsenal found himself in front of a handsome wooden structure, one story high, where the principal wild animals resided. Of course, the residence of the sea lion was known to everybody. On the inside of the garden the stately giraffe occupied a somewhat large enclosure, and adjacent were a number of pelicans, intermingled with several specimens of the ostrich tribe. The bears were in isolated cages on the green sward, near the common pedestrian route from the Fifth Avenue entrance.

THE PROMINENT ANIMALS

in the quadrangle nearest to Fifth Avenue were the bison, the nylghau, the zebu, the sacred bull, cow and calf, the zebras, the young elephant, the capybara, the guanaco, the fat-tailed Syrian var, the aoudad and the fallow deer. In the valuable monkey collection were the sooty mangabey, the bonnet macaque, the Toque monkey, the pig tailed monkey, the Arabian baboon, the black handed spider monkey, the brown Capuchin, the Teetee and the blackeared marmoset. Such was the scene before

THE TERRIBLE EVENTS

of yesterday—the bursting forth of the most ferocious beasts within the menagerie of the Park, the awful slaughter that ensued, the exciting conflicts between the infuriated animals, the frightful deaths that followed, the destruction of property and the fearful and general excitement—making an era in the history of New York not soon to be forgotten. How singular that Sunday, of all days in the week, should make the occasion of such great panics as mark the record of the past four years. It was a Sabbath morning that witnessed the destruction of Chicago and Boston and a Sabbath afternoon beheld the streets of New York given up to the fury of a drove of Texan cattle. It was on a Sabbath that the *Westfield* exploded her boiler. But yesterday capped the climax of unthought possibilities, and it was the Sabbath, too, that deepened the significance of the great disaster.

As everybody knows, the Central Park on Sunday is the popular resort of all classes—the rich and fashionable in their carriages, and the poor and humble on foot, alike sally forth to enjoy its beauties. It is safe to say that at least 20,000 people filled the various walks, drives and avenues yesterday. To nine-tenths of the pedestrian visitors the menagerie is a chief source of attraction. That it contained the elements of a sanguinary disaster to a multitude of human beings hardly entered into the philosophy of anybody. It would be vain of the writer to presume himself capable of picturing the harrowing scenes of which he was the distressed and involuntary spectator. To give, for instance, an adequate description of the frightful incident, where Lincoln, the Numidian lion, urged to indescribable fury by the bullets that pierced his flanks and shoulders, jumped into a landaulet occupied by a nursemaid and her four young charges, mangling the delicate little things past all sign of recognition, would be a difficult task. But let me endeavor to describe the fearful scenes with some attempt at order. My head is so confused and my nerves so unstrung with the fearful scenes through which I have passed that I confess I am hardly equal to picturing them.

FIRST OMINOUS SYMPTOMS.

The writer stood within a hundred yards of the menagerie when the first ominous symptoms of the approaching catastrophe were heard. The doors of the main structure, wherein the principal wild animals were confined, were closed at five o'clock. Hundreds of people, men, women and children, were still lingering in the vicinity. Five or six of the Park Police were stationed in the neighborhood. One stood at the entrance at Fifth Avenue and Sixty-fourth Street, making a record of the number of visitors passing in. Another was stationed for a similar purpose on the roadway approaching from the south-eastern entrance, at the corner of Fifty-ninth Street. Within the arsenal there appears to have been a number of the Park Police. The captain was off duty and did not appear until later at night. Mr. Conklin, the director of the menagerie, was at his post, like a good soldier. It was

A CALM, PEACEFUL AND PLEASING SCENE

in the early hours of the afternoon. Children ran around from cage to cage in the perfect fulness of delight. A stream of people released from the cares and labors of the week wandered through the grounds, pausing to admire the beautiful zebras and stopping there to laugh over the amusing antics of the monkeys. The idea of danger could only be suggested to create laughter and derision. Certainly nobody seriously contemplated the possibility of peril where seemingly massive cages restrained the wild and savage instincts of the various beasts of prey. The rhinoceros appeared the

PICTURE OF STUPID AMIABILITY,

the Numidian lion wore a look of the grossest indolence, the Bengal tiger seemed as harmless as a prostrate forest tree, the bears invited a caressing acquaintance, the boa constrictor might have been petted with the hand, the elephant eating biscuits from the fingers of a little child, suggested an extreme condition of tameness and docility. In all the rest, saving the restless and savage eyed hyena, the spirit of the day appeared to dwell.

THE ORIGIN OF THE AWFUL CALAMITY.

In a very few moments the whole aspect was destined to be changed. It is now well authenticated that Chris. Anderson, the keeper, one of whose charges was Pete, the rhinoceros, in walking around after the public was excluded, stopped in front of the den of the huge animal above mentioned. He was seen to poke his cane through the bars at the great beast, and was warned by keeper Miller to desist. The latter was leaving the building at the moment he remonstrated with Anderson, and to this circumstance, doubtless, owes his life. He says that keeper Hyland also called out to Anderson. The latter had a fashion, it appears, of teasing the animals although he was often known to eject persons from the building for similar practices. Anderson paid no attention to the warnings of his fellow keepers, and, it is thought, a heedless thrust must have entered the eye of the rhinoceros. A number of boys who were peering in through the windows on the north side of the building attracted the attention of the writer by their cries.

"LOOK, HE'S BREAKING OUT!"

There was a crashing heard within and the boys were seen to flee precipitately. I rushed to the window, drawn by a curiosity which was irresistible. My example was soon followed by others, many women struggling for a place. It was some moments before I could make out what was transpiring within. A keeper was standing in the middle of the open space apparently spellbound. Another was standing further down, grasping a crowbar, his gaze directed toward the pen of the rhinoceros. The short, angry, squeaking cry of the rhinoceros, like sudden blasts on a fish horn, was heard amid the sound of snapping bars and crashing planks. It at once struck me that the huge animal was breaking down the walls of his pen in the endeavor doubtless to reach his tormentor. Not aware of any cause for this sudden exhibition of rage, none of the fascinated crowd at the windows measured the danger of their position or the object of the infuriated beast. The keeper, afterward found to be Anderson, now rushed forward and struck at the animal. We could not see whether his blows reached the rhinoceros or not, but their effect was soon told. A crash which shook the building followed and the front of the pen fell outward and the horrid, mis-shapen mass of Pete, the rhinoceros, rushed out, his double-horned head close to the ground. Anderson made a spring sideways, to avoid the monster's onslaught and might have succeeded in gaining at least temporary safety by this means, but he was too close to the animal, for the latter, swinging his unwieldy body toward him, knocked him down with a touch of his shoulder, and an instant after had trampled him out of recognition. Backing down from the mangled body with a swiftness almost incredible for his bulk, the rhinoceros plunged his horrid horn into the dead keeper, dashing the last possible spark of life out against the walls of one of the pens, which likewise gave way. All this tragedy transpired in an instant. Horror-stricken, I tried to push my way from the window, but the crowd was now dense behind me and I could not stir. I cried:

"For God's sake, let some one run to the police station for help!"

I struggled to get out, putting my hands against the window and my feet below it, and pushing with all my might. An accursed curiosity in the crowd, who were only vaguely conscious of what was transpiring, made my efforts useless. When I looked in through the window again the destruction at the further end had increased, the rhinoceros breaking open the dens of the animals on the left hand side.

THE KEEPER HYLAND

whom I had first seen standing spell-bound, was advancing, pale as marble, and a navy revolver in his hand toward the enraged rhinoceros. The animal saw him, turned and made for him in an instant. He sprang aside and fired. The ball hit the rhinoceros on the left shoulder, for he swerved over for an instant; but it can scarcely have more than hurt him a little, as he turned with a whiff, whiff, whiff snort, his head down toward the keeper. The latter, with cat-like agility, retreated toward the lions' and tigers' cages, evidently making for the space between them, but too late. The horrid horn impaled him against the corner cage, killing him instantly, tearing the cage to pieces and releasing the panther, who landed in the middle of an open space with a spring. The cries of all the animals were now joined in horrid chorus by the loud and long-sustained roar of the lion and lioness, the tigers and all the wild beasts, that doubtless had their carnivorous instincts whetted by the smell of human blood and the sound and sight of the bloody struggles outside their bars.

"THE WILD ANIMALS ARE LOOSE"

I yelled, and the savage chorus within bore out my words. At last curiosity seemed to give way. The crowd fled in all directions, women falling as they ran, and no one staying to help them out of the way of the coming danger, which was then shaping itself so swiftly. I ran to the police station in the Arsenal building, and found that the sergeant on duty was dozing quietly. I shook him up, told him in a few words what was the matter and ran round to the space in front of the Arsenal. There I found keeper Miller calling to the policeman who was just coming off duty. Miller laughed at my story.

"Come around," I said earnestly.

"Too thin, young fellow," said the policeman.

"Don't you hear?" I said, as the roaring of the animals sounded ominously in our ears. The sergeant now came running out in search of the policeman.

"Anderson and Hyland are killed," said he to Miller. "Why don't you stir yourself?"

Miller is a tall, stalwart man of about thirty-three and it is but just to say that from the moment the sergeant spoke he sprang into action. He rushed into the keeper's room and grasped a sixteen shooter rifle, which is kept loaded for such emergencies and ran out through the central door to the rear of the Arsenal to the window the crowd had just deserted. What he saw evidentally appalled him, as he let the butt of the rifle fall to the ground and continued gazing in through the window like one in a dream. From his own lips I have learned what he saw. He said:

"An attentive glance through the window revealed the fact that

THE HUGE RHINOCEROS HAD BROKEN LOOSE."

He had apparently made no more of the massive barrier that enclosed him than a sheet of pasteboard. I saw the dead bodies of Hyland and Anderson, the former nearer to me than the other. The panther was crouched over Hyland's body, gnawing horribly at his head. I recognized his body by the striped shirt which I could just see hanging tattered from the arm. It was growing dark and this made everything look twice as fearful. I saw the rhinoceros plunge blindly forward against the double tier of cages where the black and spotted leopards, the striped hyena, the prairie wolf, the puma and the jaguar were lying. Judging from the condition of the cages, the onset of the powerful and infuriated rhinoceros must have been tremendous. In some cases the bars were only bent to an elbow, but, as a rule, they snapped asunder like kindling wood before the smashing weight brought against them.

THE RELEASE OF THE ANIMALS

mentioned angered still more the lions and tigers and all the rest within the building. The rhinoceros in the meantime was busy in the work of destruction. In a few moments more he had broken down the pens of the wild swine, the manatee, the American tapir, the two-toed sloth, and the pair of kangaroos. Just then, too, Lincoln, the Numidian lion, escaped from his cage, through some unfortunate oversight committed at feeding time. The bolt of his prison door was insecure, and when the raging rhinoceros butted his head against the bottom, it flew wide open. Hardly had Lincoln, the lion, bounded into the centre aisle of the building when the three cages containing the black and spotted leopards, the tiger and tigress, the black wolf and the spotted hyenas were sprung open by an overpowering charge from the now desperate rhinoceros. The noise of this crash might have been heard several blocks away. It was followed by a series of fights between the liberated beasts. Close by a window on the western aisle of the building the black wolf sprang upon the flanks of the Bengal tiger. The lion stood a little distance away pawing the floor, awaiting rather than offering an attack. Between the wolf and tiger the conflict was brief. The latter, shaking off the feeble hold of the other, turned quick as lightning on his hind legs and falling with open, gleaming jaws upon his less muscular foe, rolled him over in the dust. The great fight ensued

OVER THE BODY

of poor brave Hyland. There was evidently a fight over the body of Anderson, but I could see nothing more than a mingling, gleaming mess, whence arose the most awful cries. Nearer to me where Hyland lay, the lioness, the panther, the puma, and presently the Bengal tiger, were rolling over and over, striking at each other with their mighty paws. The lioness tore the skin off the puma's flank with one blow. The coming of the tiger was something terrible. I never shall forget the awful, splendid look of him as he landed with a spring in the thick of them. I could not move. It was too awful for anything. Oddly enough, while the fight was going on, now one furious beast tugging and crunching at the arms or legs of the corpse, now letting go with his teeth to plant his paws upon the bleeding remains and snap with his dripping jaws at another beast, writhing and awful as they were, I could not help looking at Lincoln, the lion, who was standing behind them pawing the ground, roaring and lashing his side with his tail, every muscle in uneasy tension. All of a sudden I had a flash.

"BY GOD, HE'S LOOKING AT ME"

I said to myself. It seemed to me I felt him looking at me. I saw him crouch. I turned and ran. "My God, I had no idea there was anybody near me." Miller had not been a minute and a half at the window when I saw him running towards me shouting at the top of his lungs:

"THEY'RE COMING, THEY'RE ALL LOOSE."

It is necessary to explain Miller's statement, "My God, I had no idea there was anybody near me." Those who ran from the window in the first instance had not run far before they looked back. There was, of course, no pursuit, and a great many lingered by, but at a safe distance. The coming of the keeper, however; his standing listless looking before the window for over a minute, had had the effect of inspiring a return of confidence in the more curious, and when Anderson, frightened by the eye of the lion, ran precipitately toward the Arsenal, there were perhaps a dozen persons near the window. He only sped a few paces when, with a terrific roar

LINCOLN, THE LION CAME CRASHING THROUGH THE GLASS.

I saw a young man fall from a blow of the awful paw, and another crushed to earth beneath the beast's weight. The crowd fled in all directions, but the lion did not pursue. Planting his paw upon one of the bodies he filled the air with the fearful rumble of his roar. I started to run, but Miller called on me to stop. I turned and saw him kneel down deliberately and take aim. There was a good chance for a shot, as the lion stood almost facing him, but with the right shoulder more toward him. I have no reason to doubt the steadiness of Miller or his reputation as a shot, but I waited with inpent breath as he took aim. He had hit him. I could not see where, but the wound was far from fatal. The bellowings were renewed, his mane erect, his tail switching his sides, while he pawed the earth and swung his huge head from side to side. Drawn by the report of the rifle and the roaring of the beasts, crowds of people were entering the enclosure from the Sixty-fourth Street entrance. I saw that already a number of Park

POLICE ARMED WITH REVOLVERS

and citizens with rifles were on the ground. I had no weapon and so ran down the incline, by the refreshment stand, toward Fifth Avenue; and almost at my heels as it were, came the Numidian lion with a series of bounds. So sudden, fierce and powerful was the leap he made into the midst of the storming party that he paralyzed the coolest calculations and scattered half a hundred armed and unarmed men like chaff before the wind. Springing in the air over the stooped form of policeman Murray, who ducked in time to save himself from the possible death, Lincoln landed in a fast widening

CIRCLE OF FEAR STRICKEN PEOPLE,

of fainting women, screaming children and terrified men. Lincoln paused for perhaps a second, lashing himself with his tail and glaring horribly around him. On the ground before him were two young men who had tripped and fallen in the precipitate retreat from before the building. They were struggling fast to rise, and had nearly succeeded when Lincoln, with another awful roar that echoed over the Park, pounced upon the nearest, and with one stroke of his fore paw, tore clothes and flesh to pieces. A shout of horror went up from the distant witnesses of the deed, but they were given little time to meditate upon it. I was just in the angle between the two aviaries, which contained, yesterday, the doves and the eagles respectively, when the last mentioned deed of blood was enacted. I was about to escape by rushing past the house where the wild animals were caged, and had just reached the path near the sea lion's tank, when what I had feared most came to pass. The rhinoceros, in his infuriated career, had at last found a gate and crashed through it. Had he done so at first there would have been less lost lives to count. A storming party which had been formed by Colonel Conklin, of keepers, citizens and police near the Fifty-ninth Street entrance, and which was powerfully aided by the arrival of a platoon from the Nineteenth Precinct under Captain Gunner and Mr. Hunt of Ninety-third Street was within a hundred yards of the building when the rhinoceros emerged, giving his short, vicious cry. His appearance was the signal for a misdirected volley, which, of course, did little or no execution on his thick, tough hide and double horn protected proboscis. It confused him momentarily, however, for he turned and re-entered the building on a sort of ambling trot. Misled by this retreat, a cheer went up from the firing party, and they rushed forward, Colonel Conklin leading, to secure the door. Had the great brute deliberately planned an ambuscade, it could not have better succeeded. When the party were within a dozen feet of the door the puma sprang through the shattered portal into their midst, overthrowing several, doubtless injuring some. Almost on the heels of the puma came the black and spotted leopard, followed by the jaguar, the African lioness and tiger. The latter came forth with a slow and stealthy tread. Archambeau, one of the keepers, had the temerity to try and lasso the beast, knowing that there was none more dangerous and blood-thirsty in the whole collection.

THE TIGER SAW THE OBJECT

of the keeper and without a moment's warning, sprang fifteen feet in the air and caught Archambeau by the right shoulder. The two went down together, the tiger on top. Instant preparations were made to save the poor fellow when, unfortunately, the rhinoceros came lumbering at a half trot out of the entrance and drove the rescuing party from their purpose. He also drove the tiger before him, but at the same time planted one of his enormous feet on the prostrate Archambeau and squeezed the breath from his body. The storming party was for the moment completely disorganized. The animals were running in various directions, and the attacking forces and the curious spectators were fleeing in every direction, scaling rocks, climbing trees, falling in their flight, and a case is reported of a citizen stabbed at this moment by an Italian over a quarrel as to which should first ascend a tree. The wounded man, Calvin Morley, of Flatbush, L. I., is at Bellevue Hospital but cannot give any description of

THE MAN WHO STABBED HIM.

I mention this terrible incident from a host of others to show how overwhelming was the fright and how blinding the stampede. The lion had escaped the bullets of the firing party in the front enclosure, or rather being maddened to further desperation by them, careered wildly through the Fifth Avenue entrance, and was followed shortly after by the Bengal tiger, a number of demoralized Park policemen, who still had a sentiment of duty, pursuing them with halloes, as if they were sheep, not sheep devourers.

CONFUSION AND DESTRUCTION.

From this point it has been found extremely difficult to gather anything like a coherent or complete story of the depredations of the uncaged beasts. From a number of statements made to our reporters by eyewitnesses, many of these statements abounding in patent impossibilities, but all of them given with apparent conviction of truthfulness, the following continuation of the story is given. The writer of the preceding, on the pell mell breaking forth from the animals, ran to the Seventy-fourth Street entrance and hurried down to the Windsor Hotel whence he telegraphed to the *Herald* office for assistance.

THE CONTINUATION OF DESTRUCTION.

The rhinoceros, after trampling down the keeper, Archambeau, made directly for the cage of the brown bear, which stood on the grass recently. The ease with which he overturned the structure well illustrated the vast muscular power of the brute. The brown bear escaped with some bruises. The grizzly bear, upon being knocked out of his house, advanced to give fight, but was bowled over on the grass three times in succession.

THE LEOPARD,

after killing a little child and mutilating several women, made his way into the inclosure containing the pelicans, the pea fowl and ostrich and killed all before him. The terror among the storming party lasted long enough to give ample time to the escaped animals to spread havoc all through the Park and the city besides.

THE JAGUAR

had been forgotten at meal time, and, made desperate by hunger, jumped over the fence surrounding the tall and gentle giraffes, and in less time than it takes to tell it, had slaughtered one of the noble but helpless animals.

OVER ONE HUNDRED SHOTS

were fired at the rhinoceros in vain. His sides appeared to be covered with slabs of wrought iron. "Shoot him in the eye," was the general cry, but no one was lucky enough, as all were nervous with fright, to strike that particular organ. A long reaching crowbar, however, struck him in a sensitive spot under the jaw, not with the effect of checking his headlong career, but only to drive him onward to

WORSE DEEDS THAN EVER.

In the same half trot with which he issued from his quarters and swaying like a ship at sea, he struck over to the cages near Fifth Avenue, where the herbivorous animals were stationed. The havoc made in this direction was frightful. All the cages tumbled to pieces, and, to add to the destruction and confusion, the liberated elephant joined forces with the rhinoceros and the joint attack on the weaker animals, such as the camel, the zebras, the sacred bull, the guanaco and the llama was simply irresistible. The sacred bull was killed instantly and one of the mild eyed zebras was crushed without pity. The other escaped into the park and ran toward Eighth Avenue. He is reported to have kicked and badly beaten a number of daring boys who endeavored to effect his capture. He is still at large.

THE BIRDS.

The destruction of the bird cages was marked by terrific screaming. The eagles fought gallantly for their eyries, but nothing could withstand the united charge of the elephant and the rhinoceros. It was late in the evening before the organized force of the menagerie subdued the former of these two powerful animals which had ruined a vast deal of property. The rhinoceros, the parent of all the destruction, made away toward the Mall when

THE ELEPHANT HAD BEEN LASSOED

by the hind leg, a huge log being tied to the end of the stout rope with which the leg was lariated so as to impede his progress, while other parties with ropes similarly hampered the other legs until they were able to throw him on his side and effectually "hobble" him so that he could not rise. They were about to shoot him point-blank, when the strange sight was presented of the elephant's keeper, with streaming eyes and outstretched arms, planting himself between the pointed and cocked rifles of the angry crowd, who had seen the deaths and mutilations, and the pros-

These figures capped the front of the Herald Building. The two men struck the hours

Now on the grounds of the New York University

trate beast, whose trumpetings of defiance were still ringing on the ear. The keeper would not move, and, with many curses, the great brute's life was saved.

THE RHINOCEROS

escaped, as we have said, toward the Mall. Here he attacked a party of young girls, killing the sewing girl, Annie Thomas, and frightening the others terribly. One of them, subject to heart disease, Ellen Schubert, has received such a nervous shock that her death may be looked for at any moment. The beast left the park at one of the upper Eighth Avenue entrances, and gored a horse at Ninetieth Street, overthrowing the heavy wagon to which he was harnessed, and dislocating the shoulder of Isaac Parker, milkman, who was driving. In this neighborhood he overthrew a shanty on the rocks, which fell before him like a house of cards. The wretched inmates were at supper, and the falling planks took fire. All the family escaped except a child in the cradle, which was burned to a crisp. Continuing on his career until he reached Eleventh Avenue, he was followed by a crowd of men and boys, who were evidently unaware of his ferocious nature. He must, too, have been nearly spent with his terrible efforts, but continued on toward the North River. A fortunate accident put an end to his career. It was now very dark and he was seen to fall into a sewer excavation at the Boulevard, fifteen feet deep. Had it been a week day and at an earlier hour, he would no doubt have ended his life in killing, by falling on them, some of the men at work. As it was he fell ingloriously.

The park from end to end is marked with injury, and in its artificial forests the wild beasts lurk, to pounce at any moment on the unwary pedestrian.

THE LEOPARDS AND WOLVES

made short work of the deer and all the blood for which they are responsible is not even yet fully computed. The subsequent fight between

THE LION AND TIGER

when they met on the open space at Fifty-ninth Street, outside the Park wall, in the presence of a thousand terrified spectators, was the great combat of the day. The lion tore away at one bite half of the tiger's flanks, while the latter, with characteristic ferocity, buried his teeth in the lion's neck until the King of beasts howled with the keenest anguish. Now it was the lion underneath and the tiger on top. The next moment positions were reversed.

BLOOD COVERED THE AVENUE

and in the distance the awestruck spectators looked on in breathless fear. Finally, the two sanguinary brutes rushed from each other as a bullet from the rifle of General [George W.] Wingate, who came promptly on the ground, whistled between their ears. Lester Wallack took aim at the same moment from behind the unfinished iron building on the East side, and perforated the tiger to some slight degree. Many other gentlemen came rushing to the scene in the meantime, among them ex-Mayor Hall, Erastus Brooks of the *Express;* Manton Marble and Mr. Bangs of the *World,* who had been visiting Governor-elect Tilden, and were on their way uptown in a carriage; Judge Daly, Judge J. R. Brady, General Chester A. Arthur, Hugh Hastings and Prosper Wetmore. But they were all a trifle nervous from running and the beasts escaped on their raid downtown, where, as everybody knows by this time, they had a bloody and fearful carnival.

TRAGIC DEATH OF THE BROWN SEA LION.

When the ponderous rhinoceros plunged through the sea lion's cage, the latter was in an apparently profound sleep. Awakened by the startling noise around him, and struck with terror at the appearance of his visitor, the poor seal uttered one long, piercing howl, partly resembling the shriek of a locomotive, and the next moment tumbled into his tank and disappeared. The rhinoceros, breaking down the whole structure, was soon floundering in the tank also. Then it was, that the sea lion, driven to bay, showed fight; but the conquest was as unequal as a ferryboat in conflict with an iron-clad man of war. For a time the seal seemed to stand a chance for his life. Being lithe and slippery he easily avoided the unwieldy attacks of his visitor. Indeed, he had every hope of safety, but for an unfortunate slip made by the rhinoceros, who, keeling suddenly over, fell with all his immense weight on his prostrate foe and killed him. During the fight the roars of the sea lion were incessant and painful to hear. It was unlike any other cry of beast, bird or fish. It was something strange and weird, and had a half human sound that struck the ear with a singular impression. The little seal escaped by hiding under the water.

DEATH OF THE ANACONDA.

In the destruction of the various cages the anaconda was roused from his torpor, and pivoting himself upon his tail, made a spring at the neck of the tall and beautiful giraffe that occupied the adjacent cage. Only a few boards separated the two. The long, slender neck of the giraffe bending over the partition proved a tempting mark for the anaconda. The graceful neck was quickly bowed to the ground in the coils of the powerful constrictor. The giraffe made but a feeble struggle and death speedily ended his sufferings. Then it was the awful spectacle was seen of the anaconda seeking to swallow the body of his victim. He had but commenced this disgusting task when he was observed by Dr. F. A. Thomas, of Eighty-third Street, who attacked the reptile, armed with a sabre, and at one blow severed the great snake's body and then departed in haste.

IN THE MONKEY HOUSE

when the elephant smashed the cages with his trunk and drove the monkeys into every hole and corner the scene of disorder and noise was perfectly indescribable. The monkeys screamed and laughed and laughed and screamed. Two green monkeys perched themselves upon the elephant's back, but for a very short time. Over twenty monkeys escaped from the house and made off in various directions. Two of them climbed into a carriage standing outside the Park on Fifth Avenue. One was killed by the laughing hyena, several were wounded by the black wolves; but considering the risks they ran and the familiarity they made with many of the liberated beasts of prey, they escaped very well.

THE NEWS OF THE PROCEEDINGS

in the Park, and the terror excited throughout the city at the prospect of having a visit from wild animals at the domestic fireside, drew an immense number of sporting men and Yorkville fast boys and rowdies in the direction of the menagerie. There was dangerous sport enough for everybody, as far as hunting down the fugitives went. They pentrated everywhere. The African lioness, after saturating herself in the blood of eighteen victims—men, women and children—was finally killed at Castle Garden by a party of emigrants. She lay down under one of the great trees in the Battery Park, having leaped the rails. Although followed at a safe distance by a large crowd, she was allowed to remain in this position.

A PARTY OF SWEDISH HUNTERS

who had arrived on the *Thuringia* on their way to farms in Nebraska, undertook to kill the beast, although bears were the only large animals they had practised on. Ten in number and armed with rifles, they scattered themselves in a semi-circle in pairs, and advanced, crawling on their bellies, until within a few paces of the recumbent lioness. Her head was turned toward Broadway, but suddenly suspecting danger, she arose and shook the heart of the onlookers with her sounding roar. It was at this moment that Jansen Bjornsen, the leader of the hunters, blew his shrill whistle, and five rifle balls were buried in the body of the lioness. She fell with a dull thud, evidently dead, but the five hunters whose guns were still charged, rushed up and emptied their pieces into the prostrate carcass. This was the signal for a deafening cheer. The hunters were carried around on the shoulders of the First Warders, and the proprietor of the Stevens House, Nicholas Muller, headed a subscription list with $50 each, as a testimonial to these brave children of the Norseland for their maiden service to the great Republic. It is announced that Superintendent Webster of Castle Garden will receive subscriptions. It is said that nearly $500 is already down on the lists. Commissioner Lynch has put his name down for $10; Whitelaw Reid subscribes $50; C. A. Dana adds $50 also.

THE BENGAL TIGER

having counted up a score of victims, surrendered his life to the trusty rifle of our aged Governor John A. Dix, who shot him as he rounded Madison Avenue and Thirty-fourth Street. This was an extremely fortunate occurrence. The Governor, a splendid shot, was in town in the nick of time. This gallant act will be remembered by the citizens of New York, although it is now too late to mark that esteem at the ballot box. It may be mentioned as a fortunate circumstance that a minute after the death of the tiger, Archbishop McCloskey's carriage drove up. A fright or injury to the horses by the ferocious beast might have ended the career of the aged prelate. Hearty congratulations were exchanged between the Governor and the Archbishop.

FRIGHT ON FIFTH AVENUE.

The crowded condition of the Fifth Avenue sidewalks on Sunday afternoon is well known to all, and the effect upon the host of elegantly dressed promenaders when the breaking loose of the beasts was made known, was curious. When the beasts made their escape from the building mainly devoted to the great *carnivoræ,* a number of excited people rushed down Fifth Avenue, shouting as they ran. It caused a general stampede of the fashionables, who ran in various directions down side streets and into the churches, which thus received full congregations long before the hour of service. The Hon. Richard Schell, who was standing near the Brick Church, on Murray Hill, and who first believed the report of the breaking loose to be a cruel hoax, told one of our reporters that the rapidity with which the avenue was cleared beggars description. The excited shouting party

SEEMED TO SWEEP THE AVENUE

before them. In ten minutes there was not a soul visible in either direction from the Park to the Fifth Avenue Hotel. It was puzzling to think where they had gone. Mr. Schell proceeded to state that he turned and walked up the avenue, but met no one for three quarters of a mile. He felt then fully convinced it was a hoax. As he neared the Park, however, he heard a number of shots fired. He in turn became excited, and commenced running toward the Arsenal. On his way he was met by a party

BEARING A DEAD BODY,

that of a youth fearfully disfigured about the head and face. A terrifying roar was heard behind them, when the party let the body fall and fled precipitately. Mr. Schell ran too, and jumped in some shrubs off the main road. The incline leading to the Arsenal is unfinished, and up this road he saw some animal of the tiger species come with a light, swift movement. The beast was evidently following the blood trail, for he went straight up to the abandoned corpse, and after striking one paw upon the breast, and touching it with his head, as if smelling, he gave forth a series of horrible howls. "I felt my blood run cold," said Mr. Schell, "but kept perfectly still lest the beast should be attracted to me from

THE HORRID MEAL

he was evidently about to commence. I soon heard a number of shouts and saw a party of citizens and police, running toward the animal, but unconscious of the fact. They were running away from danger in their rear. I shouted to them. They suddenly halted and looked back. Two of the party fired revolvers at the animal, which to their relief and mine, uttered a howl of anguish and ran, pursued by men who themselves were running away (from the lion, they said). I ran until I gained the entrance to the Park, and made down Fifty-ninth Street as the animal was proceeding at a limping trot down Fifth Avenue. I had not proceeded far when I saw a large object careering madly toward me. I recognized it as a buffalo bull. I turned to run back toward the Park, when, to my horror, I observed an animal ambling toward Fourth Avenue. I saw it was a brown or black bear. I rushed up the stoop of one of the houses and tugged at the bell. I saw as I turned that the buffalo and the bear had met, and that a fight was in progress. I cannot tell which got the better. The fight was short and I heard that the bear was seen to limp away. I got into the house, but was almost summarily ejected, although I made an urgent appeal to be allowed to remain." The animal first referred to by Mr. Schell is doubtless the one that

ENTERED THE CHURCH OF ST. THOMAS

of which Dr. Morgan is pastor, at the corner of West Fifty-third Street, causing such a deplorable panic with injuries to many. A party carrying one of the wounded down Fifth Avenue to St. Luke's Hospital, at Fifty-fourth Street, was attacked by him. Just as the bearers neared the corner a deep bass growl was heard behind them, and losing their presence of mind, they ran down the avenue and past the hospital. Descrying the church a little ahead, they hurried toward it and entered the edifice with fright on every countenance. The sight of the wounded man caused the greatest consternation. Shrieks were heard on all sides. The women grasped their protectors and the utmost confusion succeeded. The church door must have been left open, for a minute after, the animal, with his head down, to the blood trail and growling gutturally. His presence once discovered, a frightful scene ensued. Men and women rushed in all directions away from the beast, who sprang upon the shoulders of an aged lady,

BURYING HIS FANGS IN HER NECK,

and carrying her to the ground. In the haste to get away over the seats many injuries were sustained, Mrs. Catherine Ransom, of West Forty-fifth Street, breaking her leg by falling between two pews. Some one ran to the Windsor Hotel for assistance, and one of the guests ran with a loaded rifle to the church. The beast was in the middle aisle, sitting crouched over the form of his victim, when a tall, fair man, with a rifle in his hands, entered. Without a moment's hesitation he brought the weapon to his shoulder and fired. The beast stumbled over and the rifleman ran up and struck him over the head, driving the hammer through the brute's skull. When the aged victim was examined life was found to be extinct, although the flesh wound in the neck was in itself not of a very dangerous nature. Up to this hour the remains have not been identified. An inquiry at the hotel as to the name of the rifleman elicited the single word

"RIGBY!"

In several parts of the city the greatest danger resulted from people firing rifles and pistols from windows. There is no instance reported of any of the animals having been hit, while it is believed many citizens were struck by the missiles. One policeman, Officer Lannigan, of the Seventh Precinct, was wounded in the foot near Grand Street, by

A SHOT FROM A WINDOW,

during a chase after the striped hyena, which was mistaken by the crowd for a panther. This cowardly brute was finally killed by a bartender armed with a club. He was treated as a second Sampson by the entire neighborhood, and is undoubtedly a young man of courage. His name is Dan Brenan, and he is a native of the Nineteenth Ward. Counsellor Spellissey distinguished himself by stopping a causeless stampede in the Fourteenth Ward.

THE FERRYBOAT CARNAGE.

Perhaps the most deplorable of all the incidents of the terrible evening was that which took place on the ferryboat of the Twenty-third Street Line, North River. Several of the animals made their way down Fifth Avenue. Among them was one of large size (almost the only description now obtainable). It is thought to have been one of the tigers, but on its passage along West Twenty-third Street, appears to have been unnoticed in the general amazement. At any rate, just as the gate keeper on the Twenty-third Street ferry was closing the gates he saw a fierce animal bound past him and rush on to the ferryboat. The boat was well loaded. Some horses attached to light wagons were seen to rear, and show every sign of terror, and then rush forward

INTO THE RIVER

carrying their human loads with them. Several people were mangled by the ferocious brute in a few minutes. The boat had just begun moving as the beast leaped on board. When the pilot saw the horses and wagons going overboard, the boat was not quite clear of the dock. He immediately

RUNG TO REVERSE THE ENGINES

and put back. To this providential circumstance must be attributed the saving of so many lives. Numbers were seen to plunge overboard, to escape the beast, which at last sprang into the water after a young man. The wonderful escape of Larry Jerome is an incident of breathless interest. Overborne by the crowd, he was forced into the river, and although a heavily built man, is a splendid swimmer. He was seized around the neck by a desperate man, whom he shook off with the greatest difficulty. Striking out for the shore he touched against a female, who appeared to have given herself up to death. He piloted her to the spiles near the dock, and both were rescued by the fast gathering crowd. The tide was running at swift ebb and it is feared most of the bodies have been carried out to sea. This is one of the cases where days must elapse before the full list of fatalities is known.

THE HOSPITAL HORRORS.

In Bellevue Hospital many touching sights were seen. The doctors were kept busy dressing the fearful wounds, and the cries of the unfortunates in the accident ward were most painful to hear. It was necessary to perform a number of amputations instantly. One young girl is said to have died under the knife. Few of the victims were visited by their families last night, but the ministers of the gospel of all denominations took their place by the bedsides of the unfortunates. The handsome face of Rev. George H. Hepworth was seen bending over a moaning street Arab. Bishop Potter, Rev. Mr. Morgan Dix, Rev. Mr. Armitage, of the Fifth Avenue Baptist Church, and Fathers Farrelly and McGlynn, were seen moving among the sufferers, ministering to the souls of the suffering and the dying.

The following is a partial list of casualties:

KILLED

James Hadley
Owen Reilly
Peter Ryan
Michael Murphy
Peter Kerr
Thomas B. Styles
James Hewson
Ellen Lalor and
three children
Stephen Long
Mary Brady
Fred McDonnell
Alex H. Henderson
Pedro Velasquez
John Judge
Christopher Anderson
......Hyland
William Meredith
Jaccb Kuhne
Benjamin P. Steiner
Thomas Fagan
George Cross
John F. Coleman
Abel Garrett
P. D. Comstock
Annie Thomas
Fred C. Gamble
George Handley
Stephen Bruce
William Mapes

LIST OF WOUNDED

John Morrissey very slightly
General Butler
Alexander O'Leary
James Hayden
Michael Rafferty
George D. Bancroft
Silas Hammersmith
Julien D. Brown
Amos Hardy
John Connors
Mark Habelstein
Jacob Wort
Julia Denison
Anne Cushman
Sarah White
Mary Ann Gough
Pat Byrnes
George Seaver

Of the number actually killed it will be impossible to tell for some days. Of those wounded no full list can be ascertained. The charge of the savage beasts was the most unexpected in the history of cities. They tore through the leading thoroughfares with all the freedom they might have enjoyed in their native wilds.

LIST OF SLAUGHTERED ANIMALS:

1 Rhinoceros
1 Zebra
6 American deer
2 Giraffes
1 American bison
1 White-haired porcupine
1 Prairie dog
1 Sea lion
2 Leopards
1 Grizzly bear
1 Brown bear
1 Striped hyena
1 Ocelot
2 Brown Capuchin monkeys
1 American tapir
1 Anaconda
1 Woodchuck
4 Syrian sheep
1 Pine snake
1 Derbian wallaby
1 Dorcas gazelle
1 Sacred bull
2 American eagles
1 Two-toed sloth
1 Great kangaroo
1 Alligator
2 Water turkeys
4 Pink-footed geese
2 Pelicans
1 Trumpeter swan
1 Clapper rail
1 Bengal tiger
1 Chacma baboon
2 Camels
1 Sambur deer
1 African lion
1 African lioness
1 Redbreasted mergan
1 Pied-bill grebe
1 Nvighan
1 Guanaco

ANIMALS AT LARGE.

The following animals are at large in various parts of the Central Park and city, and, of course, are extremely dangerous: The cheetah, the manatee, the Cape buffalo, the panther, (a most ferocious beast, supposed to have killed the two policemen near the Belvidiere tower and eaten the goats whose skeletons were found on the Ramble), the opossum (not dangerous), the wild swine, the paisano, (a vicious beast, supposed to be on the west side of town, in the neighborhood of Manhattan market, and credited with killing the young lady found near Sir Walter Scott's statue), the mangabey and the puma lion (a very savage animal) destroyed most of the deer in the northern enclosure and bit a large piece out of the shoulder of Henderson, the policeman; supposed also to have killed the nursery girl found in the Carrousel. Three snakes escaped and are believed to be hid away in the grass near the Casino. More than a dozen monkeys are playing truant through the Park and are not to be depended upon when they become hungry. The black leopard, whose fight in the building with the Bengal tiger disabled him considerably, is limping about the upper end of the Park. The polar bear that killed the two keepers, Ryan and Murphy, is said to have been shot by Recorder Hackett near the upper reservoir. There is a sharp lookout for the black wolf. He escaped into the city, but looks so much like a Dutchman's dog he may evade detection until he has committed some lamentable tragedy. The musanga paradoxure and many other beasts of prey whose names are not immediately available are scattered over the island. Five or six bald-headed eagles escaped and many valuable tropical birds. The prairie wolf is not to be found, the suricate is also missing and no tidings have been received of the brown coatimundi.

GENERAL DURYEE

by the excellent disposition he made of the police, saved hundreds of children in the vicinity of Thompkins Square from being devoured. Had the same precautions been taken on the west side of town, the American buffalo and brown bear would never have accomplished so much fearful havoc.

NATIONAL GUARD PRECAUTIONS.

General Shaler deserves credit also for having orders promptly issued to turn out the National Guard, as the danger from the wild and savage animals at large in all the thoroughfares, proved too much for the police. The scene at the Fifth Avenue Hotel when the Malayan tapir that killed the two policemen, burst in among the mob of gentlemen standing in the portico, can never be forgotten. John Morrissey escaped with a flesh wound. General (B. F.) Butler, who had come on in the morning, was in conversation with General Gilmore, and received a bite in the calf of the leg. Major Bundy of the *Mail,* and Mr. Stone of the *Journal of Commerce,* assisted to calm J. Jones, the button manufacturer, who was thrown into a paroxysm by the appearance of the animals. Secretary Robeson and Alderman Vance were thrown violently against a pile of baggage. Leonard Jerome pursued the animal two blocks after it disappeared from the hotel, and made some excellent practice with a revolver but failed to bring the brute down. The buffalo overturned Earl Rosebery's carriage in front of the Brevoort, and subsequently ran into another carriage, containing Moses Hanz, of Forty-first Street, but without doing any serious damage.

It would be impossible at this late hour to describe the numberless scenes of dismay and disaster. The hospitals are full of wounded. There are fifteen bodies at the morgue, and several in the various precints. A sentiment of horror pervades the community.

THE GALLANT POLICE.

It is now time to say that the police deserve the greatest credit for their courage, if not for the success in dealing with this unheard of danger. Everywhere they are at the front, and among the slain and mutilated they count heavily. General Duryee's order to clear the streets was a master stroke of policy. It gave the rapidly gathered off platoons work they could undertake without further direction, while it gave the squads of officers he dispatched to the angles of the leading thoroughfares a chance to deal efficiently with the animals running amuck and without further danger to citizen life. There was only one case reported of a citizen shot by a police bullet, and, as the unfortunate victim had been warned to leave the streets, the officer cannot be blamed.

THE MORAL OF THE WHOLE.

Of course the entire story given above is a pure fabrication. Not one word of it is true. Not a single act or incident described has taken place. It is a huge hoax, a wild romance, or whatever other epithet of utter untrustworthiness our readers may choose to apply to it. It is simply a fancy picture which crowded upon the mind of the writer a few days ago while he was gazing through the iron bars of the cages of the wild animals in the menagerie at Central Park. Yet as each of its horrid but perfectly natural sequences impressed themselves upon his mind, the question presented itself, How is New York prepared to meet such a catastrophe? How easily could it occur any day of the week? How much, let the citizens ponder, depends upon the indiscretion of even one of the keepers? A little oversight, a trifling imprudence might lead to the actual happening of all, and even worse than has been pictured. From causes quite as insignificant the greatest calamities of history have sprung. Horror, devastation and widespread slaughter of human beings have had small mishaps for parent time and again.

The genesis of the hoax came through Thomas B. Connery, the managing editor of the *Herald,* who had succeeded Frederic Hudson. It seems, in his afternoon walks through Central Park, he had noted the rather frail character of the cages, and it appeared to him that there was a real danger in their condition. Some suggestion that they should be strengthened went unheeded by the authorities. It therefore occurred to Connery that an article on the outcome of a general escape would bring about the desired repairs. He set Harry O'Connor, a careless reporter, at the task, who did it badly and his "copy" was turned over to Joseph I. C. Clarke, the night editor, to lick into shape. Clarke was an Irish exile, who had done fine work as a reporter. Between his hard working hours he built up the tale and handed it over to Connery, giving it no further thought.

Connery was not the least bit of a fakir, but a most serious-minded, trustworthy man, with what seemed a rather timid personality. I came to know him as a member of the Authors Club after his retirement from the *Herald,* and he was certainly the last person to be suspected of a deliberate fraud on the public. His was a serious motive, but the result rocked the town. The article had been turned in to Connery, presumably to show Bennett. He had held it for a week and then ordered its insertion. Mr. Clarke recites in *My Life and Memories* that when the *Herald* was brought up to Bennett in bed along with his morning coffee, a glance at the page containing the tale caused him to lie back on his pillows and groan!

For once in its career the *Herald* failed to rise to the occasion. It was obviously abashed. The "hoax" had been overwhelmingly successful, but the next day's issue echoed no note of triumph. Instead, an article of less than one column in length headed "Wild

Beasts" tamely recited the need of a better zoological garden than the Arsenal and its sheds afforded, contrasting the Zoos in London and the Jardin des Plantes in Paris with the city's shabby outfit. An editorial supported the article and urged the city to make proper provisions. The suggestion did not bear fruit and had probably been forgotten when the magnificent Bronx menagerie was established twenty years later through the exertions of the New York Zoological Society.

Even members of the *Herald* staff were fooled. Doctor George W. Hosmer, a celebrated war correspondent, who later became Joseph Pulitzer's secretary and physician, appeared at the office girded with two big navy revolvers, remarking: "Well, here I am!"

The other newspapers had allowed themselves to be "sold" as well as the public. Major George F. Williams, city editor of the *Times,* receiving the *Herald* at his house, went forth frantically and, engaging a coach, picked up a load of reporters at their homes and drove to Police Headquarters in Mulberry Street, to berate the officials for allowing his paper to be so gorgeously beaten. He was turned away a broken and foolish man. Of course, the *Herald* was roundly objurgated by its rivals, who sought to play up the incident to the paper's discredit. They failed to make a dent in its prestige. Indeed, the incident helped rather than hurt the paper. It had given the town something to talk about and jarred it as it had never been jarred before. The public seemed to like the joke. Comic broadsides by peripatetic humorists were issued which showed the affair in its aftermath.

That the scare should have been so general and

lasting is not so queer as would now appear. There were no telephones, radios, "L" roads or subways. Getting about was by means of slow horse cars and slower omnibuses. People heard of things only through the newspapers. Those published in the afternoon came out late and were poorly circulated. Not until the next morning was the city reassured, but it was a fortnight before the excitement died down.

The authorship remained secret between Connery and Clarke until the latter revealed it in his recollections, printed in 1926. The cages were repaired!

CHAPTER XIV

A GOLDEN DECADE

From 1873 to 1883 the *Herald* was probably the most profitable and potentially the most powerful newspaper in the world. It printed more exclusive news than any other and if its owner did not influence events it was only because he did not care to bother with them. Aiming only to print the news, he outstripped all competitors. Plus this he engaged again in an exploring enterprise of the first magnitude.

The North Pole was the goal of many expeditions during the nineteenth century. Bennett fathered one that came to a tragic end. Lieutenant George W. De Long, of the United States Navy, who, after an experience in search of the *Polaris* survivors, had become fascinated with the Arctic, sought support from Henry Grinnell of New York for a further venture. Mr. Grinnell had backed Doctor Elisha Kent Kane in his search for Sir John Franklin and seemed a likely sponsor. Grinnell refused however, saying:

"I am too old a man and I have done my share. Younger men must take the matter in hand. There is Mr. James Gordon Bennett. He is the man to undertake such an expedition. You should apply to him."

This was on November 1, 1873. Accordingly De Long wrote to Bennett, then abroad. He held the matter in abeyance until the following spring when he returned to America and took it up in a personal interview. Nothing came of it for a time. The negotiations went on until November, 1876, when Bennett finally undertook to father an attempt to reach the Pole and authorized Lieutenant De Long to select a suitable ship. *Pandora,* a yacht owned by Sir Allen Young, seemed most suitable. Sir Allen had done some amateur Arctic voyaging in this vessel, which was built for rough work. Bennett purchased the yacht and Lieutenant De Long applied for the necessary leave of absence. This being granted, he went to England where *Pandora* was refitted and renamed *Jeanette* after Bennett's sister, Mrs. Isaac Bell whom he always held in great regard.

Mr. Bennett took an active interest in the preparations. It had been suggested that balloons might be used to advantage. He investigated the idea personally, but concluded that the unruly bag could be of no use, except possibly in a captive state for observation purposes. So none was taken along. The refitting was done at Deptford. Then *Jeanette* was moved to Cowes where her crew was shipped. From Cowes she crossed to Havre, reaching that port on June 18, 1878. Here she lay for a month, welcoming crowds of visitors. On July fourth she was formally christened. On the sixth Bennett sailed for New York and on the fifteenth *Jeanette* headed for the Pacific via the Straits of Magellan, it being De Long's purpose to approach the Pole from Bering Sea.

Jack Cole, the boatswain, and Alfred Sweetman, carpenter, had served with Bennett on *Dauntless.* "You will find Jack Cole," he wrote De Long, "one of the best sailors you ever have had under you. In times of danger he is worth his weight in gold and his tact with men is wonderful.'"*

The trip to San Francisco took one hundred and sixty-five days. But one hundred buckets of coal were left in the bunkers when *Jeanette* tied up to the buoy at Mare Island, December 27, 1878. It was necessary to secure an American register by act of Congress. This was approved March 18, 1879. The vessel was also put under the control of the Navy Department which was to provide a specially enlisted crew, to be paid by the government, but to be refunded by Bennett. Contrary to his habit Bennett was to foot the bills while the government was to have all the authority. In this dual relationship *Jeanette* became pretty well wound up in red tape and it was six months before she left Mare Island for the North.

It was not certain for some time whether the Navy Department would let De Long command. He finally convinced Secretary R. W. Thompson of his fitness, Bennett joining in the persuasion. The vessel had been rebuilt at the owner's expense. She was commissioned at last on June 28, 1879, a second act of Congress having been needed to clear the way. Some able men made up the company. John W. Danenhower was navigator and Charles W. Chipp executive officer. He had served with De Long on the *Polaris* search. Doctor J. M. Ambler was surgeon and George W. Melville, engineer. The latter was a notable person. Jerome J. Collins, who had brought the *Herald's* weather bureau up to a high state of efficiency, went along as meteorologist. Raymond L. Newcomb of

---

*From *The Voyage of the Jeanette,* by George Washington De Long. Courtesy of Houghton-Mifflin Company.

Salem, Massachusetts, was the naturalist, William Dunbar of New London, Connecticut, its pilot.

When, on July 8, 1879, *Jeanette* sailed out through the Golden Gate, never to return, Bennett cabled this farewell message through the *Herald*:

Regret exceedingly I cannot be there to bid him [De Long] God-speed, but hope to be on hand to congratulate him upon successful return. Tell him I have greatest confidence in his energy and pluck and I thank him sincerely for his fidelity to me. Say, also, he may push forward to north next spring with perfect confidence, for if ice-bound, I shall spare neither money nor influence to follow him up and send assistance next year, so neither he nor his men will be in danger. I wish this to be an American success. Tell him in case he returnes next year, unsuccessful, which I don't believe possible I shall most certainly send another expedition the following year, and continue doing so until successful, but had rather the victory be his than another's. Should De Long not return next year, or in fact never, the widows of men belonging to the expedition will be protected by me. Should like him to tell this to his men upon their departure.

"Thank God," remarked De Long, "I have a man at my back to see me through when countries fail." He had indeed. Bennett had shown amazing patience with the provoking government delays and had not shirked expenditures. Under date of July 20, 1879, De Long made this note in his journal: "At 10 A. M. inspected ship and held divine service. Informed the crew of Mr. Bennett's intention to follow us with a ship next year, and that he would provide for all widows if anything should happen to any of us. This seemed to have a good effect on the spirits of all hands."

It is not necessary to retell the story of the unfortunate expedition. *Jeanette* was sunk by ice off the Lena delta, June 12, 1881. The subsequent sufferings and death of most of the company, including the commander, added a poignant chapter to the long list of arctic tragedies. While all hands made shore, only a few eventually survived. Bennett was much in the commander's mind during the days of disaster. He named one Siberian dot in the sea "Henrietta Island" and another "Bennett Island."

Engineer Melville gives this account of the christening of the first named:* "The ground was then named Henrietta, in honor of Mr. Bennett's mother, and baptized with a few—a very few—drops of corn extract from a small but precious wicker bottle that had been placed in the boat-box for medicinal purposes."

Of the discovery of Bennett Island Melville writes, after describing a desperate dash over the ice:

> Suddenly, as we approached, the sun, as though by an extraordinary effort, rent the cloud veil in twain, and lo! before us, so close that it seemed we might step on shore, uprose and towered to a height of 3,000 feet the almost perpendicular masses of black basaltic rock, stained here and there with patches of red lichens, and begrimed with the decayed vegetable matter of unknown ages, the bold projections fissured and seamed, and the giant rocks split and powdered by the hand of time. The sight was glorious. Involuntary exclamations escaped from all. It infused new life and vigor into us; and each man straightway became

*From *In the Lena Delta,* by George W. Melville. Courtesy of Houghton-Mifflin Company.

a Hercules. Now or never, thought we, and so seized the boats and sleds, rushing them upon a tongue of the ice-foot which our main floe grazed in passing. At last! The ice-foot rested on the beach, and now many of our company set foot on terra firma the first time in two years. A sorry looking set we were, too, gathering together our weather-beaten traps; sunburned, lean, ragged, and hungry. We had appeared quite bad enough while on the ice; but now, after our late terrific toils camping under these great mountains, the tents looked not unlike ant-hills; while we, a group of vagabond insects, tugged away at a heap of rags, bags, and old battered boats as spoils. Supper over, we formed a procession, and with colors flying marched to the island, which Captain De Long took possession of in the name of God and the United States, naming it Bennett Island.

How the company became separated and how two stout seamen, William F. C. Nindemann and L. P. Noros, found Melville in the waste is another tale of wonder. The two led Melville to De Long's camp. He and all his companions were dead. Melville managed to reach Belun, a Siberian village, where he sent telegraphic messages to the Secretary of the Navy at Washington, the American Minister at St. Petersburg and to Mr. Bennett in Paris.

In all thirty-three officers and men were on the *Jeanette* when she was wrecked. They were divided into three parties, Commander De Long in charge of one in the first cutter, Lieutenant Chipp of the second cutter and Melville of the whale-boat. Nindemann and Noros alone survived of De Long's party. Chipp and his men were never heard from again. Melville's party were all saved thanks to encountering Siberian natives.

Subsequently the bodies of De Long and his companions were brought home. Cole, of whom Bennett spoke so well, was with Melville. He afterward became insane. Sweetman perished with Chipp.

Following the long silence of the *Jeanette* after she vanished in the arctic the government had, in June, 1881, sent the U. S. S. *Rodgers* to seek her out. She was burned in winter quarters on St. Lawrence Bay, Siberia, in December. The main body of her crew found its way back to San Francisco, but Colonel W. H. Gilder, Lieutenant Berry and Ensign Hunt remained and effected a meeting with Melville. Bennett had also secured from the government the services of the U. S. S. *Alliance,* Commander George H. Wadleigh, to scout the region between Greenland and Iceland. The government further sent a party to the Lena delta under Lieutenant Giles B. Harber who also connected with Melville.

When Bennett heard from Melville he at once dispatched John P. Jackson of the *Herald* staff to the delta with money and supplies. He found Melville, who, judging by his own account, was not very gracious. He had received word that two Americans were in his vicinity at the village of Tamoose. He records:

Thither I drove, on a sled, thinking that I was about to meet the naval officers of whom I had heard, but picture my surprise when, instead, I beheld Noros, who had set out for home in January with Mr. Danenhower. He was accompanied by a Mr. John P. Jackson, correspondent of the New York *Herald,* who, journeying to the Delta to "write up" the *Jeanette* disaster, had met the Danenhower party at Irkutsk, and telegraphed their stories to his journal. He had

The late Chief Engineer, George W. Melville, U.S.N.

then secured permission from the Secretary of the Navy to take Noros along with him to the Delta as companion and *aide*, and here they were with all the paraphernalia of Oriental travelers. Noros had shed his deer-skin rags, and was clothed in purple and fine linen, so to speak. Jackson had a Cossack escort and two covered sleds filled with toothsome foods and other good things.

I invited him over to Jamaveloch where he learned from Bartlett and Nindemann the details of the search, and how and where we buried the dead. . . . Mr. Jackson desired that I would detail either Nindemann or Bartlett to accompany him; but, as I had no authority to detach any of my party for such service, I declined to do so, greatly to the displeasure of Mr. Jackson who seemed to imagine that he had only to order in the name of his master, and I would obey. The egregious egotism of this kind of person is amusing in the extreme. At our first meeting he told me, with a great show of importance, that he would be obliged to me if I would turn over to him for his perusal and inspection the log-books and journals of Lieutenant De Long and Mr. Collins; that Mr. Bennett had so ordered, etc.; that if there was anything I wished to have done, he would be pleased to forward all my projects, etc., or if I wanted any money he was empowered to draw on Mr. Bennett, etc., etc. In short, he was prepared to take me in charge and complete in a proper manner the work I had almost finished.

Very much to his astonishment I was in need of no assistance, and not at all inclined either to surrender myself into his keeping, or to be captured by force. Had I supposed it was the intention of this ghoul-like party to break into the cairn-tomb, I would certainly have accompanied them, and prevented such a desecration. But I never dreamed that a person born in a Christian land would so far forget the respect due to our honored dead as to violate their sacred resting-place for the purpose of concocting a sensational story, and making sketches, or out of idle curiosity. Yet this, I afterwards learned, was done, and the timbers were sawn off and tumbled down, and the structure left so weakened that it no longer served the purpose for which it was intended.

The doughty engineer to the end of his days disliked newspaper men. Yet Jackson was representing Melville's real employer and a few days later he was indebted to him for bringing about a meeting with the naval officers of whom he had heard, Berry and Hunt. After that they traveled together, the naval gentry dubbing Jackson "dismal John" and hazing him a good deal on the journey back.

"From the wholesale manner in which he grumbled about his eating, drinking, sleeping, about everything that was around him, the sky and the earth beneath,—I seriously doubt if his halo would fit him should he succeed in edging his way into Paradise, which I must say, however, is, in my opinion, utterly improbable," was Melville's comment on his journalistic companion; adding, "and what if he were possessed of all Heaven itself, its fancied comforts and glories? Would he not fret and complain and pine for a portion of Hell as a diversion? My language is plain and strong simply because in all the miles of my travel or days of my life, I have never encountered such a fault-finder."

Melville had, indeed, performed heroic service and felt vexed, perhaps, like Hotspur, when worn by rage and extreme toil, "to be so pestered by a popinjay." He had found and buried the remains of De Long and his companions who perished as near to aid as he was himself, but missed out. Melville became chief engineer of the Navy and received proper honors for his courage and constancy. He led a vigorous row in the Navy over the long troubled status of "staff" and "line" but lives beloved in the memory of all who knew him, of whom I am one.

Nindemann was for years an employee in the Brooklyn Navy Yard. He played on Sundays and holidays with a boat anchored in old Mill Creek on Jamaica Bay, New York, where I came to know him. In a political shake-up he was dismissed. I had "pull" enough with the then Secretary of the Navy, Benjamin F. Tracy, to have him put back.

Jackson, during the *Jeanette* hunting period, had been installed in a house in St. Petersburg. Thence he was ordered to locate in Paris. He did so. When Bennett noted the locality he said it was not the sort of neighborhood a *Herald* man should live in. Jackson moved higher up. He was hardly settled before a cable came ordering him to New York. Protesting to Bennett, he was coolly told New York was the place that issued all commands. Accordingly he packed up and departed, to find upon arrival that he had been made managing editor of the *Evening Telegram*. Later he became cable editor of the *Herald*, leaving that position in 1891, to hold a like post on the staff of the New York *Recorder*.

After a year or so Bennett took him back, violating his rather rigid rule that "deserters" should never be permitted to return. Jackson knew how to pad out cables and to expand foreign news from slender outlines. This made him valuable and accounted for his restoration. He could always be relied upon to keep the foreign page, opposite the editorial, full to the brim.

Jackson, besides being an invaluable foreign editor, was no small personage as a correspondent and news-getter. While acting for the *Herald* in Berlin he succeeded in getting the verdict of the celebrated trial of Count von Arnim for treason in advance of the German press, so that it became known first in the *Herald.*

Despite the disaster of the *Jeanette,* Bennett never lost his interest in the arctic. He paid Doctor Frederick A. Cook twenty-five thousand dollars for his story of finding the Pole on the celebrated gum-drop expedition to the land of fancy that preceded Commander Peary's reaching the right spot on the polar ice.

Beside Bennett Island in the arctic, and the Bennett Mountain and River in Africa named by Stanley, Bennett became a further feature in geography as a by-product of an exploring expedition to Alaska headed by Frederick Schwatka. The latter, reporting to Edward Townsend Flynn, then managing editor, from San Francisco, wrote under date of October 9, 1883, apropos of discovering a large body of water hitherto unknown: "This lake was also deprived of its Indian name and put down on the chart as Lake Bennett, named in honor of James Gordon Bennett of the New York *Herald.* The explorers say it is one of the finest lakes they ever beheld. About midway of this lake, on the Western side a river of more than ordinary pretentions flows into it. There being no civilized name attached to it and it being one of the great tributaries of the Yukon it was set down on the chart as Flynn River in honor of the managing editor of the *Herald.*"

Before the United States had a weather service, the *Herald* had a good one of its own, which added to the importance of its ship news department. For a long time a nephew of Lieutenant Matthew Fontaine Maury, the pathfinder of the sea, was in charge of the department. The *Herald's* weather reports were among its best features and were followed with interest by the public. The later development of this weather service, as already noted, was due mainly to Jerome Collins who was to lose his life in the luckless *Jeanette* expedition. The weather was a matter of constant interest with the younger Bennett. He had a score or so of thermometers hung from trees in his garden at Versailles. These he was for ever consulting and comparing. *Herald* correspondents everywhere were constantly queried concerning the state of the climate in their vicinage.

Just as his father had initiated the "money" column so Bennett the younger began the first "real estate" department in the *Herald* about 1880. He saw the time had come for suburban booming and wanted to develop his large Washington Heights interests. The move gave the paper a lead in real-estate advertising which it never lost in his time. Lehmann Israels was the capable editor for many years. He also expanded the Sunday paper with a "Sunday News Supplement" full of reachings-out beyond the routine.

The policies of the father descended to the son. He would not allow an editorial opinion to be expressed in a case before the courts, nor permit news to be colored to fit editorial opinion. Of his foreign policy he once said: "My attitude on foreign affairs is often called changeable, and is, I believe, frequently misunderstood. It is simply this: If a nation is friendly to this country I wish the *Herald* to be friendly to that nation, but if a nation shows an unfriendly policy I wish the paper to adopt an unfriendly tone. This may not be patriotism but it is the course I wish the *Herald* to follow."

Bennett made his boyhood companion, Edward Townsend Flynn, managing editor late in 1882. Thomas B. Connery retired on a handsome pension dating from December twenty-third. Connery was but forty-seven but he had served twenty-five strenuous years on the *Herald*, thirteen of them in the trying position of managing editor. Men wore out fast on the job. Flynn was only thirty-three. Respecting his duties Bennett wrote him a lengthy typewritten letter from Paris under date of November 27, 1882. It contains so much of his newspaper creed that it is reprinted in full:

Paris, Nov. 27, 1882

Dear Mr. Flynn:

In addition to what I have already written you I want to impress more fully upon you my views in regard to your new duties. First of all I wish you to particularly consult economy. Try to carry out in the *Herald* the same principles of economical management combined with enterprise and thorough condensation of the news that you practised so successfully with the *Telegram*. Avoid the expense of supplement triple and quadruple sheets as much as possible without sacrificing the news. This can be done by judicious condensing so as to get all the points of the day's news without the verbiage. In doing this, however, be careful not to fall into the habit of mere routine summaries. Make some good lively feature every day, either local or general or both. Whenever there is any important piece of news always make that the feature of the day and "spread" upon it as much as you think it is worth. All this can be done without going to the expense of triple sheets except, of course, on very important occasions provided you give matters your constant personal attention and remain in the office until the paper goes to press ready to cut down, condense and leave out, as occasion requires, at the last hours. You can find out, by talking with Mr. Howland, exactly the point at which a supplement or triple sheet "pays" and you will please always bear that point in mind, remembering that whenever you go below it, without being justified by the pressure of news, you will be subjecting me to a loss. Your work on the *Telegram* has proved to me that you understand the value of news, i. e. what is important and what is not, what the feature of the day should be, what to condense and what to hold over or sacrifice altogether, and I have great confidence that you will be able to carry out my ideas about the *Herald.*

For your convenience I will classify what I have to say about the different departments under their respective heads:—

CITY NEWS.

While I have no special fault to find with Mr. Meighan I notice that he has been getting into a rut and that his work in other respects has not been up to the standard I require. Mr. Smith is, I believe, a good executive man and fully wide awake to what this department ought to be. As you are familiar with city news I should like you to keep an eye on it and, when you think necessary, make suggestions or changes as you see fit. Let me know fully and frankly what you think of Mr. Smith's ability as City Editor. I have selected Mr. Meighan and Mr. Gilder (who is on his way to America) as his assistants and wish them to be on duty alternate nights or alternate weeks, as you think best after consultation with Mr. Smith. Mr. Howard will have a desk in the City room and will be ready for special assignments, besides being subject to your orders for special duty outside the City department. I want the local part of the paper to be enterprising, lively and thoroughly condensed (excepting the "features") and edited carefully down to the smallest items. Have particular attention paid to Wall St. so as to have good local articles whenever there is a chance, but take care not to let the paper be used either by the writers themselves or by outsiders who may influence them for this purpose. Let there be a local feature of some sort every day, not a mere flimsy sensation worked up out of whole cloth, but the chief topic of the town, whatever it may happen to be, thoroughly well written and edited so as to make it fresh, lively and readable.

FOREIGN NEWS.

I consider Mr. Potter a very competent man in foreign news and should like you to consult him occasionally about the management of his department, but keeping a general supervision yourself over that part, as well as all the other departments of the paper. Mr. Potter has been, by my order, working up a fresh and well-selected lot of clippings from the foreign papers, but in future I wish these selections used more in subjection to the general news, so as to give two or three available columns on the foreign page in case the foreign news is dull and the home or local news crowded and important. Take as an example the *Herald* of Nov. 13 last. There were nearly three columns of small type, excellent in their way and for which I think Mr. Potter deserves credit, but which should have been left over, as I consider that the paper of that day should by careful editing have got along with, at least, a single supplement sheet. Mr. Potter knows my ideas about making features, etc., and will I think readily adapt himself to the new requirements.

GENERAL DOMESTIC NEWS.

Mr. Connery will give you a list of the correspondents in the various cities throughout the country. Make free use of their services whenever there is a chance to make a good feature or to get a "beat" but avoid the habit they are apt to get into of sending dribbling, unimportant dispatches which only increase the bills for telegraphing and cumber up the paper. I want you to treat the *Herald* exactly as if space were as much an object to it as it is to the *Telegram.* You always managed to get all the news into the *Telegram.* Use the same judgment and economy with the *Herald.* Don't consider that because the *Herald* is larger it has any more waste room than the *Telegram.* This will apply not only to the general domestic news but to every part of the paper. Never, however, spare expense or space when the news justifies it. Whenever there is an important piece of news I want the *Herald* to have the fullest and best account of it. Another point which I think you understand is letting a thing drop the moment public interest in it begins to flag. The instant you see a sensation is dead drop it and start in on something new.

SHIP NEWS.

The Ship news is never to be left out, or rather should be the last thing to leave out. Probably there will never be an occasion when you will find it necessary to omit it, though that *has* been done, in Mr. Hudson's time.

THEATRICAL NOTICES.

I want the notices of theatres to be brief, lively and always frank and fearless. Have these details assigned to good men in the City department, making the assignments yourself, instead of leaving them to Mr. Nicholas or whoever may occupy his desk. You will soon find out who are the most competent men for this work and you will keep them at work in rotation so as to avoid having a regular "critic," which I consider a mischievous and bad system in many ways. Mr. White can help you in this, and he can, in addition to his editorial duties, occasionally do the operatic and musical notices, for which he is well qualified. He can also edit the theatrical news.

J. G. BENNETT.

Please return a press copy of this. It can be copied on any letter press.

The new managing editor took hold vigorously and evoked this characteristic letter from Bennett, written on the stationary of *Namouna*:

Nice, Feby. 8, 1883.

Dear Mr. Flynn:

I was very much pleased with your letter of Jany. 27. It has the right sort of ring and I feel satisfied you will succeed in making a good paper. Already I notice a great improvement—— I beg you will continue in the good work. If Mr. ——'s sickness (?) is from drink, remove him at once and put a good man in his place. And any reporter found to be drunk or under the influence of wine while on duty should be suspended three months without pay. How are O'Connor's habits now? I see he is at Albany—sent there by Mr. Connery I suppose. Find out from Cummings, and if bad suspend or remove him.

Faithfully yrs.
J. G. Bennett.

"O'Connor" was Harry O'Connor, a *Herald* veteran of long standing. Let us hope he stood the test. "Cummings" was Thomas J. Cummins, the paper's Albany correspondent, another old hand. "J. G. Bennett" was the usual signature. He would sometimes sign social notes to Flynn "Jim." "Mr." was always employed in addressing men in the offices. More than once he sent his managing editor off on *Lysistrata* to Corfu or the Nile, when he himself went elsewhere. Friendly as they were the best part of their lives, a split came. It lasted twelve years. Then Bennett sent a cable asking Flynn to rejoin the *Herald*. The

Nice
Feby 6. 1883

Dear Mr Flynn

I was very much pleased with your letter of Jany 27 — It has the right sort of ring and I feel satisfied you will succeed in making a good paper — Already I notice a great improvement — I hope you will continue in the good work — If Mr Gilders sickness (?) is [illegible]

Courtesy of Miss Claire Wallace Flynn

Facsimile of handwriting of James Gordon Bennett, the Younger

drink remove him at once
And put a good man in his place
. And any
reporter found to be drunk or under
the influence of wine while on duty shall
be suspended three months without
pay— How are O'Conners habits now?
I see he is at Albany sent there by Mr
Connery I suppose— Find out from
Cummings and if bad suspend or remove
him

Faithfully JGBennett

after months of fighting, the *Herald* gave in, having suffered great financial loss and a large drop in circulation. Meanwhile, the *World* flourished like a green bay-tree. The bulk of its gains came from the *Sun* which "went foolish" during the Cleveland campaign of 1884 and lost half of its readers to Mr. Pulitzer, who always gave Bennett and Charles A. Dana the credit for presenting him with the New York field.

Coincident with the cut in price Bennett increased the *Herald's* advertising rates, thus further contributing to Mr. Pulitzer's support. He had become arrogant during the 1873-1883 decade and insolent in his use of power. Moreover, the character of advertising was about to undergo a change, though this did not get under full headway until the 'nineties when the department store development began in New York. These stores used larger space and display, something discouraged by the *Herald,* which stuck to logotypes and would not break column rules. The *World* allowed any kind of type and cut the rules but charged an extra price for the privilege. This was cheerfully paid and left the *Herald* at a disadvantage. In 1895, as advertising manager of the *World,* I equalized the rates and abolished the extra charges with expansive results to the paper. The *Herald* was compelled to follow suit. It also abolished logotypes and substituted outline letters in their stead. This improved its position for the time, especially as Mr. Pulitzer, whose eyes were always on the *Herald,* forbade the use of black-face and compelled us to use outline until a dry-goods combine forced a change in policy.

In 1894 the coming of William R. Hearst to New York gave Bennett a breathing spell, as the young

Californian devoted his entire time to the *World,* taking away many of its able men and shamelessly imitating all it did in bigger type and with louder noise.

Meanwhile, Bennett had made a master stroke by moving up-town and out of the welter. He selected the large triangle on Broadway between Thirty-fifth and Thirty-sixth Streets and there constructed from plans by McKim, Mead and White one of the loveliest buildings ever erected in New York. Where Pulitzer had aimed to touch the skies, Bennett kept close to the earth in what was a replica of the Palazzo del Consiglio of Verona. Here the *Herald* was housed in 1894. The press-room was made visible from the street by plate-glass windows and the business office was a thing of beauty. Within, the building was a model of good taste, but not convenient. Situated on an island, so to speak, it had no room for expansion such as was soon needed. The composing-room, up under a hip roof, was hot and low. The typesetting machine operators had to sit under the eaves. Besides, the building was on leased land with but twenty-five years to run. Pulitzer once told Bennett in Paris, when he heard this, that he could not sleep nights with his building on another man's land. Bennett dryly replied that he would not be on hand to worry about it, which became true, though he worried a good deal just the same.

The *Herald's* up-town move gave it a boom. It also boomed up-town. Great stores and hotels sprang up around it, and in due time the huge terminal of the Pennsylvania and Long Island railroads added importance to the center then named and still called Herald Square.

The warfare between the *World* and Mr. Hearst was on down-town. The *Herald,* out of it all, prospered amazingly, and its Sunday paper, by pushing a series of Christmas and Easter supplements, passed the *World* in city circulation. The Hearst Sunday sheet was far behind. All this brought big business, and it looked as if the paper were invincible. It made around a million a year. The *World* and *Journal* on a one-cent basis had a struggle. Pulitzer's profits were more than cut in half, and Hearst's loss climbed into the millions.

Bennett had need for money. He lived at great expense in Paris. His country seat at Beaulieu and his steam yacht cost a fortune each year, while his liberal use of the cables totaled a pretty sum. Besides he had a steady one hundred thousand dollars a year loss on the Paris *Herald,* started in 1887. To increase this seepage in 1889-1890, Bennett essayed the establishment of a London *Herald.* It did not fit into the English atmosphere, and, as English libel laws were very strict, holding proprietors responsible for the acts of their editors and reporters, it was not long before Bennett found himself barred from Britain.

The London *Herald,* besides vexing its owner, lost a lot of money. It was finally discontinued, save on Sunday, lingering thus for a little before finally shutting up shop. Bennett carried its first-class talent from New York—Robert Hunt Lyman, Ervin Hawkins, James Creelman, H. W. J. Dam and Thomas Fielders. All had a hand in it, while on the editorial page, former Mayor A. Oakey Hall and Louis J. Jennings, who, as managing editor of the New York *Times,* exposed the Tweed Ring and sent Hall to exile, came together across the years in this queer fashion. The New York gentlemen could not get by the English police and court system. After most of the men had been badly bumped they gave up trying and cultivated the barmaids, all save Creelman, who made an assault on Scotland Yard, with results that made his comrades rock with laughter.

In 1893 Bennett incorporated the New York Herald Company and took down "James Gordon Bennett, Proprietor" from the head of the editorial page and substituted therefor: "E. S. Drone, editor; G. G. Howland, general manager; George J. Taylor, news editor; William C. Reick, city editor; John Henderson, night editor."

Joseph Pulitzer had some time before placed his name at the head of the *World*. Bennett was reported as taking his down in consequence and putting up what he called the names of his "hired men" instead, not in recognition of their responsibility but in contempt! At any rate, Pulitzer's name also came down from the top of the column and was not replaced.

The change gave rise to the rumor that Bennett was disposing of his holdings, Reuter's Agency circulating the report in Europe. Bennett charged this as libelous, incidentally adding in an editorial that the *Herald* could be made to pay a dividend on twenty million dollars by curtailing its cables and cutting out some of the five thousand dollar salaries paid. These looked large then.

Once, however, Bennett signed an agreement to sell the *Herald* to H. H. Kohlsaat, of Chicago, who, after making a fortune in bakery-restaurants, lost it in trying to run a Chicago *Herald*. He had sold his bakery

business for a large sum and sought to be a Napoleon of journalism. The next day Bennett called him in and begged off. He had lain awake all night and repented of the bargain. Kohlsaat tore up the contract.

Save in a single instance Bennett never departed from his rule to have no other business than the *Herald.* This was in his partnership with John W. Mackay in establishing the Commercial Cable System. Mackay, starting as a prospector and handpick miner, had wrested an enormous fortune from the silver in the celebrated Comstock Lode in Nevada. His wife lived abroad. The size of her cable bills attracted his attention. At the time (in the 'eighties), the Western Union held the monopoly from Ireland to Heart's Content in Newfoundland, thence by land straight to New York. Jay Gould had given the Western Union, of which he was the chief holder, a sinister name. It was interlocked with English cable ownership. The French cable was purely foreign. Rates were exorbitant. Mackay, visiting in Europe, noted the facts. He thought there ought to be an all-American cable system.

Knowing Bennett to be the best single cable customer Mackay enlisted his interest. The two united to lay the Commercial cable, now a vast enterprise under control of Mackay's son, Clarence H., crossing the Atlantic and the Pacific, supplemented by the Postal Telegraph service all over America. The Mackay-Bennett cables soon made their way, disdaining to cut prices below twenty-five cents a word and were supreme after the Western Union system had lost much money at half this rate in an effort to kill competition. Mackay was a bold venturer to defy Gould, but he did it successfully. For one thing his capital was all solid. He had no water to pay dividends on, no financial sins to expiate. The Mackay-Bennett cable was paid for with the real money of two partners, plus that of a few minor investors. They did not go to the public and never "financed" the property.

One of the outcomes of this warfare was a bitter personal attack on Bennett by Jay Gould, which was sent to all the New York papers except the *Herald.* Julius Chambers was then managing editor, and feeling that the best way to meet the assault was to print it, succeeded in getting a proof from the composing-room of the New York *Press.* The attack in all its viciousness therefore appeared in the *Herald* the same day as in the others. He did this without consulting Bennett, who was highly pleased at the performance. Gould's assault fell flat. Indeed, to assail the character of the *Herald's* proprietor was a waste of time. It had long ceased to be an asset.

In 1894 New York was stirred as it had not been since the days of William M. Tweed by the revelations of the Lexow Committee, a legislative body headed by Senator Clarence Lexow, of Nyack, which dug deeply into vice conditions that had developed under six continuous years of Tammany rule. The testimony of Doctor Charles H. Parkhurst, head of the Society for the Prevention of Vice, and that of other witnesses brought out under the skilful examination of John W. Goff, counsel for the committee, aroused public opinion which in turn created a Committee of Seventy for the purpose of bringing about a fusion of the various political elements against Tammany Hall. That astute organization selected as its candidate for mayor in 1895 Nathan Straus, a member of the firm of R. H.

Macy and Company, the pioneer department store of the city, whose record for philanthropy and public spirit was relied upon to take the curse off the ticket. He was opposed on the fusion side by Colonel William L. Strong, a wholesale dry-goods merchant of good standing in the Union League and elsewhere. The *Herald* stated the merits of both candidates but took no stand editorially, contenting itself with the remark that both gentlemen had revealed their purposes and it would leave it to the voters to make their choice. This was a *Herald* habit in most political situations, but something happened to bring it into the open. Mr. Straus had been nominated on October tenth. On the sixteenth the following appeared at the top of the *Herald's* editorial page:

SIXTH AVENUE, FOURTEENTH STREET AND TAMMANY.

TO THE EDITOR OF THE HERALD:—

We and other large patrons would esteem your support of Mr. Straus a personal favor. He will give you a business administration.

EHRICH BROTHERS

TO THE EDITOR OF THE HERALD:—

Retail furniture dealers will appreciate your support of Mr. Straus. He is fearless, independent and capable.

BAUMAN AND CO.

We are sorry, very sorry, that we cannot comply with these requests, and also that Mr. Straus should be a Tammany candidate, for even if George Washington came to life the *Herald* could not support him if he were Tammany's standard bearer.

Ehrich Brothers were conspicuous Sixth Avenue merchants. Bauman Brothers were the biggest installment-plan furniture sellers in the city. Both firms were large advertisers. The Macy store was at the corner of Fourteenth Street and Sixth Avenue, which thoroughfare, from Fourteenth to Twenty-third Streets, was then the retail center of the town. The letters were printed in the customary editorial page type, the comment in news-face nonpareil. Not much space was consumed but it carried consternation into the Tammany camp, bearing, as it did, the tidings that the *Herald* would be against the Hall.

Not to be outdone in independence the *World* commented thus on October seventeenth:

ADVERTISING AND POLITICS

Two business concerns, both large advertisers, appealed to the *Herald* to support Mr. Straus for Mayor. One of them said it would regard such support as a "personal favor," the other, assuming to speak for its line of trade, said it would "appreciate" the support.

This is a very bad innovation in politics and it cannot be too strongly condemned. It follows naturally the nomination of Mr. Straus by a ring of discredited and unprincipled office-holders, partly because of his admirable charities and partly, no doubt, because the concerns with which he is connected are large advertisers.

The calculation of these politicians was that Mr. Straus's charities could be capitalized in votes and that his "patronage" of the newspapers would insure their support or at least their silence.

This was a very poor calculation worthy only of the low cunning of men who proceed upon the theory that "everybody has his price," and that selfishness rules the world. If they had been possessed of more knowledge and sense they would have understood that any newspaper whose support is worth anything would resent an attempt to influence it in any way.

Mr. Pulitzer, then at Bar Harbor, was the father of this editorial. He went further the next day and described Mr. Straus as "a mask for Tammany." As the result of the opposition of the two most powerful papers in the United States, Mr. Straus withdrew from the race, and the Hall named Hugh J. Grant who had already served two terms, previous to that of Thomas F. Gilroy, then under fire. He was badly beaten by Colonel Strong and New York enjoyed a house cleaning that brought Theodore Roosevelt forward as a member of the Board of Police Commissioners in which place he showed his teeth conspicuously and kept before the public thereafter.

If Mr. Straus resented the *Herald's* stand he did not show it in cutting his advertising. Neither did the others. But the *World's* action was bitterly resented, and Mr. Straus soon organized a "combine" of retail stores which twice fought the paper over rate adjustments and won a victory both times. The two battles pulled something like six hundred thousand dollars in advertising out of the *World*.

To preserve his satrapy in perfection Bennett would not recognize the various trades unions whose members got out the *Herald*. He avoided negotiations and submission by always paying a little more than the established scale of wages. For years John R. O'Donnell, night editor of the *Herald*, was president of Typographical Union No. 6, but officially Bennett never knew the organization existed.

Through the influences of the Publishers' Association the several New York offices got on good terms, after 1895, though the *Herald* never became a member. This was thought due to Bennett's haughty nature, but it was not true. He gave his consent, but the various factions in his management did not care to come in. Before this, however, an entente had been established by which the *Herald,* though a non-member, would not act in any matters of general concern, until the Association had agreed upon its course, which the former would regularly accept. Usually, when consulted by his staff officers the Commodore would cable: "Follow the *World.*"

Gardiner G. Howland, the business manager of the *Herald,* was a very precise and punctilious gentleman, an aristocrat to his finger-tips, who owed his place more to his social position than to his abilities. On one occasion, however, before the Association was in effective shape, he "cornered" Charles M. Palmer, manager of the Hearst papers, and myself delightfully. The mail hands had organized a union and established a scale. Mr. Palmer thought the *World* and the *Journal* should take the matter up with the *Herald.* Agreeable to this purpose we called on Mr. Howland, who was stately, but receptive. He agreed to stand with us and not recognize the new combination. A few days later John E. McLaughlin, the labor organizer who had been acting for the men, informed us that the *Herald* had surrendered. Very stupidly, without notifying Mr. Howland, we conceded the demands.

A few days later Mr. Palmer, as spokesman, received a note in icy terms, calling the *World* and the *Journal* to account for breaking the agreement. Not knowing how to reply we decided to call. Mr. Howland received us coldly. Palmer explained awkwardly that we had perhaps been inconsiderate, but McLaughlin had been so positive that we concluded the *Herald* had decided to act independently and so had recognized the Union.

"Quite to the contrary," said Mr. Howland. "The *Herald* has done nothing of the sort."

"Hold on," I said to Palmer. "I am not sure that McLaughlin said the *Herald* had recognized the Union. Didn't he say it was paying the scale?"

"Oh, as for that," replied Mr. Howland, "as for that I did make sundry recommendations to Mr. Bennett involving an increase of about twenty thousand dollars a year in the pay-roll, to which he consented. But we didn't recognize the Union."

With a strong desire to kick each other we departed from his lofty presence. Some time after the incident, I called on Mr. Howland with W. E. Haskell, who had succeeded Palmer, on a similar errand.

"Really," he said, "my experiences with the *World* and the *Journal* have been so unfortunate that I hardly feel like making further agreements with either of them."

Forgetfulness of sins has always been one of my valued possessions. For the life of me I could not recall what he was driving at. However, we managed to appease him and gained consent to our purpose. Once outside I recalled the mailers' incident and invited Haskell to kick me in a due desire to do penance.

Though started by Bennett himself when a young man, the *Evening Telegram* had never been anything but a starveling. Late in 1897 he determined to put an end to its puny existence, announcing the fact in the *Herald* of Sunday, November twenty-first. The announcement was made on the editorial page and headed in full-face type with this quotation from Abraham Lincoln:

You can fool all the people some of the time and some of the people all the time, but you can't fool all the people all of the time.

The announcement continued:

The *Evening Telegram* ceases to appear from yesterday for the time being in accordance with Abraham Lincoln's wise saying that "you can fool all the people some of the time and some of the people all the time, but you can't fool all the people all of the time."

And he was right. The public also can fool publishers all the time and advertisers can fool publishers some of the time and they seem to be continuing to fool them all the time. But the *Evening Telegram* doesn't propose to be fooled all the time.

An up to date evening paper at one cent doesn't pay. Therefore those who are publishing evening papers at one cent are either fooling the public or fooling themselves. As the *Evening Telegram* doesn't intend either to fool itself or fool the public it has ceased publication until the time becomes ripe when it can stop being fooled and stops fooling.

The men in the office were aghast at the ukase, and Albert Fox, the *Herald's* advertising manager, then in Paris, joined them in a protest the force of which caused Bennett to rescind his determination, thereby making a great mistake. New York is not liberal to papers printing morning and evening editions. In the case of the *World* and *American* the morning issue is the one that suffers. It was then the reverse with Bennett's properties.

On his insistence that the office managers make good as the result of their persuasions to keep the *Telegram* alive, the gentlemen proceeded to put life in its veins by pumping ichor from those of the *Herald.* Selling at one cent it had doubled the circulation of its three-cent parent. The managers at once set to coaxing the *Herald's* hitherto invincible classified columns into those of the anemic *Telegram,* giving twice the publicity at half the rate. Results count, and soon the *Herald,* which had resisted a determined assault on its classified columns by the *World,* began to lose to its junior. Had Bennett killed the *Telegram,* kept the *Herald* at three cents and saved his classified advertising, evil days would hardly have followed as they did. No paper can successfully compete with itself. The "Wants" had made the *Herald,* as much as its enterprise. Their loss undid it while enterprise slackened with diminishing profits.

In handling the war with Spain in 1898, the *Herald* quite won the honors. The *World* and Mr. Hearst tried to outdo each other with the effect of thoroughly disgusting their public, and the *Herald* carried off the palm, so that 1899, the year following the war, was credited with being the best in the paper's history. The *World* dropped to a low point from which it finally rallied, while Mr. Hearst went gloriously on to new expenditures and greater exhibitions of energy. He came near to a Waterloo level when the assassination of President William McKinley was laid, quite unjustly, to the door of his morning edition. A boycott resulted that cut his city circulation down from over a quarter of a million to half that amount, and his sheet was long in a groggy state.

Just as his father was the first journalist to appreciate the invention of the telegraph by Samuel F. B. Morse, so Bennett was the first to recognize the merit of Marconi's wireless. After experimenting at Sorrento the young inventor transferred his activities to Ireland and Newfoundland, seeking to ride the Hertzian waves across the sea. Milton Snyder was sent to follow the experiment. He brought the tale of the new wonder back to Bennett in Paris. He seized upon the amazing invention at once and brought Marconi to America to utilize his device in reporting the *America's* Cup yacht race in 1899. The inventor was paid five thousand dollars for the service—a sum that came in very handily in enabling him to perfect wireless. Capital was chary and he had slow work in making his way. Bennett established a wireless station at Sankaty Head, and also encouraged the efforts of Lee J. De Forest at radio development in its application to the transmission of news. In this Lieutenant-Commander J. D. Jerrold Kelly, the *Herald's* naval expert, lent important assistance.

When William R. Hearst ran for governor of New York in 1906, Bennett ordered the *Herald* to oppose his candidacy. This it did with vigor. Mr. Hearst alone on the Democratic state ticket was beaten by Charles E. Hughes and held the *Herald* to blame for a fair share of his defeat. His manager, S. S. Carvalho, seeking vengeance, found a means for satisfaction in the *Herald's* "Personal" column, a valuable feature founded by the elder Bennett. It usually filled the first column of the front page, at that time given over wholly to advertising, but on Sundays it covered the page and often overflowed. At this time the *Herald's* Sunday circulation in New York was the largest of all, the page of "Personals" no doubt aiding greatly in its sale.

The character of the advertising had undergone a great deal of change. When Doctor Parkhurst's crusade drove houses of ill-fame into hiding, their owners took to using *Herald* "Personals" as guides to their lurking places. Ingenious anagrams were much employed with the result that some horrible obscenities crept in, escaping the vigilance of proof-readers and laying the paper open to prosecution. Mr. Bennett was advised of the danger but replied that the "Personals" had always been a *Herald* feature and would so continue. The avenging Carvalho caused the United States Grand Jury to look into the matter, with the result that the *Herald* and Bennett were indicted and convicted. Fines aggregating twenty-five thousand dollars were paid and the "Personal" classification was discontinued. Mr. Pulitzer, with whom I was then associated, asked me if I did not think the *Herald* would suffer from a moral reaction growing out of this episode. I said it would suffer from leaving the "Personals" out of its columns. He professed to be greatly shocked by this wicked view on my part. It was correct, however. The "Personals" were fascinating reading. When they were killed the paper's Sunday circulation soon dropped to third place. Mr. Hearst bought away some of its best Sunday comics and used them to advantage, but the real decline came from the killing of the "Personal" column.

After this disastrous encounter with Hearst, the Commodore ordered that the latter's name should be excluded from the *Herald,* a rule that was obeyed though it often required considerable ingenuity to print the news and omit it. One incident of embarrassment follows. When Bennett sold his old residence in

Twenty-first Street, one of the Hearst papers printed an offensive item about the transaction apropos of which I received the following letter from William C. Reick:

The New York Herald.
December 6, 1906.

Dear Mr. Seitz:

The *Evening Journal* had a very disagreeable article the other evening about Mr. Bennett selling his residence 28 West 21st Street and saying that he had decided to leave New York permanently. The facts are that Mr. Bennett has sold his house downtown in order to buy the property 37 West 47th Street as his permanent residence. He does not care about replying to the *Journal*, but in case you think this is of sufficient news interest its publication in the *World* might explain the *Journal's* story.

Yours truly,
W. C. Reick.

Mr. Bennett had sold the family mansion at 435 Fifth Avenue to Austin Corbin, in 1896, and then purchased the Twenty-first Street house. The Forty-seventh Street dwelling remained his New York residence until the end. It was always kept open on the chance of his coming. So was his villa at Newport. He maintained the big Washington Heights house also, and owned besides a palace in the Avenue d'Iena in Paris. He also rented an apartment in the Avenue des Champs Élysées, whence he was wont to edit the Paris *Herald*.

Incidentally the *Herald* had an *index expurgatorius* that was the despair of its editors. To leave out a man's name was to extinguish him, in Bennett's opinion. One victim of the expurgation rule was Roger A. Pryor. He had been a firebrand of the rebellion in Richmond and was a member of Congress during the hot days that preceded secession. For some reason he took umbrage at the *Herald* and in a fiery, secessionist speech echoed some of the false assertions concerning Mrs. Bennett. He became a brigadier-general under the Confederacy, but after the war removed from Richmond to New York to hunt for a living. In time Tammany gave him a seat on the bench. Remembering the insult to his mother, Bennett excluded mention of him from the *Herald's* columns. Until his death in 1884, Colonel James Watson Webb's name also was banned.

On a famous occasion, Mrs. Stuyvesant Fish, a social arbiter of the day, gave a grand ball. It was fully reported in the *Herald*. Unfortunately for the story of the event, a prize-fight came off on the same evening, and the make-up man got the names of those present at the one transferred to the other. Mrs. Fish was in a mighty rage and sent her husband to Gardiner G. Howland, general manager of the *Herald*, to see about it. Now, the Howlands ranked socially with the Fish family and after failing to convince Mr. Fish that it was an accident, he told him future mix-ups of the sort would be prevented by omitting all reference to Fish affairs. This did not suit. The ban went into effect nevertheless, but was later lifted. Incidentally, Mrs. Fish's kindness in taking Mr. Reick into society may have had something to do with Mr. Howland's sternness.

The New York *Sun* set up the motto, "If you see it

in the *Sun* it's so," and the New York *Times* followed it with, "All the news that's fit to print,"—blandly printing all the news it could get. Bennett adopted both mottoes, placing them conspicuously in the "ears" on either side of the *Herald's* heading. He was persuaded to drop them when some one proved to him that "it's so" was a powerful aid to the collection of damages in libel suits, covering as it did the whole contents of the paper and vitiating any covering of "alleged" and "it is said" that otherwise might have been protective.

Bennett's sympathies at the outbreak of the World War were firmly with France. Long before America entered the conflict he had taken the French side strongly. Indeed it was he who first applied the contemptuous term "Bosch" to the onrushing Germans.

The war worried and oppressed him. James L. Ford in his *Forty Odd Years in The Literary Shop* reports asking a *Herald* veteran fresh from Paris in 1915 how Bennett was, and received this reply:

"He's dead. The old, drunken, money-spending Jim Bennett is dead. In his place has come a Scotch miser."

The Paris *Herald* kept on publishing and denouncing the Kaiser. Other prints in English suspended—this of course before our entry into the war, after which things changed and more were started. Bennett's autos, horses and carriages were commandeered and he walked to his office, where an editor kept track of the armies by sticking pins in a map, but when they came too close to Paris the editor fled. Bennett stayed though fearful of being driven out of France, and the *Herald's* revenues suffered severely. He felt the crimp

James Gordon Bennett, the Younger

From a snap-shot taken on his last visit to America

in his income, having never troubled himself to accumulate a fortune as he might readily have done. By odd chance, when America entered the struggle, the Paris *Herald,* which had been good for a loss of one hundred thousand dollars per annum, took to making that much or more. The parent paper, however, did not rally as the other New York newspapers did in the flood-tide of prosperity that followed the ending of hostilities.

Joseph Pulitzer had a superstition about the number ten. He was born on the tenth of May, 1847, bought the St. Louis *Dispatch* on December 10, 1878, and the New York *World* on May 10, 1883. He cultivated the habit of working in "ten" wherever possible in his doings. Bennett might have done the same. His birthday was May 10, 1841, and though presumably a confirmed bachelor, he was married on September 10, 1914, in Paris, to an American woman, formerly Maud Parker, of Philadelphia, widow of the Baron De Reuter, a scion of the great European newsgatherer.

On May 10, 1918, he was fatally stricken after a period of disability, at the Villa Namouna, Beaulieu, France, and died the following Friday morning, May fifteenth, at four forty-five o'clock. The day before his marriage, although born a Catholic, he had been received into the Episcopal faith. His body was brought to Paris where funeral services were held in Trinity Church. He was buried in the cemetery at Passy. The elder Bennett was seventy-seven when he died, the younger stopped at the same mile-post.

From 1909 to 1918 the *Herald* establishment showed a profit of $1,940,992, but this covered losses in 1917 of $151,870 and in 1918 of $138,203. During his long ownership he probably drew and spent $30,000,000 from the property. During 1917 Mr. Bennett felt the paper slipping in his hands and had under way a serious negotiation with Adolph S. Ochs of the *Times* to take it over, and consolidate with the latter. Nothing came of it however. By his will he required annuities aggregating $142,500 to be paid by his executors, Rodman Wanamaker and the Guaranty Trust Company of New York. The executors found the property losing so heavily that they were forced to sell the *Herald* and *Telegram* to Frank A. Munsey, on January 17, 1920, for four million dollars, of which one million dollars was in cash and the balance notes. On January 30, 1920, the *Herald* appeared for the last time from its own plant. It was first merged with the *Sun,* then operated as the *Herald* by Mr. Munsey, to be finally sold by him to Mrs. Whitelaw Reid for five million dollars and combined with the New York *Tribune.* Bennett's will decreed that the name "*The New York Herald*" should always stand. So it precedes that of the *Tribune* on the consolidated sheet. The *Evening Telegram* became the property of the Scripps-Howard Chain in 1926.

The estate in its final disposition was willed to found a home for the relief of indigent *Herald* employees and journalists generally, the former to have preference. Its condition did not warrant the enterprise as of early date, the income being nearly all consumed by the annuities, so the "home" is still on paper, with a good while to wait, though some *Herald* men have been taken care of who were in special need. There was once an impression about that Bennett would leave the newspaper to his lieutenants, but none survived the tests he was always making long enough to be recorded in the book of gold.

Through the initiative of Professor James Melvin Lee, head of the Department of Journalism in the New York University, some scant relics of the great newspaper have been salvaged. These include bronze and marble busts of the elder Bennett, portraits of the father and son, a group picture of editors, and other items of historic value taken from the Herald Building when abandoned after the sale to Frank A. Munsey. These were donated by William T. Dewart, Mr. Munsey's successor as head of the *Sun*. They are housed in a "Bennett" room in the Washington Square Building of the University and under the care of the Department of Journalism. The collection has also been enriched by contributions from Hamilton Peltz and a file of the paper donated by the *Herald-Tribune*.

Mr. Dewart also presented the University with the great ornate clock that stood on the Thirty-fifth Street façade of the Herald Building, which cost Bennett two hundred thousand dollars, together with the bronze owls that blinked down upon it when the two heroic figures with hammers struck the hours, to stand near the Hall of Fame on University Heights looking across to the Washington Heights section the elder Bennett so much loved.

THE END

INDEX

INDEX

www.ingramcontent.com/pod-product-compliance
Lightning Source LLC
LaVergne TN
LVHW020554110826
845149LV00002B/268

* 9 7 8 1 4 1 8 1 8 8 4 2 9 *